Sell The Meeting: Set Discovery Calls & Sales Appointments To Close New Accounts

A Lead Generation Process With Phone Script Samples For B2B Appointment Setting & Cold Calling

SCOTT CHANNELL

Also by Scott Channell

7 Steps To Sales Scripts For B2B Appointment Setting:
Creating Cold Calling Phone Scripts For Business To Business Selling, Lead Generation And Sales Closing

Setting Sales Appointments:
How To Gain Access To Top Level Decision Makers

© 2019 by Scott Channell.
All rights reserved.

No part of this publication may be reproduced, stored in a retrieval system, or transmitted in any form or by any means, electronic, mechanical, photocopying, recording, scanning or otherwise, except as permitted under section 107 or 108 of the 1976 United State Copyright Act, without the express written permission of the author.

Published by New Mark Press. July 2019.
ISBN: 978-0-9765241-8-2

Limit of Liability/Disclaimer of Warranty: While the publisher and author have used their best efforts in preparing this book, they make no representations or warranties concerning the accuracy or completeness of the contents of this book and specifically disclaim any implied warranties of merchantability or fitness for a particular purpose. No warranty may be created by any sales representative or written materials. The views expressed are those of the author alone. The advice and strategies contained herein may not be suitable for your situation. You should consult with a professional where appropriate. Neither the publisher or author shall be liable for any damages arising herefrom. The reader is fully responsible for his or her actions. Adherence to all applicable laws, regulations, and business practices in any jurisdiction is the sole responsibility of the purchaser or reader.

All product and company names are trademarks™ or registered® trademarks of their respective holders. Use of them does not imply any affiliation with or endorsement by them.

Names, company names, characters, places, and incidents either are the products of the author's imagination or are used fictitiously. Any resemblance to actual persons, living or dead, businesses, companies, events, or locales is entirely coincidental.

Bonus Scripts And Materials
Thanks for your purchase. I'm offering 25 scripts (Set the appointments, objection response, gatekeeper, voicemail, and email) and additional supplemental material to readers of this book. You can access this information free at
https://www.scottchannell.com/STM-book-extras

Introduction

Sell The Meeting

Sell a meeting, and you have a chance to sell a new account.
No meeting? No chance to close a new account.

The buyers are out there. They are meeting with, evaluating and signing checks to others, right now, and they haven't met you.

For many, when you or your team can get a meeting or discovery call, you can close.
But if you can't get in...

The good news is that some industries and many sales reps are very good at setting sales appointments, discovery calls, and demos. There is no reason why you or your team can't do the same.

This guide is about two things.

1. How to earn attention and interactions with top decision makers within accounts that are clones of your best accounts.

2. When you earn that often momentary attention, communicating something substantial enough to enable someone who is going to write a big check to conclude you are worth more of their time.

That's it.

Work a system that gives you the opportunity to pitch a top dog. Then don't screw it up when you do. Have something worthwhile to say.

I set more than 2,000 C-level sales appointments. My paycheck used to depend upon setting appointments that ended up closing in both B2B and B2C markets — still training teams and coaching reps on these strategies 25 years later.

Learned how by sitting in a cube, dialing the phone and experiencing the monotony, frustration, and euphoria of high-level sales prospecting. I have seen what works in many environments and adapted to the changes over time.

What used to be a true "cold call" is now a process of interaction which includes multiple touch points and technologies.

The buyers are out there.
Let's get em.

Scott Channell

Table Of Contents

Part One
Before You Even Think Of Calling

1. Introduction: No First Meeting, No Close   1
2. Why Do This?   11
3. 31 Key Drivers   23

Part Two
Setting Up Your System

4. Six Core Concepts   55
5. Know Your Goals   59
6. Selecting Your Targets   65
7. CRM/Contact Manager Setup   79
8. Call Process   95
9. Your "Pile of Words"   105

Part Three
Messaging And Phone Script Paths

10. Crafting Your Scripts   117
11. Your "Identify the Decision-Maker" Script   129
12. Your "Set The Meeting" Script   135

13. Your Voicemail Scripts   149

14. Sample Email Touches   153

15. Objection Response Concepts   161

16. Objection Responses   171

Part Four

A Day In The Life Of An Appointment Setter

17. Intro: Managing Your Day   187

18. Your Launches: Part One Of Your Day   191

19. Your Follow-Ups: Part Two Of Your Day   199

20. Spending More Time With Those Worth More Time: Part Three Of Your Day   207

21. Calling A Suspect: From First Call To Last   209

Part Five

Beyond The Call

22. What If It Is Not Working   229

23. How To Find A Good Appointment Setter   239

24. Compensation and Incentive Systems   245

25. Management and Marketing Integration   253

26. Selling With House Money: Do You Make More Sales By Focusing On Overall Process Or Individual Outcomes?   265

27. Managing Your "Sales Debt"   273

28. Tips From Top Appointment Setters   277

Set 3,022 meetings

"Our CEO announced a goal to become a national player in the managed service space within banking, healthcare, and manufacturing. We had a great solution set and best-of-breed engineers who could deliver. Like many companies, however, we hadn't yet cracked the code on how to get our consultants in front of enough decision-makers. I was the inside sales manager of a newly hired team and had no idea how to obtain these meetings. Fortunately, I read Scott's first book, "Setting Sales Appointments" and in December 2009 started religiously leveraging the system outlined in those pages. By September 2013 we had set 3022 meetings, 85% of which were with C-level decision-makers. We also saw less than a 13% cancellation rate. AMAZING! Those stellar results and the substantial business that followed happened because we stayed true to the process, made adjustments along the way, and a lot of hard work. This process helped us overcome hurdles such as efficiently identifying decision-makers, getting past gatekeepers, and turning "Call me back" responses into meetings. With this book, you will avoid some very costly mistakes. It is an expansion and update of the strategies that worked so well for us. I highly recommend this book to anyone engaged in a high-ticket complex multi-step sales process. No matter how good you are, you are not going to make a sale if you can't sell the first meeting.

-MORGAN CHAPMAN

Essential for the salesperson in today's market

I am happy to write this, my third recommendation for Scott's effective and motivating books. All salespeople go through downturns in their business, and all suffer from the negativity that is brought to the table, sometimes by the very person we are selling to. Scott teaches how to overcome those stages and prosper. The hard copy can be marked and used over and over again. All said this is the one book that I would consider an essential for the salesperson in today's market, no matter what you sell.

-STEPHEN SCHIFFMAN, AUTHOR OF 53 BOOKS ON SALES AND SELLING TECHNIQUES

We noticed closing rates increase an average of 16 – 34%

Scott Channell's sales strategies have been instrumental in building my career. His no-nonsense approach to script writing and making the most of every touch has been duplicable and easy to train. While working with my sales team, we noticed closing rates increase an average of 16– 34%. Those who applied Scott's approach were making appointments and closing sales. Scott knocks it out of the park with this book. He is masterful in handling questions and getting the appointment. You can feel the authenticity of Scott and the sincerity in his words. It's obvious that Scott has done this work. My team and I have tested his techniques and they work!!
Of all the sales books I have read, this is the best!

-EVIE DiPIAZZA, VP BUSINESS DEVELOPMENT, LANTZ TECHNOLOGIES GROUP, FORMER VP BUSINESS DEVELOPMENT, IPEC COACHING

Helped us grow at +20% in an industry that is flat

Inside sales have always been the thorn in the side of our business… until we worked with Scott Channell! Scott's book and his consulting advice allowed us to create a system that works! Now we have a top notch A+ inside sales division of our company, and that has helped us grow at +20% in an industry that is flat. Scott's system WORKS!

As an added benefit, we have found that it is easier to attract and keep inside salespeople when they are working in a proven system. Good people know this.

If you want to dramatically outgrow the competition, read the book and implement the Scott Channell program. It'll be the best investment you have ever made for your business.

-DOMINIC GENTILE, CEO

Grown from three hundred customers to over nine hundred

I would highly recommend your methodology to any company that has an inside sales function. Before adopting your processes and training materials nine years ago, our inside sales function felt like they were trapped in the endless cycle of trying to find that needle in the haystack. Lots of frustration. We now have a consistent process to continuously identify high-value leads (the customers that we really want) and a trackable touch system that is effective in persuading potential customers to give us a face to face meeting. The results speak for themselves. We have grown from three hundred customers to over nine hundred."

-DAVID T. BURNS, PRESIDENT OF SALES

Our appointments skyrocketed, and it helped lead us to national recognition within our organization

After 10+ years of business to business sales and sales management, I knew something had to change. I was living the definition of insanity with my appointment setting team. I got tired of beating my head against the wall and decided to think outside of the box for a solution, not just another band aid! I hit the internet one night and found Scott Channell. I was peaked with curiosity as I read the Amazon description of his first book "Setting Sales Appointments," so I ordered it thinking I had nothing to lose.

Much to my delight upon reading the book, I found myself intrigued by Scott's No Nonsense No BS approach and although I initially disagreed with some of his methods, I was forced to look in the mirror and say, "What do I have to lose?"

I used Scott's formulas and examples to sculpt killer custom crafted scripts just for my team, utilizing my companies strengths and differentiators.

CONFESSIONS OF A SOUTHERN GIRL: I was convinced that "sales are different in the south," so I was a little (or a LOT) skeptical about a few of Scott's ideas, but I'm now a believer! I had to be willing to humble myself a little to either prove myself right or wrong and let me say ... I've never been so happy to be wrong. Feeling right doesn't pay the bills; success does!

By consistently applying Scott's methods and dedicating myself to rebuilding my inside sales/ appointment setting program around this system, our appointments skyrocketed, and it helped lead us to national recognition within our organization.

This book "Sell The Meeting" is an updated and expanded version of his first book which helped my team so much. I highly recommend it.

-SUNDAE SISCO JOHNSON, VP SALES

Taught me his "3 Cycles of 3" call process and the importance of "ear candy"

Using the strategies in this book, I learned the importance of a script to deliver my message like a crystal clear radio advertisement—no more rambling or being caught off guard by objections. Instead of getting bogged down and demoralized by "being persistent," I learned about "diminishing returns." Scott taught me his "3 cycles of 3" call process and the importance of "ear candy" to showcase my offering. Prospects are bombarded with sales calls making it easy for ours to get lost in the shuffle. Dusting yourself off and getting back on the phone is a fraction of what is required to succeed; leveraging Scott's insights from booking meetings with more than 2,000 C-Suite Executives is the balance. It is the X Factor that will propel you to stand out and shine."

-SEAN FISET, VICE PRESIDENT, DEVENCORE, COMMERCIAL REAL ESTATE INDUSTRY

Whether you're getting on the phone or your team is getting on the phone, get this book

I hadn't been this scared since I was in a foxhole watching machine guns shoot at enemy aircraft. No, I wasn't in combat. At least not the death-and-destruction kind.

This was the combat of business. And my enemy was the telephone. Anyone not trying to sell you on the latest social media scam will tell you that the telephone is the single greatest weapon in the War of Business. And anyone who's said "will that be Visa, Master Card, or AMEX" on the phone knows the fear that can get the best of the strongest of people. For me, staring at that phone was like staring down the business end of an AK-47. I could either fight through or get some help. I'm no dummy - so I got help.

I bought Scott's stuff, trained my people, and got to ring the register in less time than I could have ever done on my own. Look, it's not complicated. Forget all the fancy stuff. It's just math! Do the math. You'll see that the telephone beats any social media, digital wizardry BS all day (and twice on Sunday). Whether you're getting on the phone or your team is getting on the phone, get this book.

-MACEO JOURDAN

Time-tested and extremely effective

Scott Channell's strategies and methods are time-tested and extremely effective. Technology may change, but his proven philosophy has not. He has helped me build a plan over the years to increase engagement and sales while developing a daily prospecting strategy to stay focused.

-SEAN FITZGERALD, LIAISON INTERNATIONAL

Insights hit me like a soft surprise snowball in the face

Scott's insights hit me like a soft surprise snowball in the face. His perspectives changed my views on sales prospecting and lead generation. From the impact of credibility to helping prospects open-up about their needs, to who should even be on your radar in the first place – no one has impacted my professional career more. If you've been struggling with sales prospecting these strategies will put you on a successful path.

-RICHARD SLATER, MARKETING DIRECTOR

The only one who has actually practiced what he preaches

If you sell B2B…and want to deploy a sales process that produces real results and real income…you need to read Scott Channell's latest and greatest book. I've read literally hundreds of "sales" books over the years, and Channell is the only one who has actually practiced what he preaches (writes)! Using Scott's processes, I have built a very successful direct mail marketing business. We all get sales burn out occasionally, so when that happens I go back to the well and re-read Scott's books…it's like a double shot latte.

-FRANK FURGIUELE, CHIEF REVENUE OFFICER,
SOS DIRECT MARKETING

Steadily rose to within the top 10 producers of an over 250 member global salesforce

A few years ago, I switched from an operations role to a role that required marketing and sales. I found the plentiful advice from well-meaning friends and colleagues to be of little help towards creating the sales process I needed to find desirable prospects and convert them to customers. Luckily, I came upon the strategies and techniques taught by Scott Channell. Using his methods, I steadily rose to within the top 10 producers of an over 250 member global salesforce.

Scott has consolidated his teachings into his new book, "Sell the Meeting - Set Discovery Calls & Sales Appointments To Close New Accounts." It's a powerful but easy book to read. If you're involved in selling and desire stronger outcomes, Scott's book is filled with multiple examples demonstrating the right and wrong way to apply your craft.

-WM. DAVID LEVESQUE, PRESIDENT,
LEAN PERFORMANCE DEVELOPMENT, INC.

Directly contributed to the 5X growth of our organization

Our company has used a combination of Scott's materials and in-person consulting to grow and develop our prospecting programs. Scott has provided systems, materials and coaching that we have implemented and stood by for many years, and have directly contributed to the 5X growth of our organization. Qualified appointments with potential buyers are the lifeblood of our company, and Scott's methods have had a substantial contribution to the steady growth of our opportunity pipeline. We would highly recommend this book to anyone looking for guidance on how to generate first meetings with solid prospects.

-MATTHEW WARRILOW,
DIRECTOR OF SALES & MARKETING

A must-have resource for anyone in B2B sales

Scott Channell did it again. Sell the Meeting is a must-have resource for anyone in B2B sales! Follow what he teaches and getting meetings with the top decision-makers will become second nature.

-GEORGE ATHAN, AUTHOR OF CLIENT MACHINE

Salespeople will quickly value the step-by-step framework

The Master of Scripts, Scott Channell does it again! In, "Sell The Meeting," Channell loans salespeople of all walks, decades of successful and proven techniques for pinning down meetings and securing appointments with ideal clients. Eager salespeople will quickly value the step-by-step framework that Channell lays out clearly; from what to say, to how to say it; and even how often and by what means. A "must-have" for any Sales VP to invest in for their sales forces!

-JAKE WEGNER, VICE PRESIDENT OF SALES

Bulk Orders And Customization
This book is available at a discount when purchased in bulk for corporate use or sales promotions. In larger quantities, this book can be modified with customized covers, content, and corporate logos. For information, go to
ScottChannell.com or call 978-296-2700.

Speaking, Training, Coaching
Scott Channell is available for speaking engagements, training sessions and executive coaching.
See ScottChannell.com for contact information.

Bonus Scripts And Materials
Thanks for your purchase. I'm offering 25 scripts (Set the appointments, objection response, gatekeeper, voicemail, and email) and additional supplemental material to readers of this book. You can access this information free at
https://www.scottchannell.com/STM-book-extras

Dedication And Acknowledgments

To Sadie and Anna
For The Endless Joy They Bring

Thank you ...

To the many clients, sales pros and colleagues who have collaborated with me and provided the opportunity to practice the craft of sales.

To Bonnie Lizotte for her exceptional organizational skills and ability to keep the office humming.

To Beth White for constant support and encouragement.

Cover Design by Al Feuerstein
Editing by Gail Lowe

In Memoriam
Troy Duguay
An accomplished entrepreneur, family man
and a genuinely nice guy.

Chapter 1
No First Meeting?
No Close.

Why a System for First Sales Conversations?

Because when you can get a substantive first interaction with decision-makers, you can close accounts.

No first meeting? No first sales conversation?
No close.

For many businesses, the core of gaining net new business starts with gaining access to those that drive strategy, make decisions, sign checks. For those businesses, the key is to sell the meeting.

For others, the ability to set meetings may be a small part of a larger marketing plan. They may use these tactics a bit more strategically. They may seek to set discovery calls to gain a foothold or more market share in strategically important verticals. Or, to land a few larger sized accounts. Maybe to temporarily provide leads if other marketing methods are falling short.

Whether it is core to your "close new business" efforts or just part of a larger plan, you need to do it right.

Without a system to get shoulder to shoulder with top dogs within "A" type prospect opportunities, you spend a lot of time with mid-level "Seymours." Managers who don't drive decision-making and can't cut checks.

Many invest time booking discovery calls or face-to-face first meetings and fail. You can invest time with drastically different results if you have a system that works.

That is what this book is all about. Giving you the core strategies and walking you through a step by step process of creating a workable system to book first sales conversations.

What You Can Do With This System

Meet with more of those referred to you.
Meet with more people who could make referrals to you.
Meet with more current accounts to renew them, sell them more, generate referrals.
Meet with dormant accounts to reactivate them.
Close more strategically valuable accounts.
Gain entry into new verticals.
Gain access and close more "whales." Accounts that buy volume and generate a disproportionate share of profits.

And oh yeah, almost forget, this system will help you get more appointments with "strangers." People/companies that have never heard of you, don't know you and have not referred.

Strangers that will write checks to you and be grateful to have found a capable service provider that delivers value.

Strangers That Are Clones Of Your Best Accounts

You want to work a process that enables you to meet buyers within accounts that look just like your best accounts.

This same system can be used to meet with dormant accounts, referrals and those that could refer. The same set of skills, call process, script structures, touch system and follow-up that works with strangers is what you will use to resell, cross-sell, reactivate, close those referred and generate more referrals.

Some of you will use this system in start-up situations looking for those very important first clients. Some of you will have in-house teams and feel a need to lift results.

Some of you used to be able to depend upon personal networks and referral sources for new accounts, but those sources don't generate what they used to. Now you need to reach out to strangers.

The system is the same in all these circumstances. Different circumstances might mean more or less emphasis on steps within the system. But it is the same system.

SELL THE MEETING

The Elephant In The Room

Calling stinks. Cold outreach stinks.

The good news is that a lot of people do it successfully, so there is no need to reinvent the wheel.

The bad news is that once you discover what works, you have to do it. Over and over again.

It's boring. Repetitive. When you mix repetitive tasks with really smart people, you have a recipe for disaster.

To consistently set sales appointments, you are going to have to make phone calls, leave messages and send emails. You won't want to, and any activity other than dialing the phone will be more important than making calls. That is a reality.

I teach the process but do not love making calls. Even after all these years I still don't. But if you take a deep breath, if you just follow the process for 60-90 minutes at a time, good stuff results. You have conversations with top people. Some agree to meet now or tell you when to be back in touch. Some return your calls, emails, and touches. You get "recon" info on the needs and plans of those you call. You start to fill your pipeline and close deals.

The best advice I can give you is to acknowledge the beast. Calling stinks.

If You Have Other Marketing Tools, Use Them.

If you have other options that will deliver the meetings you need, I recommend you put them in play. If you don't have options, or if your options won't deliver what you need then you will have to make calls.

No calls. No opportunities. No closed deals.

Aside from the fear of consequences if you don't sell enough, there is something else that should provide an incentive for you to set appointments. There are a lot of buyers out there. There are a lot of companies and individuals that are right now buying what you offer from others. There is no good reason why they wouldn't buy from you.

Right now there are active qualified prospects of what you offer looking for the right provider. They are gathering information, meeting with competitors, evaluating their options. Right now.

It is the most normal and natural thing in the world for these future buyers to meet with you. It is the most normal and natural thing in the world for you to ask them to do so.

You Are Doing Them A Favor By Reaching Out

Assuming that you have a quality offering, you are doing them a favor by doing so. Many of these buyers will make the wrong decision. They will choose to work with a company not as good as yours, select a product or service not equal to yours. They will get less value for their time and money, and they will suffer the consequences of not being fully informed on all their options and factors relevant to their buy decision.

Why? Why will they select a less worthy competitor or offering? They didn't meet you. That's why. You didn't call at all. You didn't reach out. If you did try, your effort was partial, haphazard, and your value message fell short.

Fear of the consequences of no sales or few sales should drive you partially, but the biggest motivator should be that there are buyers out there. They are buying from someone else right now because they never met you.

Lots of people set sales appointments and discovery calls effectively. That wheel has been invented.

Take it step by step. Get comfortable with a few steps at a time before you move on to the next. Within 4-6 weeks you will be coordinating a total process of touching top-level decision-makers that will lead to more meetings, better meetings, more closed deals.

Shortly, when you ask, "Would you have some time in the next week or two?" you will hear... "sure."

B2B vs. B2C. Companies vs. Individuals

Common misnomers of high-level prospecting are that what works B2B won't work B2C, that what works for companies won't work for individuals, that what works for big companies won't work for smaller companies, what works in one industry won't work in another. What works in the South won't work in the North. That companies on the left side of the street are different from those on the right side of the street.

SELL THE MEETING

All 100% wrong.

I set more than 2,000 C-Level sales appointments with pure cold calling, just smiling, and dialing. B2B. B2C. All sorts of industries, big and small companies. The process to gain access to top-level decision-makers is remarkably the same.

There are nuances to every project, but what drives success are the core strategies and behaviors acted upon consistently.

Get your core engine up and running powerfully first. Get experience and comfortable with foundation practices and behaviors before you even start to think about exceptions to the rules.

The "Cold Call" Has Been Slurred.

"Cold call" is not a four-letter word. It is two four-letter words.

It is a tool. A step in a process. Neither good or bad.

Like any marketing tool, it is right to use in some spots, not others.

Like other marketing tools, mail, email, PPC, TV, radio, postcards, dancing hotdogs and clowns holding signs on street corners, it works when used in the right places and is a disaster when used in the wrong places.

No marketing tool is right for everyone. If you use a marketing tool, use it right.

If you ignore the lessons learned and science of direct mail and send out lousy letters to the wrong people, you are not entitled to conclude that mail is dead. If you send out lousy emails, it is not correct for you to conclude that email is dead. And if you make phone calls as part of a prospecting process and suck at it, as many do, you are not entitled to state that "cold calling is dead."

A "cold call" is part of the appointment setting process. It is not THE process. Using this resource, when you reach out you will be doing it right.

What Has Changed In The World Of Appointment Setting

When I started to set sales appointments in 1994, it truly was "cold calling." The decision-maker either picked up the phone or didn't. I pitched them. They agreed to meet with a representative of my client or they didn't.

That was about it.

That was how it started, but that is not how it ended. Over the years as I made tens of thousands of calls the core process that worked was improved. Yes, it started with a "cold call" but also came to include "recon" questions, call back strategies, follow-up methods, plan "B" strategies, and much more. By the time I wrote the book "Setting Sales Appointments" in 2004, it was a total system of interaction and follow-up. To say it was merely cold calling would be a misnomer.

But, A Few Things Have Changed

It has become in vogue to declare that there are "new" rules of selling. "What used to work doesn't matter," say many. The great unwashed are quick to conclude that you can throw out everything that used to work. "Today it is a brand new ballgame with new methods, techniques, and strategies." What crap and a disservice to sales professionals.

Can you tell I feel strongly that selling is a craft? You learn it. You practice, practice, practice it. You try, you test, you fail, you try again, you learn. You don't make the same mistakes two, three, or four times. That experience gives you a decided advantage when new technologies come along or the selling environment changes.

Realize something about top producers with today's "new" rules. Most of them were the top producers under the old rules — skill and experience matter.

Before the Great Recession, when the economy was lifting all boats, there were a lot of order takers, talkers, and yappers walking around making money, thinking they were solid salespeople.

But then things changed, and the order-takers, who thought they were salespeople, didn't have the skill set to adapt and change. They didn't have the depth of knowledge and experience even to survive, never mind excel in new realities. But guess what? The top producers under the "old" rules survived and many thrived under the new realities.

Having A Firm Grasp Of Selling Fundamentals Is Critical To Success

If you are smart, capable, hard-working, and just not getting the traction you need with sales prospecting and sales conversion, salvation will not be some flavor of the month, a new idea, or finding the one thing that will save you (the answer is never one thing. It is always multiple things coordinated well.)

The root cause of poor performance is often lack of mastery of the basics. I see far more quantum leaps in sales productivity when people and companies take a step back to reassess, rebuild, and make sure the basics are right than I do because they jumped on the latest greatest new idea that just went viral.

Doing The Basics Right Provides More Quantum Leaps Than "New" Strategies Or Technologies

New ideas are not worth spit if you have not mastered the basics and are implementing them, practicing them, improving them consistently. You build upon strong foundations. You build upon the basics.

Why this rant? Because there are two things very significant that has changed in selling that you must be prepared to confront head-on when you seek to gain access to top decision- makers.

First, your best prospects are better informed. They are just a few keystrokes away from the information they need to solve their problems. With a quick, easy online search, they can identify qualified vendors and consultants they feel are worth their time.

Second, your prospects don't trust you. They have had too much time wasted and been snookered too often with fake sincerity, overstated claims, and half-truths. Unless you are perceived to be rock solid and head and shoulders above the rest, the risk/reward calculus works against you.

Why Should They Spend Time With You - A Person Or Company They Don't Know?

Why should they take the risk, again, that some unknown entity will be worth their time when fairly quickly they can let their fingers do the walking over their keyboard and find top-notch credible vendor options worth a meeting?

They won't unless you give them very good reasons to do so.

They can easily, or have already, identified some potential vendors, suppliers, consultants that they feel will meet their needs well. Why should they meet with you and take the chance that you will waste their time?

That is what has changed.

It doesn't mean that you use a totally new approach to get face to face with buyers. It means that you do what used to work, but you do it better, and you have to go deeper into the process to get sustainable results.

Build Upon The Basics And What Used To Work. Do It Better To Thrive In New Realities.

Under the "old" rules it was important that you pick the right suspects to call. Today, your suspect pool has to be even tighter to win.

Under the "old" rules you had to use a contact manager or CRM. Today, not only must you use one, but you must set it up with custom fields, segmentation coding, template documents, emails, and automated follow-up.

In the "old days" you could be far less than perfect with your scripting, how you communicated credibility and value, and the interaction process you used, and still get results. In the old days, you could still be sloppy and make money — not today. Your messaging, your call process, the efficiency with which you work has to be better and much tighter to set appointments today. There is far less wiggle room if you are not totally prepared, very efficient, and quickly and succinctly communicate value and credibility.

For those you discover are your very top prospects, they are worth more of your time and money. For that very top segment of prospecting targets, it is wise to integrate other marketing tools, both offline and online, to gain access and establish credibility and value. Tools and marketing methods that would not make economic sense among average or lower value targets generate high ROI when used with higher value targets identified through your calling efforts.

Value Communication

Perceptions of greater value are necessary today. What you say must have even more impact. If you are perceived to be "another one," you are toast. You must communicate more credibility and benefits than the rest, or your prospect will let their fingers do the walking over their keyboards to select potential new vendor options.

SELL THE MEETING

Messaging. You only had a few seconds to convey your message under the old rules. With the new rules, you have fewer seconds. Scripting structures and word selection were always important. Today there is even less room for the vague, the ordinary and yada, yada, yada.

Resolve to be exceptional at the fundamentals, and you can be a top producer in this "new" age of selling. Master the basics, and you can build upon them to move from the bottom of the pack to the middle, from an average producer to a top producer.

If you skip the basics, you are building on sand. If you follow the herd, you will get mediocrity at best; you will be doomed to again and again trying the latest "new" thing that changes it all or the "one thing" that will make all the difference. Your personal results needle won't move. You will still be in the middle or near the bottom of the pack.

Awareness and mastery of the basics of appointment setting can drive a sales advantage. With a solid foundation in place, you can adapt and thrive in almost any environment.

Let's review the basics.

Then let's build upon them.

Worksheets, additional scripts, and periodic updates
are available to readers of this book at
ScottChannell.com/STM-book-extras

Chapter 2
Why Do This?

How You and Your Team Benefit From a System that Generates Appointments and Discovery Calls

Quality appointments and discovery calls improve your forecasts, budgeting, cash flow, and profit margin.

You avoid sales peaks and valleys.
You don't miss out on opportunities anymore.
You can reduce reliance upon your personal network and referral sources.
You can generate qualified leads from strangers when leads from your personal network and referral sources slow down.
You add another tool to your sales toolkit.
You cross the prospecting chasm.
You gain control over your sales life.
You gain value from those who are unreachable or have no immediate need.
High-value prospects will start to call you.
Your close ratio improves.
You can easily follow-up for future sales.
You can scale faster.
You have another way to interact with top prospects.
You improve the mix of your interaction.

Bottom line, being able to set qualified discovery calls and face-to-face first sales conversations generates more accounts, revenue, profits, and higher margins.

When your other marketing and social media efforts are not delivering, you have another option: Go directly to the buyers.

Let us review all the benefits that come to us when we can consistently and cost-effectively generate substantive first sales conversations, with the person who can authorize a check that would clone our best and most profitable clients.

You Avoid Peaks And Valleys

How many times have you had this problem? You either have more business than you can handle or are dying for dollars. When you are in that boom or bust cycle, something very bad is happening.

When you're dying for dollars you take business you should not take; you make price concessions you shouldn't make, and you make promises for delivery and quality that are unrealistic — a guarantee of dissatisfied clients, more client churn, and lower profits.

When you're in a rush to book business, you often short-circuit your production or service processes. Before you know it, you have no processes, just chaos. The odds of a dissatisfied client and unexpected problems go way up.

When you can generate a steady stream of first sales conversations, you won't feel pressure to cut your profit margin to seal a deal. You won't be tempted to make unrealistic promises or work outside of your service delivery systems.

You Won't Miss Out On Opportunities Anymore

Good clients are just waiting for your call. Great clients are searching their emails for messages from you. But you are nowhere to be found.

A sad reality is that there are a lot of really great accounts out there, buying from competitors unaware that you exist. They don't know you.

So they buy from a competitor that provides them with less value.

They don't know the benefits you deliver or how credible you are. They don't know what you can do for them. It is only that lack of knowledge that is denying them the opportunity to benefit from your services.

You didn't identify them or get their attention. You were not there at the right time.

SELL THE MEETING

If you did speak to them or get their attention briefly, your messaging did not adequately communicate your value or credibility. That opportunity to clone your best accounts was lost at "hello."

Those great prospective accounts, soon to choose a new vendor, will not have the opportunity to work with you. A provider they would have been thrilled with.

You lost the opportunity for a great account who would pay well and provide a steady stream of profits for you over a long period. Simply because you were not there or did not communicate sufficient reason for a next step when you had the chance.

You Can Move Beyond Your Personal Network and Referral Sources

This is a call I get a lot.

Companies that have grown and done very well relying on repeat business, word-of-mouth, their personal networks, and referral sources now have to reach out to strangers for new business.

Sometimes the repeat business slows down. The referrals just don't come in like they used to. The marketing that used to work does not deliver what's needed anymore. Sometimes the Rolodex and personal network have no more to give.

Now what?
Talk to strangers?
Yikes.

What is sufficient to close a deal with those who know you or referred to you will not close a deal with strangers.

What you said to get a meeting with those familiar with you will not be enough with strangers. You will need to move through a larger group of targets systematically to have any chance of success. You will have to **prepare** new things to say. Strangers will cut you loose much faster if they don't perceive value. This will be new to you. Working a new process will not be easy. You will need to be disciplined in ways you never had to be.

But the good news is that the methods of gaining traction with companies or with people who could be great accounts have been invented. It is rooted in rock solid basic marketing and sales principles that can be learned. Lots of companies and individual reps are doing it well.

You Add Another Tool to Your Sales Tool Kit

Outreach to set appointments and discovery calls is not for everyone. It's not for every business. It makes sense in some places and is foolish in others.

For some businesses being able to set discovery calls or in-person appointments is the core of new business development. For others, it is just part of a larger picture.

For those of you new to this, you add another option to your sales and marketing kit. For those of you already setting appointments, you get to sharpen a tool you are already using.

Think of appointment setting as a tool to be used as needed. You might use it very strategically to infiltrate a new vertical. You might use it to avert trouble when business slows down. You might use it day in and day out as the core of your new business process.

It is neither good nor bad. It is a tool.
Use it if it is the tool you need.
Use it in the right place.
If you use it, use it correctly.

You Cross The Prospecting Chasm

When you implement an appointment setting system that works, here's what happens every single time. In about six weeks, you will have booked a ton of good solid appointments. But you'll also create a problem.

Not only do you have to prospect for appointments, but you also have to show up at their office or conduct those calls. And then, because they are good, worthwhile appointments with qualified people who can afford your product or service, you are going to end up going back 2, 3 or 4 times to close a substantial size deal.

SELL THE MEETING

And once you book the business, of course, you have to service it.

You will shortly have to cross the "Prospecting Chasm" where you have to prospect, sell, and service accounts. It is extremely tough for you to do all three functions superbly.

You have to be very focused and ruthless about weeding out the "no's" and the "maybe's." You also have to be very good at time management. At some point, you may have to delegate substantially most (if not all) of your appointment setting and generating discovery call functions to a lower level person who can perform those tasks adequately. You may not believe this person can prospect as well as you. They don't have to. They only have to prospect adequately.

You'll have to consider that as an option down the road. If you set up a system that generates plenty of opportunities for your pipeline but only you can set the appointments, your whole prospecting system will collapse. You're just not going to have enough time to prospect, sell, and service. Prepare for this.

Gain Control Over Your Sales Life

You are in charge. Not your prospects. Not your clients. You.

When somebody wants you to take 10% off, or they threaten to go to a lower priced competitor, you'll tell them to take that deal. You won't care.

When somebody asks you for impossible delivery times or tells you that they have expectations that are not realistic, you'll walk away. You have lost nothing but problems and headaches.

You'll have the option to drop small accounts that are a pain in your neck. Cast aside the low-margin accounts you currently service.

You see, when you know (really know) and have confidence that new leads and inquiries will continue to come on schedule as a result of your system, you're going to be far more selective about whom you choose to do business with. You'll know from experience that a certain percentage of those leads, inquiries, and appointments/calls will convert to new accounts.

You'll know how long it will take and what the average size and profit margin of those new accounts will be. You'll have a base of experience from which you can intelligently allocate your time to gain the highest return. You will have the confidence to say "no" to business that isn't what you want.

Time Allocation Is Key

As you develop a steady stream of inquiries and appointments, you will learn which are most likely to convert to profitable accounts. You can make a conscious decision as to where to allocate your time for best results.

Maybe there will be a certain segment of your market that contains longer term, larger revenue more prestigious type accounts. You will identify these prospects, and you will decide how much time to devote to them.

There may be another class of account consisting mainly of your mid-range, bread and butter type clients that can be counted on for decent profit and revenue regularly. You will decide how much time to spend on those accounts.

You may have yet another class of business account that sucks every bit of mental energy and motivation out of your business because you constantly have to listen to complaints, whines, and impossible demands while working for mini-money or no profits at all. You will learn to identify, avoid, and discard these bloodsuckers.

You Will Gain Value From Those That Are Unreachable Or Have No Immediate Need

This concept is a major factor in managing an appointment setting process that works and generates qualified appointments consistently over time. If you do not fully leverage all the value you can obtain from your calling efforts; you leave a lot of money on the table.

What do you do with the majority of people you cannot initially reach? What do you do with the majority of people who you do reach, yet don't immediately agree to see you? Are those calls wasted? Far from it.

SELL THE MEETING

When I started setting appointments with high-level decision-makers in the mid-1990s, the game was simple. Call targeted organizations. Identify the top decision-maker, and get them on the phone. Then slay them with a powerful 30-second script. They either agreed to a meeting, or they didn't. That was it. Next.

There were very simple short-term economics to meet. I had to book enough appointments that would convert within a reasonable time, to an acceptable average sale, so that the prospecting efforts would justify the time and money invested.

But, over some time, as I tracked what was happening, I realized that in a big-ticket sales environment most people I tried to contact were unreachable. Most people I did speak with said "no." I also realized that many of those people, within a reasonable period, would have a need and be prime candidates for the services or products my clients had to offer.

A very big part of appointment setting success is determining which targets are qualified or not — determining if they are of "A" value (your highest potential value range) or lie on the opposite side of the spectrum. You want to find out if they are "E" value, likely below an acceptable value range so that you waste no further resources on them. And of course, you have "B" (above average,) "C" (average) and "D" (below average, but acceptable) values in between.

You are making the calls anyway. You must have a strategy and make an effort to determine the potential worth of those you call, **even when you do not speak to your target.**

More on this later, but here is a top tip. As important as it is to identify qualified and high potential worth accounts, it is even more important that you proactively identify and stop investing time with low or no potential value accounts as early as you can.

And when you hear "no," "no," no" from a decision-maker within a qualified account, does that end it? Nope. Many of those that say "no" will write major checks to a competitor within 3 to 15 months. How many times has it happened that you prospect someone that says "no," "we are all set," or "we love our vendor" only to call back 6 months later to find out they just switched and you just missed the chance? It has happened to all of us. Oh well.

A big part of success is enabling those who say "get lost" now, to invite you to call in the future. You need to have a strategy for that. And let me say this, the strategy is not saying "OK, can I call back and check in in a few months?" Only a prospecting knucklehead would say that. Stay tuned.

Higher Value Prospects Will Start To Call You

You should think of your set the appointment get the discovery call system as part of an overall effective means to cost-effectively generate solid opportunities and meet your goals for business growth and profitability.

When you invest time and effort into a well set up system, you will book more appointments and discovery calls. You will also, if you are doing things right, identify companies that have above average value and some that have plans to buy what you offer shortly. At times you get the double whammy. A company that has above average value potential and shares that they will be reviewing vendor options within a few months.

So as you call, call, call, and your pot of qualified targets with above average value grows larger and larger, what do you do? Just call them back sometime? Not if you want to make mad money and fat stacks.

With very little additional work (and very little expense, I might add), this system is going to enable you to easily and cost-effectively manage a communication system that will have prospects calling you when they have a need.

Inexpensive, consistent touches delivered to a high-value, high-probability audience will generate you outsized rewards for a small additional investment of time and money. Even simple letters, well written and sent out consistently, deliver major rewards when targeted to that very small segment of your target group that has the most value and potential.

Those marketing strategies that were duds when shotgunned into a larger group. When you rifle shot them into the right places, it is ka-ching and ka-ching.

SELL THE MEETING

Your Prospects Can Be Qualified, High-Value And Be Calling You

When people are touched by you consistently over some time, they become better educated about the benefits you can provide them. When they hear a consistent message over that period, you create a perception of credibility in their eyes.

Who do people buy from? Those they are comfortable with and trust. Comfort and trust are not created overnight. It takes interaction. It takes time: basic marketing and common-sense 101.

Those you identify that have the highest potential value and those that indicate a buy decision shortly are worth a little more time and effort. To get the full value for your efforts, you must be set up to deliver "touches" consistently to this group.

They should hear from you consistently. Good prospects will come to recognize your name and perceive you as a potentially valuable and worthwhile resource. They will think of you and call you when they have a need. They will be more receptive to meeting you when ready to buy.

Your Close Ratio Improves

Better closing ratios are determined, in part, by the quality of the prospects, the quality of the sales process, and the quality of the messaging.

To set appointments and discovery calls effectively you need a crystal clear vision of your top value highest probability targets. You are no more trying to dial faster among the sludge pile trying to find too few qualified prospects. You need to fully develop all the most important verbiage, name drops, reasons why people buy, success stories, benefits, proofs, and more, so that at the moment of truth when you have mere moments to activate something positive in the minds of top prospects, you can relate verbiage that most powerfully communicates your value.

The sad truth is that many companies are spending far too much time calling the less worthy. Far too many companies have stats, stories, benefits, specifics, name drops, and more that would communicate their value very effectively, yet this verbiage is sat on, not used. All of your top verbiages must be brought to the surface and used throughout the prospecting and sales process. You will hear more about this "pile of words" later.

One prospecting intervention for a $100 million company with 27 salespeople had a nice little side benefit. Within a few months, the closing ratio of this team increased by 25%. With another, the team jumped from a 30% closing ratio to 60%. It wasn't that I was so great.

The process introduced to you in this book helped them to infiltrate a much higher percentage of their ideal target group and get in front of the top decision-makers. Because they were in front of higher quality prospects, this client got more practice and became more proficient at each step of the sales process. They focused on what to do at a first meeting to advance a sale, how to better cross-sell, how to best avoid and respond to resistance, and how to improve proposals. If you get more appointments with widget sellers, you get better at knowing what to do to advance and close a widget deal every step of the way.

Plus, all that great stuff about problems they solve, benefits, success stories that existed but were not used before? They were all written down in the "pile of words" to be used by all.

You Can Easily Follow Up

The one thing I hear again and again and again from salespeople and management is: "I don't have the time to follow up."

No offense. But it is just downright wasteful and insane to spend all that time smiling and dialing, asking questions and collecting information to identify top targets to not follow up with the most valuable.

The biggest investment of time is your initial foray to the prospect. The largest dollar expense is buying the target list, getting it into the database, and investing the time to work it.

Easy follow-up is something planned for before you make your first call.

Follow-up can be simple when you have planned for it and you work with "groups" of prospects.

SELL THE MEETING

You invest a lot of time and money to make the first pass to a prospect. It takes just a fraction of that time and money to follow up when you have set up a system to do it.

Because at the same time you are calling into companies, you will be coding and segmenting those records. You will be collecting information that enables you to sort and prioritize targets as to potential worth. This is something that takes no additional time and is no expense to you. The result will be that you can launch "touches" (whether they will be letters, emails, postcards, candygrams, ravens, or something else) literally with the touch of a few keystrokes.

This small marginal additional effort will reap outsize rewards for you and your team.

You Can Scale Quickly

Sometimes you need to go from zero to 60 in seconds flat.

In some situations, you can't wait for the biggest buyers to bump into your content online. It might be too big a stretch to assume that your social media efforts will translate to qualified leads and sales in enough volume to meet the goal.

If you are in a venture-backed situation, you scale, or you don't get the next round.

Knowing how to zero in on your high-value high-probability targets, approach them systematically to maximize the odds of interacting with a decision-maker and being prepared to say what buyers need to hear to move to a next step, enable you to scale as quickly as possible.

You Get Revenues. More Accounts. Higher Margins.

These rewards are the natural result of a prospecting engine that is running smoothly. You will be meeting with more qualified prospects so you can choose to work with the best and say goodbye to the rest. You can now negotiate from strength on proposals. Why shave the margin to get a piece of business when you know from your full sales pipeline that you are already on target to meet or exceed your sales, revenue, and profit goals?

Worksheets, additional scripts, and periodic updates
are available to readers of this book at
ScottChannell.com/STM-book-extras

Chapter 3
31 Key Drivers to Appointment Setting Success
You Have To Believe In Something

You make a lot of decisions when you reach out to prospects. Who to call? When to call? What to say? When to stick to your plan? When to vary from it?

Those decisions and details are part of a larger plan and driven by core beliefs.

You must have core beliefs and act consistently with those core beliefs if you are to have a successful program.

If you have clarity about your core beliefs and what drives success, then all the smaller implementation questions become easy. Just act consistently with your core beliefs.

If your core beliefs are non-existent, incomplete or just plain wrong, you are doomed before you start. This material will solidify your core beliefs. Those beliefs will guide you in making the best decisions and getting the most results as you implement.

Example: You can't believe that "people are busy," "get to the point," "respect people's time," and "keep it short" and then open up your calls with "how are you?" "Have you got a minute?" and "I know you are busy; I will keep it short." Those actions are inconsistent with your core beliefs.

Every action, every script, every call pattern, how you purposely allocate your time, what you will measure, all must be consistent with certain rules. Know them and thrive. Ignore them, and you will waste your time and miss out on opportunities.

Having set 2,000 C-Level appointments myself, and having worked with companies to set first meetings and discovery calls for more than 25 years, let me share with you my core beliefs about what drives appointment setting and discovery call success.

1. The Buyers Are Out There

People/companies are buying what you offer right now. Shortly, a good many of them will buy, buy more, add or change vendors. At any given time about 15% to 18% of high-probability targets are "in play," meaning that they will purchase or change vendors within the next 3 - 15 months. You need to connect with those buyers and not screw it up when you do.

2. Don't Try To "Convince" Anybody of Anything

This process is not about appointment setting or lead generation. It is about closing sales.

You are not trying to instill something that does not already exist in people. You are looking for those that on some level recognize a need or dissatisfaction and will buy or change vendors shortly. Those are "buyers."

Trying to convince people is a very low-probability, low-conversion activity. Interacting with people who already recognize a need or openness to change is a much higher probability higher conversion rate activity. If you try to "convince" people, you will waste phenomenal time with meetings and proposals that don't result in new business.

If you wish to educate or convince people of something, there are marketing tools and methods much better suited and more cost-effective for that purpose.

3. Everything You Do, You Do At The Expense of Something Else

If you choose to research, you are not calling. If you call low probability suspects, you are not calling higher probability suspects. If you call low-volume, low-margin suspects, you are not working with higher-volume, higher-margin suspects.

If you choose to reach out to "C," "D" or worse, "E" value suspects, you have chosen not to spend that time with "A" or "B" value suspects. If you don't know the difference, you have also made a choice. To invest substantial amounts of time with C, D, and E grade suspects because you don't know the differences.

You have choices. Everything you do is done at the expense of something else.

Are you engaging in a higher probability, higher value action or a lower probability, lower value action? You must know the difference.

What percentage of your time is spent on higher probability actions? When I was setting appointments, I always wanted to feel confident that 80% - 85% of my actions were in the high probability zone. It was OK if 15% or at most 20% of my actions were in an unknown probability zone. But I knew which ones they were and had a plan to either move them into a high-probability zone activity or discard them or label them a low-probability or low-value record so that I would not waste too much time with them.

4. Fight Crap Creep

If you justify calls and time spent based upon "you never know," or "maybe, possibly," you are doomed. You must know the difference between high-probability and low-probability activities and organize yourself to maximize time spent in the high-probability zone.

You do not want to call crap at all, but you also want to call what is not crap in order of priority. You want to call all your "A" records before you call your "C" records, and call your "C" records before you call your barely acceptable worth less than average "D" records. If you lump them all together 80% or more of your time is spent calling "C" and "D" value records, when you could be spending 100% of your time calling "A" records.

You must fight "crap creep." If garbage is taking too much of your time, it is your fault. What is not worth your time at the moment is relative to what your options are.

Those that are best at finding gold are best at determining what is not gold. You must "actively disqualify" every step of the way. You are not trying to keep a record alive. You are trying to kill it. Be determined to identify and not call records not worth your time and reprioritize what is worth calling. The better job you do at identifying and not calling or not continuing to call low-prob, no-prob, low-value suspects guess what? The more time you have to call high-probability higher-value targets.

Do not call crap.

Crap creep kills.

5. "Bump" Into More People At The Right Time. You Must Engineer Prospecting Velocity.

Bumping into people at the right time has more to do with success than we might want to admit.

Our great scripts, our superior sales skills, our pleasant personalities, quick wit, and repartee… I have news for you. Bumping into people at the right time has more to do with success than all those things.

If you believe bumping into people at the right time is a major factor of appointment setting success, then you must engineer a call process that enables you to bump into more high-probability, high-value targets at the right time. Move through larger groups of high-probability suspects faster, and you increase the odds of bumping into buyers. You must at all times have a handle on your prospecting velocity.

If velocity stalls you lose.

6. Know Your Point of Diminishing Returns

Very important. Groups you call, callbacks you make, the info you send, voicemails you leave: All activities and actions have a point of diminishing returns. You are better off allocating time to a higher value action than to allocate time to a lower value action. Knowing when to stop or not engage in any action is key to avoiding banging your head against the wall in frustration and no results.

SELL THE MEETING

7. Think "Groups"

Do you schedule a meeting or next step with Company A, Company B, or Company C? Who cares? Don't care about what happens on any one call. For every group of 100 similarly situated suspects do you book 2, 7, or 15 meetings? Care about that a lot.

8. #1 Reason People Don't Agree to Meet with You. You Don't Give Them Enough Reason to Meet With You.

If you are connecting with people on the phone who recognize a need you can fulfill, and they are not receptive to your message, this is happening for the simple reason that you have not given them enough reason to agree. You haven't provided enough reason for them to invest 30, 45, or 60 minutes of their time with you.

Every single word you say counts. Every-single-word. And, you have a very limited time on the phone to state your case. People think ten times faster than they listen. So don't babble unnecessary words in the very limited time you have a suspect's attention. Your target is thinking while you blabber "this person is just like all the rest… a waste of time I'm going to get rid of." Once a target comes to that conclusion, nothing you say will dislodge them from the belief that you have nothing worth their time.

So what do you do? First, write down what you plan to say so that you can make every word you use as powerful as possible. The first few seconds are the most valuable. Rip out every single syllable you can between "Hello" and communicating what you do, credibility, and benefits that matter to buyers. If you fill up those precious first few seconds with groveling, apologizing, and pleasantries, you are communicating nothing of significance that enables a buyer to conclude that you are worth more time.

Don't confuse being direct, prepared, professional, and getting to the point with being rude or "too salesy."

Eliminate everything unrelated to communicating a benefit and a reason to meet. And understand this: you must provide sufficient reason to meet. And, the benefit they will get from meeting you has to be *delivered at the initial meeting.*

If what they expect to learn at the meeting is perceived to be worth 30-60 minutes of their time, you get a meeting. If not, you don't.

9. Have Reasonable Expectations.
Know the Difference Between Normal And A Problem.

A 4/5 to 1 conversation to meeting ratio is pretty good. Booking 1 meeting for every 10-25 companies you work your process on is a reasonable range. Closing 1 in 5 accounts from cold meetings is reasonable.

Do you expect to make a couple of calls and get decision-makers to pick up? If you do, you are mistaken and will short-circuit a potentially good process. If a process that will make you money requires 9 or 12 dials, and you quit at 3, you self-sabotage yourself. Not because you are not doing the right things, but because you are a stop-short. You had unreasonable expectations and stopped a process that would have delivered for you if you had followed the steps in your system.

10. If It Doesn't Make Sense On Paper, It Is Guaranteed CRAP.
Can't Realize A Profit

Cost per meeting. Cost per opportunity. Closing ratios. Conversion rates. Size of the average sale. Margins realized. Lifetime value. You need to make some reasonable assumptions. Map out a call scenario that makes economic sense. If it doesn't work on paper, it won't work when you start to call.

11. You Must Overcome Gravity.

The most common, natural knee-jerk reaction to a request to schedule a meeting is "fuggedaboutit."

Most people get way too many calls, emails, and sales touches. Most of the people who reach out waste the time of those contacted. Many of those that call do a lousy job calling and give the rest of us a bad name. Most of the people we interact with simply have no needs we can help them with.

SELL THE MEETING

Our suspects are preconditioned to reject calls in a knee-jerk manner. They are quick to conclude that a call/email/touch is a waste of time and that the sales rep is an idiot. Gravity is working against us.

Powerful gravitational forces are working against you when you seek to schedule a discovery call, demo, or first sales meeting.

For you to achieve the purpose of your outreach efforts, you must project a more powerful force than the factors that are working against you. To break free of gravity, you must punch through with a more powerful force.

Your call process must break through gravity.

Guess what? It is not easy to get someone on the phone or to earn their attention with a voicemail or email. Suspects are inundated with calls and emails and reflexively ignore the vast majority of them. Suspects have been on the receiving end of too much irrelevant and poorly worded messaging and will immediately bail the moment they sense it is a waste of time. This decision to ignore/delete you is made within moments.

Your call process must first be sufficient to get their attention for those critical few moments. If you think that a couple of calls or touches made haphazardly or a beat around the bush poorly worded voicemail or email is going to get their attention for those critical few moments, you are deluding yourself.

You must commit to a total call/outreach process that contains sequenced calls, voicemails, emails, maybe a LinkedIn message or other touch, delivered on a pre-defined schedule. You must commit to a call process which, when implemented, provides your greatest chance of earning the attention of high-value, high-probability targets for those crucial few seconds.

To earn their attention, your call/outreach process must be powerful enough to punch through all the reasons why they would choose to ignore you.

Once you get their attention, don't screw it up.

Once your process earns you a few moments of attention, don't screw it up. Say something that enables a buyer (someone who recognizes a need and is going to buy from someone within the next 3 to 15 months) to conclude that you are worth a bit more of their time. To listen a bit longer to your pitch or voicemail, to read more of your email.

What you say and how you say it must contain enough energy to overcome a decision-maker's normal, natural reaction to blow you off. You will only overcome that if you take calculated actions, are prepared, and practice.

Once you earn their attention, it is credibility and value that will keep it. Be prepared to communicate specifics within moments that enable buyers to conclude that you are worth more of their time. What you say right up front must be sufficient to overcome their reflexive action to dismiss you.

Don't fall into the trap of doing what feels most comfortable to you. Certainly, don't do what most of your co-workers or others are doing. Those actions guarantee you failure and frustration and mediocrity at best.

In those first few moments that you worked so hard to get, say something sufficient so that a busy, overworked, tired of having their time-wasted BUYER, can recognize that you are worth more of their time.

Apologizing for calling, promising to be brief, trying to be "nicer" than all the other time-wasters and drooling out words that shed no light on how you might help, why you are credible and the value you provide will not be sufficient to interrupt their normal, natural reaction to dismiss you.

12. Have a "Buyers" Only Focus. Throw Everyone Else Down the Stairs.

Setting appointments and discovery calls is about ultimately closing sales. Your prospecting efforts are one part of an overall process that generates new business cost-effectively.

People who have no needs, no money, or no time will be annoyed and bothered regardless of what you do. Their feelings are irrelevant.

Your objective - your sole objective - is to get the most out of the time/money that you invest in prospecting (to schedule the most appointments with qualified prospects as you can).

SELL THE MEETING

For your company and yourself, you cannot let those who have no needs you can satisfy dictate your actions. Focus only on how to deliver your message effectively to those who do have a need. So, at the moment of truth when you only have a few seconds to deliver your carefully calculated, benefit-rich message, those prospects will absorb it and be receptive to it.

Always speak and act as if you were speaking to someone who would be receptive to your message.

What do I mean by this?

Well, the great majority of people we speak to have no need or desire to buy what we are selling. That being the case, many salespeople water down what they say to be comfortable with prospects they anticipate will say no.

They don't want to bother or interrupt people. They don't want to annoy them (whatever that means). What ridiculous thoughts. Of course, you want to interrupt people. You decided to interrupt them when you chose to call them. You want to interrupt them and get them to focus on you.

You have to think only of those you can reach; who have a need; and who, if they can comprehend and absorb the major benefits you can deliver to them, would agree to meet with you. Ignore everyone else.

Focus only on actions that would be welcomed by those who are reachable, have a need, and would be receptive to meeting with you.

Everything you say and how you say it must assume that you are speaking to someone who has a need and will be willing (as well as able) to buy from you as soon as you've said the things buyers want to hear.

You have a very limited time to make your case before the minds of suspects and prospects shut off and they conclude that you are wasting their time.

Don't waste precious time probing to see if they have a need or interest before you unload the heavy guns and deliver your powerful benefit-laden message. Don't ask decision-makers who don't know you "if they have a few minutes"? Waste no words that don't communicate benefits to those who need what you offer. Deliver only words that communicate benefits to them.

Deliver only the words that would get someone who has a need you can fill to sit up and pay attention to you.

Those who don't recognize a need or are not buyers will reject you no matter what you say. Don't focus on them or give that group even a moment's thought.

Focus 100% on saying words that buyers need to hear to conclude you are worth more of their time. Assume everyone is a buyer until you learn otherwise.

Most of your best clients fit a certain profile. They respond a certain way to your calls and move through your sales pipeline pretty much as all your other good clients did. The more you vary from your desirable new account profile or an appointment setting or sales process that works, the fewer results you will obtain.

Assuming you have picked the right pool of targets, all you have to do is move methodically through that pool and deliver a very clear precise benefit-laden message. When you do, the ears of your future new clients will pick up, and they will identify themselves to you. If you are clearly and concisely delivering a benefit-laden message to the right audience, they will respond.

If they do not, maybe you are not clear and concise. Maybe you are not communicating enough benefits they need. Or, maybe you have cast the net far too wide, defined the pool of targets you will call too broadly, and far too many you call have no needs you can help with, so they reject what you say.

Focus solely on "buyers." Say what "buyers," those who recognize a need, have some discomfort with their present situation or are open to a new vendor relationship, need to hear to determine you are worth more of their time. Ignore everyone else and ruthlessly toss them down the stairs.

13. You Are Interrupting Those You Call. Get Over It.

Do you callus your finger dialing to get someone to pick up the phone and start a conversation with "how are you?" "have a got a minute?" or

"I know you are busy. I'll be quick?" If so, you are among the most annoying, time-wasting, least respectful of your suspect's time. You interrupt them, suck up their time, give them no clue about the call and say nothing of value to them during the first crucial few seconds. You are exactly the person you are trying not to be.

Get to the point quickly and succinctly and enable suspects to "get it." Let them say "yes" or "no." That is most respectful of a suspects time and non-salesy (whatever that means.) You are interrupting people. You have *chosen* to interrupt them. Respect them, get to the point quickly, and say something of substance rather than making them listen to you grovel and apologize.

14. People Buy From Peers; Be a Peer

Don't diminish your status. Your time is worth as much as their time. You have valuable information to share and many welcome and benefit from your offering. At this stage of the process, you can talk toe to toe with anyone at any level. Believe that and project that.

You may not have the technical knowledge or substantive background to have an in-depth conversation on the problems you can solve. You don't need it. On most of the appointment setting/discovery call projects I have worked on in my career my substantive knowledge was about 3 minutes deep. I did not know the details. I was not a subject matter expert. Didn't need to be.

**You are not selling the product or service.
You are selling the meeting.**

If people have a need that you or your company can solve, you are the best person to help them decide if a meeting or discovery call makes sense for them. When questions come up that you can't answer, that is exactly why they need to take the meeting.

Your only job is to help people decide if taking the first meeting will be worth their time. Don't apologize for that. Communicate as a peer. Put your best case forward for why a discovery call would make sense. Let them decide "yes" or "no."

15. Numbers To Keep In Mind

Fun facts. On average it takes 9 to 12 dials to a targeted suspect to have a conversation. Not 9 dials to 9 different suspects, but 9-12 dials to a particular suspect. That number is growing.

The "Rule of 7" tells us it takes 7 "touches" before people begin to recognize and grasp our message. So what does this mean? It means that your call, email, touch, and interaction process must contain a minimum of 7 touches to be even in the ballpark of success. Not only do you need multiple consistent touches, but you need a mix of touches. Not all people respond to the same things. Phone calls, voicemail, emails, snail mail, and Linkedin are the most common touches.

The volume of your efforts and the consistency of your efforts must be in this range. If not, your behaviors are not congruent with those most successful.

16. Your Most Successful Scripts, Messaging, And Emails Will Be An Annoyance, Waste of Time, And "Too Salesy" To Most

For every action, there is an equal and opposite reaction.

For every person who is on the receiving end of your most responsive scripts, emails, and touches and yells "Eureka! Where have you been, let's meet," there will be someone else who will reply "You are an idiot. Only a dolt would do what you are doing. You are wasting my time. Never contact me again, fool."

You cannot expect to work a group of suspects with messaging that is viewed positively by a segment and generates meetings and qualified leads consistently and cost-effectively without also generating an equal and opposite reaction from another segment.

Here is a bulletin. Your "great scripts" that get you the best results will be knee-jerk rejected by most.

It's Them, Not You.

Their response has more to do with their situation and their recognition of needs than it has to do with you. No matter how well your pitch is received overall, it will be rejected by those who don't have or recognize certain needs. It has more to do with their situation than it does with you. You constantly focus on relating verbiage that is helpful and welcomed at the highest rate. When you communicate a message that is clear, impactful and concise, more will say "yes" and more will say "no." You can't change that.

Rant mode: One of the biggest mistakes I see, which is a great example of sales and marketing idiocy, is to water down messaging, which decreases response from those with the greatest needs and highest probability of buying so that fewer people will be "annoyed." Focusing on "not annoying" is a fool's errand. Don't overreact when you have a bad conversation or get a negative response. Getting fewer negative responses does not get you more positive responses.

It never made sense to me that people would prioritize having more comfortable conversations with those who never are going to buy anyway and forget you within seconds of hanging up at the expense of more responses from high-probability buyers.

People don't change effective mailings even though most people trash them at a glance. Why change effective messaging when you get negative responses. You don't see mail going into the trash. You do see and hear negative responses to scripts and emails. Keep the big picture in mind. Don't overreact.

17. Value Knocks Down Doors.
Value As Perceived By Those You Reach Out To, Knocks Down Doors.

Assuming you are calling the right people, it is the value and credibility you communicate that wins.

Not whether it is too long, not whether it sounds conversational, not whether you are comfortable with it, not whether it seems too scripted, not whether it seems too salesy (don't get me going) or whether your co-workers and friends like it. Value wins.

You can do a lot of things imperfectly. If you are communicating value and credibility in the eyes of the suspect, you will win big. Smooth delivery and comfort come with time and practice — stuff as much value in what you say as you can. If you are talking to a buyer, they will listen, even if you think other things are imperfect.

18. You Alone Will Decide What You Do, Not Your Prospects

You are in charge of your time and your actions. You alone will decide what you do and for your reasons. You never let those you speak to or communicate with dictate what you do. Never.

They want you to leave a message. Get lost.
They ask you to send some information. Fuhgeddaboudit.
They ask you to call back. Do they think you are an idiot?

Put those you prospect in charge of your destiny, and you will buy ramen noodles by the case. Your objective is to set a meeting. I can guarantee you that if walk their road it will not lead to a meeting. Your objective is not their objective. You will never be rude or unprofessional, but you alone will decide what you do and what is reasonable at every stage.

19. Top Performers Do Not Model The Struggling, The Mediocre, And The Wannabes That Never Will Be.

Most discovery call and sales appointment setting programs fail.

If you do what most people do, if you succumb to common thoughts about what is the "right thing" to do, you and your team will fail.

Why would you expect to do what everyone else does and get drastically different results?

Be Different From Most. Be Similar To The Best.

True story. Might sound a bit harsh but this is the way you must think.

When I was doing my very first appointment setting project, there were a lot of opinions as to what might work. This project was calling companies with 1,000 or more employees and booking a meeting with either the CEO or an Executive Level VP. Four "experts" had come and gone before me and nothing worked. The company had a great close rate when they could get in the door. But their get in the door efforts were costly with only sporadic success.

That company was filled with really smart, hard working people who were falling short when it came to setting appointments. They were lousy at it for years before I arrived. Unless something changed, they would still be lousy at it a year in the future. The group had a ton of ideas, but nothing got much traction.

Knuckleheads

This may sound harsh, and maybe a bit jerk-like, but one of the most important decisions I made was not to listen to my well-meaning co-workers. They were trying hard for years but were mediocre or worse. Why would I take advice from them?

I thought to myself, "why listen to these knuckleheads?"

I knew the answer was to do something different than what most did.

The reality was that they had tried very hard for years to open more doors at high levels within companies, even hiring four "experts" to help them, but nothing clicked and it was holding the company back.

When I started, I wasn't sure what to do but I knew what not to do. Don't listen to my well-meaning co-workers. Despite their best efforts, they had been choosing the wrong behaviors and would continue to do so.

If you are going to model your struggling co-workers and blindly accept what most say, you will fail. Do what most do, get the results that most get.

What works works

So I went on a quest to discover what worked. I sought out those that had been successful and studied their methods. I did what those who were already successful did. Period. No exceptions.

Be determined to do what works. It doesn't matter if you like it, feel comfortable with it or if your co-workers, friends, or sewing circle like it or think it is a good idea.

It may be more comfortable to fall in line with the great unwashed, but you will never be an above average lead generator/discovery call setter.

You must clarify your own beliefs about what drives appointment setting and act accordingly.

Align your behaviors with the behaviors of those who are successful at doing what you want to do. Without variations, excuses, or rationalizations as to why you won't.

You don't feel comfortable with something. It does not matter.
You feel something sounds salesy. Irrelevant.
Your co-workers don't think it is a good idea. Forget those knuckleheads.
You think you might annoy someone. You are an idiot.

Find out what works. Do what works without exception.
Don't do what most do, do what the best do.

20. In Any Group of Suspects You Target, Only a Limited Percentage Will Be Reachable and Receptive. Know Your Points of Diminishing Returns.

In any given pool of targets, there are only going to be so many who would be receptive to your message if they got a chance to hear it.

Example: Over time, if you are working methodically and doing basic tracking, you will conclude that for every 100 targets you move through your prospecting process you end up with X number of discovery calls set. That number might be 3, 5, 10 or more. You need to know that number.

So, assume you select 100 targets that among all your choices are the highest-probability highest-worth targets you could prospect. You work your well thought out multi-step multi-touch system with well-prepared impactful messaging on that group. Let's assume on average you get five discovery calls and three quality callbacks from those efforts.

As you labor, you will book meeting #1, #2, #4, #5. As you call, you will reprioritize some records based upon the info you learn. You will delete some records as not worth your time. At some point, you have to ask yourself if you are better off calling a new pool of 100 targets that typically contains five meetings?. Or, do you continue to call this shrinking group trying to squeeze out meeting number 5, 6 or 7?

A good part of effective prospecting and appointment-setting comes down to good time management and time allocation. Everything you do, you do at the expense of something else.

When you started calling that group of 100, it was a very high-probability list. As you worked it and booked meetings, collected info and knocked some out, what was left became a much lower probability group.

There are only so many "yes's" in any group of suspects.

You will get better results working a high-probability group than a low-probability group. You need to know the difference.

You need to know at what point you would be better served by letting go, stopping the chase, and pursuing a new target. If you don't know when that is, you are doomed to failure. At some point, you have to stop beating your head against the wall and move on.

21. The Benefits You Promise Must Be Delivered At The *First Meeting*

They are much more likely to meet with you if they know that <u>*at the first meeting*</u>, they are going to get something they consider to be worthwhile, even if they don't do business with you.

Are you structuring your pitch to tell suspects (essentially) that you are great, do great stuff, and want to meet so you can find out more about them to determine how you can assist them so you can come back to them at a later date with something specific?

That is just not as powerful as telling them that you have information and strategies about how similar companies have solved the same kind of problems and achieved similar goals that the suspect's firm would like to achieve. And, the best part is that you are going to provide this information and those strategies at the time of the first meeting.

Strip out every unnecessary word. Tell them clearly and concisely how they will benefit at the first meeting. Lay your cards on the table. Let them say "yes" or "no."

22. Your System Must Be Sustainable And Duplicable

In reality, most people who start to prospect (even if they get off to a good start) stop somewhere along the way.

They get busy with new prospects and prospecting does not get done.
They get bored doing the same thing again and again, even if it is working.
They get frustrated with a lack of results. So they stop.

If you use strategies that get you short-term results but cost too much on a per inquiry or per meeting basis, you won't want to continue. If you have to spend too much time to get a meeting scheduled, the system isn't sustainable.

Your system must be sustainable in the sense that you know that if you invest a certain amount of time and money that you will cost-effectively get the result you seek. When your system is sustainable, you will know that as you progress, the system enables you to segment and code your targets and utilize the information you pick up during your calls so that you will be motivated to continue its use.

Make your system so that others can be onboarded quickly

In addition to being sustainable, it must be duplicable. It must be duplicable in the sense that you could train and onboard a new person to work the system. Such a person might take over where you left off or work the process on a whole new group of targets thereby giving your business even more opportunities.

Your system must be duplicable because it is very likely that there will come a time when you are spending so much time attending the meetings that you schedule and following up on those opportunities that you now find it difficult to make time to prospect. And, human nature being what it is, let's face the fact that if you have other things to do, it is usually prospecting that will be neglected. You can't let that happen if you want to ensure a continuous flow of solid, worthwhile new business opportunities coming to you.

If your system is duplicable, you can pass the calling duties on to someone else. You can duplicate the system and delegate to a lower level of competence.

I have seen many companies start a campaign by having some of the salespeople implement the prospecting system with success. But once results came in, they quickly realized that they needed to have the higher paid salespeople on the road selling all the time while others (paid at a lower rate) could handle the prospecting and appointment setting function more than adequately.

23. Think "Groups," Not Individuals.

Always think of success in terms of groups, rather than individual records. If you think in terms of individual records you are doomed to failure. The vast majority of people you try to communicate with will be unreachable, have no need or say "no." So, it will be rejection rejection rejection.

Example: if you select 100 targets to prospect, think of whether you set 5, 9 or 13 discovery calls within that group. Always focus on getting greater results from similarly situated groups of targets. Celebrate and focus on the results and marginal improvements you make when working through a group of targets.

Do not think of prospecting each individual in the group. If you think of prospecting in terms of results when calling a specific individual or what happens on an individual call, you are setting yourself up for failure as the vast majority of the time, you will not achieve the result you seek. So your mind is focused primarily on failure and rejection.

The big picture must be based not on how you do with any specific target but how well you do with any particular group of targets.

You have choices to make

Are you going to choose to invest 10 hours working with a group of records that you know usually contains two meetings?

Or, are you going to invest 10 hours working with a group of records that you know typically contains eight meetings?

Let's put it another way. Are you going to invest 10 hours of your time working with a group of records that results in an average sale of $50,000 or a group of records that results in an average sale of $250,000? Are you going to invest time with a group of records with a typical three-month sales cycle or a group of records with a typical nine-month sales cycle?

You must also be aware of groups that are just not responsive by nature or within which you are likely to have a lower probability of success. You must be able to identify these groups so that you can avoid them.

Beware of information requests.

A very dangerous group of suspects is the group that requests information or asks that you call them back. Many neophyte prospectors believe that these are positive signs. In reality, this lets the targets control their time and then they call call call and wonder why they are not getting anywhere close to a real appointment.

Information requests are a good example of "group" think you must have. Think of common scenarios as another type of group. When someone asks you to send information and you (insanely) just agree and do it, what happens? More than 9 times out of 10, nothing happens.

So when you encounter a common scenario, a request for information, and you agree to it, you know that 9 times out of 10 your follow-up calls and efforts will be useless. A complete waste of time or at best, a very low probability use of your time.

Only an idiot would walk into that scenario and choose behavior that wastes their time again and again and again.

You need to be able to recognize a low-probability common scenario and have a plan. In the case of an information request, rather than choose to send info and doom yourself to low-probability land you can choose another option. Include strategies in your call process to separate that group of targets who would request information to get rid of you and have no legitimate need or intention of buying, from that group of targets who request information because they do have a legitimate need and may buy.

In this common scenario, you can choose a behavior that keeps you prospecting in the high-probability zone.

Remember – think about prospecting success in terms of groups rather than individuals. Here's an example of how that would work.

You might decide that for best results you will invest 50% of your calling time on that class of targets that makes a buying decision within 90 days so that you can guarantee reasonably steady cash flow. And then you might use the other 50% of your time for that class of prospects that offers a much larger, more profitable sale but typically takes 9 months to complete a sales cycle.

When you think in terms of groups and make conscious decisions as to where you will invest your very limited prospecting time, you have greater control over your business destiny.

24. You Must Always Retain Control.

Your targets should not control what you do. You control what you do. Always be in control of the conversation. Always steer a conversation that wanders off-course back to your purpose. Always be in control of where you invest your time and your resources

If your targets are in control, you are doomed to failure. Example: We referred to the typical "send me some info" or "call me back" blow-off. Well, if you put a smile on your face and readily agree to such requests, you will have lost control. Your targets will now be in control of your time, and you will most certainly lose.

When we get into scripting and responses to resistance, you will learn strategies to maintain control in such instances. Always be in control of the conversation and how you invest your time.

25. The "Rule of 7"

The rule of 7 states that people have to be touched by us 7 times before we can reasonably expect them to appreciate, understand, and respond to our communications.

Now, the rule of 7 is not literal. Some people will respond within the first few touches. Others may have to be "touched" dozens of times before they respond at all.

The significance of the rule of 7 is twofold. First, if you are not touching your contacts multiple times within an outreach cycle, you are not touching them at all. If you think you are accomplishing something by calling them and leaving a voicemail message or emailing them once, you are fooling yourself.

Built into your prospecting system must be the core concept that you have to touch people multiple times within a very short period to have any chance of getting their attention and an appointment. If your call process doesn't plan on touching your prospects about 7 times, you have no right to expect to get their attention and get an appointment.

How do we touch them? Well, as a practical matter, we only have a few tools at our disposal. Phone. Voicemail. Email. At times, Linkedin messages.

Should you use mail as a touch?

Direct mail is not a viable mechanism to lift your discovery call results. Now read carefully as this statement has some nuance and context.

Many believe that if they mail a letter before reaching out to a suspect that it "warms up" the call and will lift response. The truth is the exact opposite.

First, most people won't get what you mailed out, those that did get it probably don't remember it, those few that remember getting something didn't read it. So it doesn't lift response.

But the second reason is the biggest reason why sending mail out is self-defeating. What do most callers who send out letters before a call do that is self-defeating? They call, call, call to get someone to pick up the phone, and they reference the letter they sent. Say something such as "following up on the letter I sent you" blah blah blah.

What does the suspect say 99% of the time? "I didn't get it, don't remember it, didn't read it. Send it again." So rather than using those precious first few moments to communicate what you do, why you are credible and worth their time and throwing in a few benefits delivered to boot, you talk about none of that. By your choice, you choose a low-probability behavior and steer the conversation to a topic that does not contribute to achieving the result you seek.

I do not recommend sending mail to "warm" up calls. I have seen many companies do that but never once seen it cost effectively lift meetings scheduled.

However, direct mail is a great marketing mechanism.

Having said that about mail as part of your active book the meeting process, let me say this. I am a huge fan of using mail as a marketing mechanism. Particularly as to your higher-worth targets a continuous drip campaign by mail calculated to get a call, response, or steer someone to a form on your website can be a very cost-effective high probability strategy. But more on this later.

How long do you have to deliver those touches?

The rule of 7 says that you have to touch people 7 times before they start to get it. But over what period should those touches be delivered?

If it takes 7 touches for your target to be impacted, and you called and left a message every couple of weeks, it would take 14 weeks to deliver 7 touches. Do you want to wait 14 weeks to have an impact and know whether your target is a viable prospect? I don't think so. Plus, 7 touches delivered over 14 weeks is nowhere near as effective as 7 touches delivered over 2 weeks. If you space out your touches over too long a period, it is like starting over again every time.

Anything done once is the equivalent of doing nothing at all.

Setting appointments is an assault. It takes constant, consistent, and calculated action to have a chance of getting someone's attention, never mind their agreement to meet with you. If you do something once, one call, one email, and think you have done something to further your business objective, you are deluding yourself.

You need a cumulative impact.

People don't remember. You need people to be touched numerous times within a short enough period so that they recognize you are trying to communicate with them. If they recognize that, you have a chance, a chance that they may absorb your message and be more predisposed to schedule a discussion.

You need the impact of cumulative touches and spaced repetition to penetrate the minds of your targets.

What works best? Deliver your touches in 3 spurts separated by 3 business days over roughly two weeks. Do this and you increase the impact of your actions. You are sending a consistent benefit rich message to your carefully chosen targets within a short period. That greatly increases the odds of them noticing you and absorbing your message.

If they need your product or service, you have greatly increased the odds that they will respond or be more receptive to your message.

You are going to make a lot of phone calls, leave a lot of voicemails, and send a lot of emails. You want maximum impact for your actions. Live by the rule of 7 and deliver those touches within a 2-week window.

Consider the law of diminishing returns

If you are sending our clear, concise benefit-rich communications to the right audience, and if they have been touched by you multiple times within a short period but have not responded, then you can safely conclude that they are not your next clients. They have no needs you can fulfill. You should move on.

You want to prospect like Goldilocks. Enough but not too much. Enough to maximize the result you seek, but not so much that you are wasting time and resources.

You build into your system multiple touches so that you can realistically expect a response from those who recognize a need you might meet. With those multiple touches, you can have the confidence to let go when there is no response. If these suspects had a need, your system of multiple voicemail and emails (and at times other types of touches) that were delivered within a short period maximized the chance that they will become aware of your core benefits and "raise their hand" from the crowd. When they don't, you can move on with confidence.

26. Scott's Rule of 50/20/20/10

I used to believe in the 60/30/10 rule when it came to booking appointments and discovery calls. That rule stated that 60% of your prospecting success would come simply by hitting the right targets, 30% will come because you have the right message and 10% will come from all other reasons combined.

With the benefit of 25+ years of experience, I think that a better rule is 50/20/20/10.

50% of the results come from interacting with the highest-probability highest-value targets you can with the time and resources you have.

20% of the results come from your process of interaction. When do you call, voicemail or email? How many times? You must work a total process of outreach from start to finish calculated to get the result you seek. The quality of that process and the quality of your execution is 20% of the reason for your discovery call success.

20% of the results come from your messaging. Does your messaging give those with needs sufficient reason to meet? Does your verbiage communicate value, credibility, and benefits clearly and concisely?

10% of your results come from everything else.

50% of your results come from just hitting the right targets. Here's the biggest mistake I see over and over again. Rather than carefully profile the best targets to call, you grab some local list that is free or easy. Or, major assumptions are made about a list that is good enough. The result of this is that your net is cast far too wide and you are pretty much doomed to fail no matter how good your call process or scripting is.

When your list is not properly selected, you and your team spend way too much time reaching out to low-probability and no-probability targets. This is a major cause of appointment setting failure. If your target list is not properly selected you and your team are doomed before you make your first call. All the odds are stacked against you and it is your fault.

Get this right, and you can screw up a lot of things and still be successful.

Even if you have an average message and screw everything else up totally, if you select the right targets, you can have a successful prospecting program. If you select the wrong targets, no matter what else you do, no matter how good your message is, no matter how efficiently you work, no matter how good your process is, you are guaranteed to fail.

How do you pick the right targets? Very simple. Make a list of your best clients. Make a list of your competition's best clients. Make a list of the specific accounts that you know would be great, profitable accounts for you to have. Then go to a database and look up those specific companies. Create a chart that notes their SIC or NAICS codes.

Every industry has a code. Do you sell to consultants, restaurants, or retail? They each have a code. Find out what the SIC or NAICS codes are of the companies you are profiling. Make a note of their revenue range or number of employees. This information can be obtained for free using publicly available databases such as ReferenceUSA.

In addition to the information you find in public databases, make a note of how your best clients/customers/accounts first found you. What needs did they have when they first became your clients?

Write it down. What did your clients tell you their problems were when they first came to you? Write them down.

Do this enough times, and you will have an accurate profile of the people whom you should be calling. That is to say, you will know the exact industry codes and the size of the businesses you should be calling. These are the only people you should be calling.

27. Do Not Focus on "Not Missing Anyone."

Let me tell you one of the biggest mistakes you can make. The phrase that I hear that tells me I am talking to someone doomed to prospecting failure. *"I don't want to miss anyone."* Surer words predicting prospecting failure will never be spoken!

The point of prospecting and appointment setting is to generate the most results for your limited time and resources.

When you start, you should call only those who fit the profile of your best potential clients. Usually, there are more of those targets than you could reasonably call in 6 months or more. So you are not limiting yourself in any way. After you contact all your targets that fit your "best suspect" profile and do it very well, then you can start thinking about contacting others.

Let's discuss a close to real life example. You make some assumptions about whom to prospect, and your list universe has 5,000 targets. If you do some basic research and analysis, you might find that about 7% of that list, 350 targets, most tightly fits the profile of your best clients. Let's call those your "A" targets. Another 7% or so, about 350 records, are close to your best target profile. Let's call this the "B" group. Then you have "all the rest," about 4,300 records that contain average, below average, and totally unqualified suspects.

Who are you going to call first? The A's, the B's, or all the rest?

If you are like most who jump in and call without knowing which targets are in the A or B group, you are going to spend 86% of your time calling "all the rest," while the A's and B's get very little of your time and attention. A scenario all too common and a recipe for guaranteed failure.

This is where the self-destructive thinking comes from. We all have clients who are great clients but don't fit the profile of our very best clients. For example: if most of our best clients are businesses that have at least $2.5 million in revenue, we probably have some great clients that are much smaller, only doing say half of a million or a million a year in business.

It may be true that there are some businesses out there that only do half a million dollars in revenue, which could be "great" clients. But, if you tried to prospect companies in that revenue range, you would lose your shirt trying to find those "great" clients.

You Want to Jackhammer Through a Solid Vein of Prospecting Gold. Not Work Through a Pile of Prospecting Crap Trying to Find a Nugget of Gold.

You are not "giving up" on anyone when you resist the temptation to dilute the quality of the suspect pool you call.

It is financial suicide and sheer madness to invest limited prospecting time sifting through sludge panning for a few small nuggets of gold when you could spend the same amount of time jackhammering through a solid vein of gold.

The more you vary from a suspect pool that most resembles your typical "great" client, the more you can expect that your success rate in scheduling appointments will be lower. Your conversion rate from appointment to sale will be lower, and your average order size of the sales you do make will be lower. Do not make this mistake. Initially focus and prospect only those companies who fit the profile of your very best clients.

Once you finish prospecting that pool and have a baseline of results, you can then selectively start prospecting other pools of suspects in some order of priority.

50% of your results will come just from communicating with the right targets.

20% of your prospecting results come from your process of interaction. How many times do you call, voicemail, or email and when? If you don't do enough, maybe call a few times or haphazardly, you will fail. If you do too much and work past your point of diminishing returns, your results will also plummet.

So assuming you are calling the right targets, you must work an effective process when you interact with those targets. That process moves you through your high probability group very efficiently and increases the odds that you will "bump" into a high-value prospect at the right time.

50% of results from calling the right targets.
20% of results from working the right process.

20% of results from effective messaging. Very simply, when you call the right people and work a system that earns their attention for a few moments, don't screw it up. Have something worthwhile to say. Communicate what you do, your credibility, and value, clearly and succinctly.

In those few crucial moments of attention you worked hard to get you must communicate words that enable buyers (those that recognize a need) to conclude that you are worth more of their time. If your message is weak, watered down, or non-existent in those moments you are toast.

50% is the list.
20% is the process.
20% is the messaging.

10% is all the rest. All the other issues that suck up your time and attention that are on the fringes of what matters have very little impact on results. I am generous when I say they impact results 10%.

Call the right people the right way and have something worthwhile to say and you are 90% there. Don't let other issues divert your attention.

28. Make Every Word Count. Ruthlessly Eliminate Every Worthless Word.

When you are trying to set a first sales conversation, you have very limited time to get someone's attention and relay benefits in such a way that they will agree to spend an hour or so with you. You have to know specifically what words are most likely to get you the result you seek.

You must brainstorm all the words and phrases that might communicate a winning message. You have to write those words down. Every word counts. If you take 50 seconds to say something that could be stated in 30 seconds, you will lose a lot of appointments. If you don't clearly communicate credibility and the most powerful benefits you offer before someone says "no," you will lose a lot of appointments.

Most people will agree with me up to this point. The next point is where people start to get fuzzy and resistant. My advice is to write down those words and master how you deliver them.

That means you are initially going to work from scripts. You have to write down the sequence of words most calculated to get you the result you seek and learn to deliver them effectively.

Creating your "pile of words" and writing out the best words to achieve your business objective is nothing more than preparation. If you don't brainstorm all the words you might use so that the best words are identified, your verbiage will not be powerful, and you will lose opportunities.

I see this all the time. Companies that have great credibility, deliver superior results, have great examples to relate that would send a powerful message of value to prospects, don't use them. Many companies have not even collected them and organized them in some order of priority so that the most powerful words could be used.

As a result of that lack of basic preparation, a lot of weaker words and filler words get used. Words that are not strong enough to break through the gravitation forces working against you.

29. The 80/20 Rule, With A Twist

Everybody has heard of the Pareto principle which states that 80% of your results come from 20% of your efforts. That seems to be true in life, and it is certainly true when you set sales appointments.

You can choose to spend substantial amounts of time engaging in activities like calling, voice mailing, and emailing that you know with certainty has a much lower chance of success when compared to other activities.

You can choose to spend substantial amounts of time engaging in activities like calling, voice mailing, and emailing that you know with certainty has a much higher chance of success when compared to other activities.

The key phrase here is "you can choose" to engage in those activities … or not.

To set appointments effectively, you must know with a relative degree of certainty what to expect from calls and contacts made to segments of your list.

You can choose to work only in the zone in which you get 80% of your results from only 20% of your time, or you can choose to work in the zone where you get 20% of your results with 80% of your effort. It's your choice. Do you know the difference?

The reason why I think so many people get frustrated by prospecting and appointment setting is that they spend way too much time in that lower probability of results zone. You can decide where to spend your time.

If you are calling suspects that closely fit the profile of your best clients, working them with an interactive process just long enough to get their attention, and using clear, concise verbiage that in just a few moments enables buyers to conclude you are worth more time, you are working in that highest probability zone.

But, if you are calling lower probability targets with a minimal effort call and touch process and deliver weak verbiage, you are working in the zone where you spend 80% of your time and only get 20% of your results. You made that choice.

30. Remove The Drudgery

Your system must be set up so that you can move quickly through a prospect pool delivering a carefully calculated message with impact and get a "yes" or "no" with certainty.

Drudgery occurs when you make wasted calls, when you enter needless notes into your system, when you engage in double shoveling (doing things twice when you only have to do them once). It is all drudgery, and you are the one creating it. Stop it.

Evaluate every keystroke, every notation, everything you do between actually making a call or delivering a touch to your suspect. Eliminate every single little thing that is not necessary.

The good news about prospecting is that a lot of people do it successfully and you can, too. But the bad news is that once you discover what works, you have to do it again and again and again — boring city.

Mixing smart people with repetitive tasks is a recipe for disaster. Remove every unnecessary keystroke, movement, and syllable you can that is not necessary.

When you call and leave a voicemail message do you type out "Called Bob wasn't in. Left a voicemail message. Try again," or do you just type a code such as "LVM" for "left voicemail message."

Do you have to open four screens in your CRM to find out the status of a record before you make a call? What a waste. Organize your screen so that what you need to know to make a call is right up front.

Do you spend too much time searching your database to find out who to call next? Work a call process and schedule every next action so that you don't waste time.

Even when you are doing the right things it becomes boring. Rip out every unnecessary keystroke and wasted moment to make it easier.

31. "No" Is A Perfectly Acceptable Result. The Maybe's Will Kill You.

"No" is a perfectly acceptable result.

Getting to a "No" as quickly as possible is a must do to excel at appointment setting.

Many people will do anything to avoid getting a "no." But, you avoid "no" at the expense of getting more clear "yes's."

Success in the appointment setting game has an awful lot to do with how quickly you can move through a pool of records effectively. When you move through those records, you need to know things with certainty. This is a "yes." This is a "no."

Or, if you couldn't reach targets, your process of multiple and consistently focused touches delivered within a short period should give you the confidence to conclude that if they had a need, there was plenty of opportunities for them to "raise their hand" out of the crowd. Once you reach that conclusion, move on.

Those who are best at prospecting for gold are best at identifying that which is not gold.

The faster you can get a clear and concise "no," the sooner you'll recognize what's "not gold." And that means you will spend less time with people who are unlikely to meet with you and more time with those more likely to meet with you.

The maybe's will kill you. Maybe's come in different forms.

It is not the "no's" you should be afraid of. It is the "maybe's" that will keep you from prospecting success. "Maybe's" are multiple conversations with someone who conveys warm fuzzies yet never agrees to meet. You must avoid the "maybe's." Be direct. Be professional. Get a clear yes or no.

> Worksheets, additional scripts, and periodic updates
> are available to readers of this book at
> ScottChannell.com/STM-book-extras

Chapter 4
6-Core Component Parts Of Your System

Before you even think of reaching out to your prospects, you need to set up your system.

If you think you'll just start with a script and neglect the rest, you will fail.

If you grab an easily accessible list such as a Chamber of Commerce directory or some top local business list and just start calling, you will fail.

If you grab the phonebook or download a large list of targets without a clue as to which are high-probability, low-probability, high or low value, and start calling because "you never know," you are clueless, and you will fail.

If you call using paper lists or Excel spreadsheets, you will fail.

If your sales manager asks you to do any of these things, you will shortly lose your job for lack of results, so you might as well quit now and find something where you have a chance of success.

Before You Even Think of Calling

Prospecting is tough and getting tougher.

You want to increase the odds of success. That means having clear goals, prioritized lists, a contact manager/CRM that enables you to segment and prioritize as you work, to maximize efficiency, work a process that increases your odds of success and words that work.

You must put 6 parts in place before you even think of making a call or sending an email.

1. Know your goals.

2. Select the right list. (Top quality among all your choices and the right size.)

3. Set up a contact manager/CRM.

4. Map a call process.

5. Create a pile of words.

6. Craft your scripts & emails.

If you seek to schedule discovery calls or set sales appointments with those who do not know you and don't do these things, you doom yourself to inefficiency and ineffectiveness.

You can do an adequate job on getting these 6 parts in place with a 10 to 15-hour investment of time.

It never made any sense to me at all, why people will spend 10 hours a week, 15 or 20 hours a week or more, week after week, trying to set discovery calls working inefficiently, on a hodgepodge basis, winging what they say. An investment of just 10 to 15 hours, done once, greatly increases the odds of success and reduces frustration.

A lollapalooza effect

Marginal improvements in any one of these areas will impact your results. Make marginal improvements on multiple parts or all of the parts, and you have a lollapalooza effect. The impact on your results will be extreme, due to the power of multiple marginal improvements working together.

If you have a sales team, the consequences of not being set up properly are multiplied. If you are weak in any one of these areas, your results will plummet. If the list is not prioritized, the wasted time on low probability or no value targets is multiplied. If the team is working inefficiently, money flies out the window. If verbiage is not prepared, you work hard and at the moment of truth, when someone picks up the phone, listens to your voicemail, or glances at your email, your words have no impact.

SELL THE MEETING

A small investment of time in each of these areas greatly increases your efficiency and effectiveness.

Let's focus on each one and get you ready to reach out successfully.

> Worksheets, additional scripts, and periodic updates are available to readers of this book at ScottChannell.com/STM-book-extras

SCOTT CHANNELL

Chapter 5
Your Goals Drive What You Do

The goals you establish for your appointment setting efforts will drive what you do, how you select records, how you track progress, how many tests you run, how many scripts you try, how often you evaluate results, and how often you make changes.

Without clear goals, you are just madly dialing trying to book any meeting without clear direction or any ultimate benefit in mind.

Let me be absolutely clear. Activities are not goals. Bottom line results are goals. Milestones that lead to results are goals. Activities are not goals.

A good goal is to move company revenue from $X to $Y within the next 12 months.

A good goal is to add a specific amount of margin dollars to your bottom line in the next year.

A good goal is to close 10 accounts worth at least $50,000 every quarter.

A good goal is specific, relates to the bottom line, is measurable and tied to a specific time period.

I keep hearing that prospecting is a numbers game. What are your numbers? The number that will be added to your revenue, your margin dollars, your profit?

Start there. Everything you do with your appointment setting program will have those numbers in mind.

Dials Are Not Goals. Activities Are Not Goals. Bottom-Line Results Are Goals.

I wince whenever I hear a caller or manager start to describe their appointment setting or discovery call goals in terms of how many dials they make a day. The number of dials to be made should not even be part of that conversation.

Understand this, this is counter intuitive, but it is the truth. There is no rational relationship between the number of dials made and the results obtained. Those who are best at setting appointments do not make the most dials. Not even close.

Programs that prioritize and measure activities, such as the number of dials made or emails sent out or records called are almost always low performing. I refer to these programs as being from the "whip them harder" school of appointment setting. As if more activity could fix that management is asking people to call unqualified lists, very inefficiently with poor CRM setup, no process, and scripts that communicate no credibility or value. I don't care how many times you dial the phone in that situation; more dials do not help.

Over-emphasis On Activities Contributes To Low ROI

Chew on this. A consistent observation I make is that within organizations that put a priority on measuring activities, the account size tends to be smaller and accounts churn more frequently.

Why would that be? Well, when activity goals are set too high and given outsized importance, there is less time to think and make solid judgments and do things that are more likely to contribute to the bottom line goal, as management is demanding a certain number of dials. So that is what management gets. Dials. Management is not encouraging thinking, judgment and behaviors more likely to lead to the bottom line result they need. They are getting what they demand, more dials.

It is certainly true that a caller has to be making a reasonable number of dials, but once a reasonable number of dials are being made consistently, if meetings are not popping out, more dials will not help.

I find this common over-emphasis on the number of dials and measuring dials to be insane. Part of the reason why I think it is nuts is that I see how destructive "activity" thinking is to improve bottom-line results.

You Get What You Measure

If you set goals for your outreach team based upon activity, guess what you get, activity. Not the results you seek. Now your callers and your whole team work to meet the daily and weekly report numbers. If you measure dials, you will get dials. If you measure meetings, closed accounts, average account size, and profit margins, those are the things you get.

Callers Will Make Dials That Are Worthless Just To Meet The Report.

They will sacrifice efforts that are more likely to lead to new business because they know if their activity report is low, they will get yelled at. So they give the manager what is asked for, dials. Those who work in such environments are among the living dead. Just going through the motions knowing it is stupid, but that is what is required. Top performers flee such environments. The mediocre and lower performers have fewer options; they will stick around.

If you like fiction, you will love reading cold calling activity reports. The numbers can easily be manipulated to look like the right things are being done.

You Must Set The Right Goals

As a team manager, or if you are managing yourself, you must set the right goals. Everything you do should be based upon meeting bottom-line goals. Meetings. Closing ratios. The average size of the sale. Profit margins. Lifetime value. Bottom line type goals.

The only thing worth tracking to get there is the number of conversations you have with targeted decision-makers, positive replies you get from emails, and returned phone calls.

Conversations with your targeted decision-maker. When a decision-maker you have targeted picks up the phone, says "hello" and you slay them with your "set the appointment pitch," that is worth tracking as there is a rational relationship between that and the number of meetings you set — same thing with positive email responses and return calls from your effort.

If you increase the number of conversations you have, replies from emails or calls back, those milestones will directly impact your bottom line results.

You should always strive to be as efficient as you can and be as effective as possible for the time you spend prospecting, but over emphasis on activities decreases your team's effectiveness.

When Do You Look At The Number Of Dials Made?

It is certainly true that when you have a successful caller or a successful program, there is a certain rhythm to success. Over time, if you are meeting your goals consistently, you will be able to say that your team sets X number of meetings, has Y number of conversations, Z number of positive email replies and XX number of returned phone calls. And to generate that they made XXX number of calls. You could look back to evaluate a successful program and see that rhythm.

But it is not true to start by saying if they make XXX number of calls they will be successful. It does not work that way. Because in successful programs you are not only making calls, but you are deciding who to make them to. In successful programs, you spend time determining who not to call so that you don't waste dials. In successful programs, there will be times when you hang on the line longer or call back to get that extra recon info that will tell you whether this is an "A" value target worthy of more effort or a "D" value target worthy of little or no effort or all. You spend more time with those worth more time when larger opportunities are identified; you will spend more time with them, not necessarily more dials, but more time that will impact the goal.

As a manager, you need to set the right goals, but you also need to know what to measure to meet those bottom-line goals. Is the most responsive group of targets being called? Are those targets being called with the process most calculated to get the result you seek? Is the messaging communicating value and credibility sufficient for a buyer to meet? Those are the things you need to know and manage to get the result you seek.

When I am actively coaching a team, I tell them I don't want to hear any discussion about how many times they dialed the phone. I could not care less how often a caller dials the phone — worthless info.

SELL THE MEETING

The only time you look at dial activity is to see whether someone is making a reasonable effort. Even then, it does not tell you the full story because a poor caller can work to the report, rather than to the result.

Set Goals For How Your Calling Efforts Are To Impact Your Bottom Line Results.

Measure meetings and discovery calls set.
Measure the number of conversations with targeted decision-makers. (When you deliver your "set the appointment" pitch.)
Measure the number of positive responses you get to emails or replies to voicemail.

Measure the conversion of those conversations, email and voicemail replies to discovery calls and meetings set.

Measure your cost per meeting.

Measure the closing ratio of meetings set, the show rate, the average size of each sale, the profitability of each sale, and have a clear sense of their lifetime value.

Know what it costs you to set appointments and discovery calls and know what that investment is generating for you.

If it is not working, do the things that will move those numbers.

Increasing activity goals will not fix programs that are fundamentally flawed.

> Worksheets, additional scripts, and periodic updates
> are available to readers of this book at
> ScottChannell.com/STM-book-extras

Chapter 6
Selecting Your Targets: Your Most Important Decision

The whole purpose of this book is to enable you to work a system so that you bump into more buyers at the right time, and then don't screw it up when you do.

The most important factor by far that will determine your discovery call, and appointment setting success is whom you decide to target.

Would you rather invest 100% of your time interacting with a group of targets that look just like your best accounts or spend that time working a group where only 10% of the targets look like your best accounts?

Would you rather jackhammer through a solid vein of gold or dive into a pile of muck and feel around for a few nuggets of gold?

Those are real choices for you. Too many unknowingly choose to work a group with very few decent targets within or jump into the muck. They wonder why they failed and declare "calling is dead, email doesn't work. They say "no one picks up the phone anymore." Or other such nonsense.

The reality is that they were pretty much guaranteed to fail before they started reaching out. They had picked the wrong targets and stacked all the odds against them.

Picking the right targets is 50% of the reason (at least) that your outreach program will be successful.

How Do You Select The Proper Targets For Your Prospecting Campaign?

You better know the answer to that question and get it right. If you don't, no matter what else you do correctly, you are sure to fail.

That is correct. You can have killer scripts, a superior offering, be working an efficient and effective call process, and yet it will all be for naught if you don't select the right targets.

Get this right and be mediocre at everything else and you can still get results.

Pick the wrong targets, and no matter how good you are at everything else, you will fail. Guaranteed. You are stacking the odds against you.

The Most Common Reason Why Campaigns Fail

Many times call centers, or in-house sales teams, will ask me to review a campaign that is not producing. Very commonly I find that 70%, 80%, 90%, or more of call activity (and expense) was allocated to targets that never should have been called in the first place.

Even more sadly, almost always there is an easily identified reachable pool of targets that are high-probability buyers who are not being touched at all. When the phones ring or emails are popping into inboxes at those buyers' offices, it's not you, and others are getting the accounts and checks that should have been yours.

There Were Enough To Keep Them In High-Probability Land For Six-Months, But…

Typically, and I'm not kidding, there were enough high-probability, higher-value type prospects to keep the sales team busy for 6 months or more. But they chose, and it was a choice, to skip the list qualification and prioritization step and ended up in the muck feeling around for a few nuggets.

You or your sales team have limited time. Every business has limited resources. You must get the maximum return for dollars and time invested.

You must make informed decisions about whom to call, in what order, and in what priority. You must at all times allocate your limited time and resources to where they will do the most good. You have to make choices.

"Not Missing Anyone" Is Not A Goal

Very commonly those choices are not made. Under the guise of "anyone could be our client," "I don't want to miss anyone," "we had a great client like that once," or equally ridiculous "you never know," the prospecting net is cast far too wide. When there are typically enough higher-probability buyers to keep you or your sales team busy for a long, long time, resources are wasted with far too many lower-probability and no-probability buyers simply because prospect pools are not properly selected and prioritized.

Rather than spend just a little bit of time profiling the best records to call in some order of priority, the choice was made to invest bundles of time, over and over again, wading through a much lower quality pool.

Huge waste and unnecessary.

Your objective is never to "not miss anyone." That is dumb. Your objective is always to allocate your resources to where they will get you the greatest return.

Common Profiling Example

Basic marketing 101 says that the people most likely to buy from you look like the people who have already bought from you. Genius.

So you start by building a profile of those who have already purchased from you. The parts of that profile will commonly be industry (SIC or NAICS codes,) revenue range, or the number of employees.

The SIC Code (Standard Industrial Classification) system was developed in the 30s and last updated in 1987. These codes classify businesses by their primary activity. NAICS codes (North American Industrial Classification System) emerged in 1997 to replace SIC codes. NAICS codes provide more detail about a company's activity and are assigned on a more consistent logic than SIC codes. SIC codes are still widely used by marketers today.

First Step

Create a list of the accounts or clients you wish to clone. Include your best accounts and your solid bread and butter accounts, but exclude the smaller accounts.

This list must be made up of only those who have written checks to you. Not those that you think should or want to write checks to you, only those who did write checks to you.

My suggestion is there should be 30 to 50 accounts on this list. If your company doesn't have at least 30 good names, then use companies you know have purchased from competitors.

Take that list and go to a business database. I have always used InfoUSA's Salesgenie product for this purpose. There is a free version called ReferenceUSA available at many local and college libraries.

Look up each company on your list. In separate columns make a note of the location, industry (SIC or NAICS codes,) revenue range, and employee size range.

You may choose other criteria as well, but the above usually suffice for a solid first cut.

Now Look For "Clumps"

Once you have looked up all the names, you want to find patterns. Very simply, what are the most dominant SIC or NAICS code ranges, revenue ranges, and employee size ranges of the accounts you would most like to clone?

As to each characteristic, ignore the stragglers above and below the dominant range.

Once this is complete, you have a profile of your current accounts you would most like to clone.

Armed with this profile, go back to your business database tool and search by those criteria in the geographic area you are targeting.

For example: If your dominant profile is companies with SIC codes in these ranges 20-23, 50-51 and 7311-7999, revenue range of $2.5 - $20 million, with an employee range of 25-100, use those parameters for your search.

Guess what? You have now identified the companies that look the most like the companies that buy from you. Call them first.

Skip This Profiling Step at Your Peril

Let's review an example to illustrate how easy it is to doom your prospecting efforts before you even pick up the phone.

If you do not create a profile of your target account, run the list counts correctly, and prioritize accordingly, you are doomed.

Here is a typical case history selected from my client files.

First, get a handle on your call universe. What is the number of businesses that theoretically might buy your product or service?

In our example, this client had a service that theoretically any business might buy, so the call universe was all businesses within their geographic target area.

Call universe: 88,667 businesses

Now we seek to slice out records that would be lower or no-probability targets.

In this case, the decision-maker is almost always found at corporate headquarters. So we would choose not to call branches or subsidiaries.

Select only headquarters or single location companies: Call universe just dropped to 77,599 records.

You just eliminated 11,068 locations that would be a waste of phone calls.

Your next cut uses the profile you created.

Your "A" profile represents those SIC code ranges and revenue ranges that are most dominant among the accounts and clients you would like to clone.

Your "B" profile represents those SIC code ranges and revenue ranges that are a bit broader or less dominant than your "A" group but very much above average.

Your "C" profile would be your "bread and butter" accounts. Average size account potential and moderate sales cycles.

Your "D" group would be records with below average potential but still acceptable.

Below that would be the dredges — your "E" group. You never want to call into your "E" Group. Calling E's is like throwing money out the window.

Can you identify your "E" records?

There Is A Super Responsive Sub-Group You Want To Identify

I call this the "A+" group.

Very simply, within your "A" group, it is very common to see a super bullseye. A sub-group within the "A's" that is even more dominant. It might be a tighter SIC code range. Maybe a higher revenue range than the rest of the A's. You look at it and think "Holy cow, never knew so many of our great accounts would be found within such narrow call list parameters."

So, when you run counts, you want to run counts of your "A+," "A" and "B" groups.

Back to our example. How many records showed up when we ran counts of these 3 groups?

> A records: 3,417 (3.8%)
>
> (A+ records found within the "A" group: 812.)
>
> B records: 6,118 (6.9%)

So out of a total potential call universe of 88,667 records, just 3,417 were "A's." Now if you were managing a team or you were calling to pad your paycheck, where would you choose to call?

Within the group that you know for a fact contains by far the highest percentage of buyers. Buyers who look just like your current best accounts you wish to clone. Or, would you choose to call a group which contains far fewer?

If you had a choice and could pick your poison, you would choose to call into the group that increased the odds that you would bump into buyers.

50% Of The Buyers Are Found Where?

Now, let's add another fun fact to the equation. In this example, and very typically, 50% of the "great and good accounts" were to be found among the "A" list. The other 50% of the accounts we wish to clone are scattered among all the rest.

Let's contemplate that for a moment. If you are a business owner, manager of a team, or someone whose commissions depend upon closing deals, and you have limited time and resources, you have choices. Would you choose to work a group of 3,417 records (your "A" group) that contain 50% of the results you seek, or would you choose to work a group of 85,250 records (your "B," "C," "D," and "E" groups) that contain 50% of the results you seek?

When you spend just a few hours creating these profiles and running these counts, you give yourself that choice.

In this example, the company had two callers setting appointments/discovery calls. On average, they could launch their call process with about 50 new records a week. So two callers would together eat 100 new records a week. If they focused just on the A+ records, it would take them about 8 weeks to do that. Two callers each eating 50 records a week = 100 per week. It would take them a little over 8 weeks to call out the 812 "A+" records.

If you were managing a call team, it would make sense to put your A+ records into play before all the rest. That is the group that has the heaviest concentration of accounts that look just like your best accounts.

Who would not do that?

After that it would make a lot of sense, to focus calls and outreach efforts on the rest of the "A" group. That group of 2,605 records (3,417 "A" records - the 812 "A+" records already called = 2,605 "A" records left to call) would keep this call team busy for another 26 weeks.

Who would not do that?

Run Counts And Set Priorities Among Defined Groups

Our example related a common, yet basic set of choices. A+, A, B, C, D and E groups.

Depending upon your business goals, competitive situation, and resources of time and money, you may want to identify groups of other potential targets before you set your priorities.

You might identify a segment of "whales." Whales are companies that buy a lot. These will typically be harder to penetrate, longer sales cycle type accounts. When they pop, they buy a lot, but they take a long time to cultivate. Having some very large accounts is nice. If you chase too many whales, you should expect to incur all the expenses of prospecting with a low probability of short-term results. So you have to make a purposeful choice of how to allocate limited resources to chasing whales.

Maybe you have an emerging segment. A class of prospects that you feel has a high potential for you, but you do not yet have a significant account presence.

You may decide to allocate 80% of time and resources to prospecting your "A" and "A+," 15% to emerging segments with growth potential and 5% to your whales.

The key point here is that you are making purposeful conscious, informed decisions based on facts, research, and basic marketing and sales principles.

This profiling and research effort gives you control over how you allocate your limited lead generation resources.

Avoid These Mistakes

Let me share a few crippling mistakes commonly made that will self-sabotage your prospecting efforts before you make even one call or send your first email.

Mistake #1:

Casting the net too wide.

You might look at your profile, note which of your current accounts fall outside of the dominant profile and say "hey, those are good accounts. I don't want to miss those." So you have the urge to call through those fringe segments so that you don't "miss anyone."

It is not unusual for a company to download tens of thousands of records thinking they are doing a good thing. They are not.

In our example, if the company decides to download 25,000 records (see it all the time) that would mean that at best 14% of outreach time (the A+ and A records) is going to the highest-probability groups. 86% of outreach time is now going toward lower probability groups.

Don't do that.

You want to keep your calling in the high-probability zone and allocate limited resources of time and money to those groups of records that are most likely to produce an account. Once you call those out, you then have the option of dropping down and calling your next highest-probability group, but not before.

Those who refuse to prioritize cast the net too wide end up calling a severely diluted quality prospect pool.

Remember, every call made, or email sent to a low-probability or low-value account is one less call or email sent to a high-probability or high-value account.

Proper allocation of limited resources is key to prospecting success. Be sure to set purposeful priorities among target groups to call. Call the most-probable before you call the less-probable or the least-probable.

Mistake #2

Buying too many records.

I strongly recommend that you not buy more records than you/your team can call in 3 to 6 months maximum.

Many times, to save a few cents per record a company will bulk buy thinking they are saving money.

Not so. Those few cents of savings per record cost you massive amounts of calling efficiency and decreased results in the future. Why? Because your database has aged so significantly by the time you get around to calling it. Lists degrade at the rate of about 2% per month. Lists of smaller businesses and mom and pops degrade at an even faster rate.

The cost of your list is minuscule compared to what it costs you to pay people to work the list.

When you buy too much, you get less and less return for the hours your team invests in prospecting as your team is forced to wade through records that are less and less accurate. By your decision to buy more than your team can eat in a short period, you guarantee a lot of wasted time and effort that you are paying for.

Also, as you start calling in an organized, systematic manner the "profile" of records you decide to call may very well change. You learn things as you call. Don't get married to a list prematurely.

Always work a fresh list. Stay flexible.

Mistake #3

Letting the crap creep in

We saw in our example that just 3.8% of the call universe were "A" group records (A and A+ records totaled 3,417 out of an 88,667 potential call universe.) That means that call records picked randomly have a 19 out of 20 chance of being of lesser quality than your "A" group.

Many companies or reps love to grab Chamber of Commerce lists or lists of top companies found in business periodicals, pull down names found from an Internet search, call companies in the news, or companies they notice from driving around their territory.

So a rep or call team could start with a list containing 100% "A" group targets. As you throw records into your call pile from these other sources, an extremely high percentage of them are going to be from your B, C, D, and E groups.

So you go from a situation where 100% of your activity is directed into a group of "A" quality high-probability targets, to letting more and more of these lower-probability records slip in. Drive by a business that looks like a maybe, throw it into the pile. Hey, the local Evening Snooze just published a list of the top 50 fastest growing businesses. Let's call them; you never know. The Chamber of Commerce just published their directory with current names and phone numbers. Some of those would be good accounts. Let's call them.

Now, rather than 100% of your outreach investment directed into high-probability high-value targets, that percentage starts to slip. 90%, 80%, 70%, 50% or fewer of your calls are into your highest-probability groups. You have lost control over your call universe and made it much harder to get results.

Remember, every call made, or email sent to a low-probability or low-value account is one less call or email sent to a high-probability or high-value account.

I am often called to conduct prospecting rescues (sometimes these turn into prospecting autopsies), and it is very common for me to see that 70%, 80%, 90% or more of call time is directed into low-probability no-probability lower-value target groups.

Sadly, it is also common for these companies to have plenty of easily identifiable "A" quality records to call, but they are not.

Mistake #4

Getting locked into major expenses prematurely.

You want to stay flexible financially until your program gets some real traction and results so that you know you are on the right track.

Many times I will see companies that feel that the "best" database or the Cadillac CRM system is what they need to be successful. They are not.

When you make major investments prematurely, you are now locked in. If that money proves to be not well spent, unless you have unlimited dollars to spend, you have severely limited your effectiveness.

If you or I could predict human behavior, I would not have had to write this book, and you wouldn't be reading it. We would be on some island we own. But we are not, as we cannot with certainty predict human behavior. We can and should make our best judgments about these matters, but we need to test, measure, and adjust.

Can't tell you how many individuals or organizations I have dealt with that make major assumptions and get locked into major expenses to find out that those tools were not what they needed. Often, they have blown their budgets or run out of time and cannot now do it right. Sucks to be them.

It is not just the wasted money on lists, data sources and CRM's I am talking about. The biggest cost is something far more damaging — lost opportunities.

Don't Prematurely Limit Your Ability to Bob and Weave, Test And Make Changes

If you allocate limited resources to the wrong places or get locked into expenses that don't produce for you, you limit your ability to bob and weave, test, and make changes to find what will work.

I strongly recommend that you stay as flexible as you can until you can see your system working.

Rather than invest thousands in an advanced database that you assume will be worth it, spend hundreds of dollars per month on something good enough for test purposes.

Rather than make a major long-term commitment to that Cadillac CRM system, start with something decent at a lower cost you are not locked into.

Stay as flexible as you can financially until you have a system that is working. Only make major or long-term commitments after you have results and proof that you are on the right track.

Other List Selection Tips

Create Your Profile With The Same Data Source From Which You Will Download Your Leads

If you can, create your profile using the same data source you will use to download selected records into your CRM. Different data sources compile records and assign SIC codes, revenue ranges, employee ranges, and other data using their own methods and algorithms. You want as much accuracy as possible and to minimize waste and call time outside of your bullseye. If you use a single data source to create your profile and download leads, the odds are good that the leads you select will be within the bullseye profile you created. If you create your profile using 1 source and pull lists from another, there will usually be less than 100% overlap between the 2 groups as they may pull data from different sources and compile them differently. Which means that you or your team end up calling records outside of your bullseye target. You want to maximize time spent interacting with your bullseye profile and minimize time spent on records outside of your profile.

Think Ahead, Think Duplicates

If you plan to be in business long term, you will be adding to or refreshing your list from time to time. I strongly recommend that you select a data source that remembers the records you have already downloaded so that you do not download them again. This is a huge source of inefficiency and massive amounts (gargantuan) of wasted time. Very simply, if you provide your team with a list that contains records already downloaded, it takes your team a lot of time to wade through them and eliminate them. That is time that could be used to call new bullseye records.

SELL THE MEETING

For many projects, not all, my tool of choice to create the profile, run initial counts, and download lists of corporate targets in SalesGenie. I like it because it has been around a long time, the data is consistent, and it includes all U.S. businesses. The interface allows for more selections when searching, so you can "slice and dice" your list in a fine-tuned manner. That means less wasted time interacting with records outside of your profile. Plus, it remembers what you have downloaded, so you don't have to waste time on duplicate records.

This is also a great place to ponder the difference between price and cost.

There are less expensive databases. The cheaper databases tend to have interfaces with fewer selection variables. That means your lists tend to be broader and a more watered down version of your best bullseye profile to call. Plus, many of the cheaper data sources do not remember what you have previously ordered, so future orders will contain a lot of duplicates that will waste time.

Now the PRICE you pay for data upfront might be less than other options, but the COST of that data, after you include paying for the hours it takes to call through broader lists that return less response, and the cost of the time it takes to deal with duplicates, will be far higher.

Those facts do not include the bigger price you pay when you choose lowest initial price data, and that is the value of the opportunities you lose when you work outside of your target profile and very inefficiently. (Plus, try to keep good callers when you make them waste tremendous amounts of time, at the expense of them doing the things that will earn more money for themselves and the company, because you were short-sighted and thought it a good idea to buy a cheaper list.)

The low price you paid for your list will be long forgotten when you factor in the cost of time wasted, inefficiency and lost opportunities.

The price you pay for lists is by far your lowest cost in prospecting. Buy solid data and think of all the costs incurred by using that data before making your choice.

Identifying Decision-makers Within Companies Targeted

A database like SalesGenie is great when you wish to build a profile and identify companies that fit that profile. It is not a great tool (in my opinion) when it comes to identifying whom to contact within a targeted company.

For that purpose, my tool of preference is Linkedin Sales Navigator. You can select a targeted company and search by title, level of authority, company size, and other variables. This has practically eliminated the need to call a company to determine who the decision-maker it.

Plus, with Sales Navigator, you can search by specific titles within companies of a certain size or within targeted industries. The keyword search capability also enables you to get creative with your searches and zero in on bullseye targets.

Select Data Sources Well

You have a lot of choices. Be aware of all the variables of profiling your targets and refreshing your list in the future. If you choose poorly, you will weigh your team down with inefficiency baked into your process. Choose wisely, and you keep your team focused on bullseye targets and enable them to prospect most efficiently.

Wish to Find Out Which Tools I Use?
Get the list of data sources for leads and emails I use
and recommend to clients.
You will also get checklists and script supplements to this book.
ScottChannell.com/STM-book-extras

Chapter 7
CRM/Contact Manager Selection And Setup

Do you strap a weight belt on before you go swimming?

Do you carry a bowling bowl when you run a road race?

Well, if you don't use a contact manager or CRM and set it up properly, you are doing the same thing prospecting.

It's Not All About Scripts

"Good scripts" won't save you if you are not talking to the right people. They won't save you if you are not talking to enough of them.

It is how you are set up, and the <u>efficiency</u> with which you prospect, that enables you to have conversations with enough qualified prospects to meet your sales goals. Can you move quickly enough through a large pool of grade "A" prospects to even have a chance for success?

If you are not set up properly, you can't.

If you are prospecting using a paper system, you are doomed to fail. If you are tracking your calls using a spreadsheet, you are doomed to fail. In either case, before you even make your first dial, you have <u>no chance</u> of success.

**Not Using a Contact Manager?
You Are Not Really in Sales.**

Your contact manager makes you more efficient, enables you to properly allocate limited time and resources, and enables you to utilize more advanced marketing strategies and touch systems.

If you are not using a properly setup contact manager or CRM, you are doomed.

Efficiency

Greater efficiency means more opportunities for time invested. But, with success comes a problem. Once you start generating meetings you have to prepare for and attend those meetings. Conduct those meetings correctly, and your pipeline starts to grow. Oh, and once they close, those pesky clients want to continue to feel the love.

That all takes time, which means you have even less time to prospect. You must create, manage and master a system now in anticipation of the day when your time is short.

You may even have to turn over prospecting duties to someone else. To do that, you need a system that can be duplicated.

Time and Resource Allocation

Time and money. When you are smiling, dialing, sending emails and more, you have to constantly improve efficiency and effectiveness to get more results from your limited time and money.

It's All A Giant Sorting Process.

You need to be in control of where you allocate your time and money.

As you call, you want to be able to control how much time you spend with those worth more and how much time you spend on those worth less. How much time spent with those who will buy now, how much time spent with those who will buy later. How much time on higher-margin stuff, those more probable to close, yada yada yada.

All those calls where you don't connect with a decision-maker can be extremely valuable to you as you can pick up valuable recon info that enables you to sort records in order of priority.

You Are In Charge At All Times, Not Those You Call.

Remember this. Those you call and speak to are not in charge of your time. You are.

You do not do things like follow up, send info or call back just because a voice asks you to. No way. That is certain prospecting death. But more on this a bit later. Suffice it to say in this "setup" stage you want to enable yourself to sort…

SELL THE MEETING

By worth

By category

By other sub-segments

Many start calling without proper setup and doom themselves to massive outreach inefficiency, lost opportunities to pick up data which would help them, and an inability to move up to more advanced techniques. What a waste. Or, some of you have an incompetent boss who thinks sales management begins and ends with exhorting people to "make more calls." I pity you.

I want you to imagine that you have called 500 or 1,000 companies. You have smiled and dialed, you have fought battles with dragons, gatekeepers, and other vermin. You survived voicemail hell, you have endured corporate phone systems, and you are still standing (or sitting) ready to dial again.

After all that work, can you, with just a few keystrokes break out your highest potential "A" type accounts? Your "B" accounts?

With just a few keystrokes could you break out suspects or prospects by current vendor, contract renewal date or what they might buy from you? Are there other criteria you would like to be able to sort by?

Have you coded the totally worthless and too small value prospects so that you won't spend time or money on them again?

As you called, did you take advantage of every opportunity to discover if they had a current vendor, the volume of their spend, the best time to reach out, and many other factors that would help you in the future?

You are making the calls anyway, so, on all those calls where you did not get hold of a decision-maker, did you make every effort to extract value from that call and improve your knowledge about their potential worth and how to reach the decision-maker in the future?

If you did do these things, is there a dedicated field for these tidbits that enable you to find it and sort by it in the future?

The worst and most useless place to record this info is in the notes. You simply cannot search and sort properly if various forms of data is mindlessly put into notes.

You should be able to do all these things.

You Have Two Objectives With Your Calls

First, connect with as many top decision-makers as you can and book as many meetings or "next steps" as you can whether they be a face-to-face meeting, phone appointment, discovery calls, webinar, or whatever label you place on your call objective.

Booking as many meetings as you can is your primary objective.

However, here is where reality hits the road. Most of those calls will never reach the decision-maker. A good number of those you reach, even in your "A" group, will not be buyers. Of the buyers, some will buy too little to be worth the effort.

The second objective of your calls is to collect "recon" info on your targets. Why?

Well, assuming you are going to be in business for more than a day or a week, you are going to be calling people back. You also probably have other marketing tools you could use to further business development.

If you make a call and can't book a meeting, you may be able to determine whether they are a buyer or not. Whether they buy a little or a lot, who their current vendor is, whether they have a contract renewal date. Maybe knowing whether they use certain technologies would be helpful to you. Knowing what side of the street they are on might help.

You are making the calls. If you are the owner or manager, you are making a large investment to make those calls. If you can't book a meeting, use the call to gather recon information that will make it more likely that you book a meeting in the future.

If you confirm that they currently purchase, you can continue to call them.

If you confirm that they buy a lot, you now have the option to invest more in prospecting them as you see fit. You could make more calls, integrate other marketing tools or have special offers for the whales you identify.

If you find out they are not buyers or buy little, you can allocate fewer resources of time and money to them. Maybe you call them less. Maybe you never call them again.

SELL THE MEETING

If you view your calling or outreach efforts as part of an overall effective marketing plan, *the calling is <u>part</u> of your process*, not the whole process.

Why not get full value from your calling investment? You need meetings, but you also need information to properly allocate resources of time and money for future success.

You want to set yourself up to collect that info during the call but also to access it and be able to sort and call up sub-groups of records in your database with a few keystrokes. That provides you with the ability to allocate time and money for the best results and also allows you to customize messaging or utilize other marketing tools for greater results within that sub-group.

But you won't be able to if you don't think through what info would help to allocate your time and what info would enable you to launch more impactful responsive marketing or follow-up efforts to sub-segments of your suspect or prospect universe.

A Tale of Prospecting Nirvana

This company sells a B2B service for a monthly fee that ranges from $300 to $3,000 a month. A few accounts are worth more. Contracts are typically 1-3 years in length. The dominant method of business development is calling for a meeting.

By far the most profitable accounts are $1,000 a month or more. With these accounts the margins are higher. Expectations are more easily met, there is less client churn and the renewal rates are higher.

Below $1,000 a month, there is trouble brewing in River City. Below $500 a month, there are red flags everywhere. Margins are tighter as these accounts are more price conscious. Accounts in this group tend to have unrealistic expectations. That combination of having unrealistic expectations and being hyper price conscious makes it harder to service them satisfactorily. Client churn is much higher within this group. They are less loyal and more likely to bolt to chase a promise of a lower price. As the monthly commitment decreases, these problems tend to increase.

As these smaller volume lower-margin accounts leave, they must be replaced. The costs of sale for smaller low-profit accounts that churn is high. Those costs mean these accounts are even less profitable.

This Strategy Is Most Profitable

This division of a national company is consistently among the most profitable, has a lower cost of sale, and ranks at the top of corporate-wide meetings booked, closing ratio, the average size of sale and account retention.

What do they do that is so different? Not a lot. But those slight differences leverage superior sales results and profitability.

This division carefully selected their call targets based upon a proper profile and set priorities. They called all the A's and some of the B's. The C's, D's, and E's were never touched.

As they made their first pass through their call list, they did everything they could to book meetings, but they also made a concerted effort to gather recon info.

Those who were determined to be low-value, no-value, low-probability suspects were dropped from further calling.

Those who were determined to be potential buyers or still viable for calling were called again.

With every call, if they couldn't reach the decision-maker or book a meeting, they dug in deep to gather all the recon info they could. Do they use the service? How often? Do they have a vendor or do it in-house? How large is the facility? When will they review options for new vendors? Is there a contract renewal date? On and on.

With no extra investment, **they are making the calls anyway**; they ask questions to get all the information they can. They use that info to sort and prioritize their calling. To launch more calls or use other marketing tools within sub-segments where it makes economic sense to do so.

They now are prospecting from a space where they have identified all the suspects within their territory most likely to turn into a good account. These "good" accounts pay a reasonable fee with healthy margins per month, they have reasonable expectations, and their needs can be satisfied. They renew at a high rate. Client churn is low.

That Is How You Make Money

Rather than call the phonebook and the 70,000+ companies that "maybe" would buy at a price is anybody's guess and likely churn for the possibility of saving a dollar, they can focus on a group of 1,200 highly targeted suspects.

That group is more than sufficient to replace their low account turnover and provide growth. As they are more focused on a smaller higher-value and higher-probability group, they can call more consistently. That leads to greater recognition of their value messaging and differentiation.

When there is a service failure with a competing vendor, or it is time to review vendor options, they are there. The increased recognition and consistent value messaging make it easier to get in the door. As they have touched these targets consistently over a period of time, there is more comfort and trust. Closing ratios are high. Once closed, as they have reasonable expectations and are paying enough to be serviced properly, they tend to renew again and again.

That Is How You Make Money.

How about the rest? The other divisions in the company that are not at the top of the list when it comes to sales, cost of sale, average sale size, and account retention. They have a great role model to follow. Why not do better?

Well, they do what most do. They call too many targets. They don't identify the high-probability from the low-probability. They think short-term immediate results only. They have not set themselves up for maximum call efficiency. They don't gather recon info as they go. They are not able to properly allocate their time or resources as they chose not to make the one-time investment of a few hours in basic list research, setup, and organization, so they are now doomed to spending hundreds if not thousands of hours calling inefficiently to lower-probability or no-probability targets that buy less, if at all.

Beware "Activity" Mode

The rest are in "activity" mode. Dial, dial, dial. They think the lack of sales and profits is due to a lack of dials. They think more activity can make up for their poor marketing planning and setup. It can't.

Your CRM/Contact Manager Fields And Coding

Here are the standard fields you see in a contact manager.

Company
Contact name
Title
Street Address
City
State
Zip code
Main company phone number
Direct dial number
Phone extension
Cell phone
Email
Website

Other Fields That Help

Status   Suspect, Prospect, Client.

Are they a suspect, prospect or client? A "suspect" is someone who fits your profile of a potentially good customer/client. A "prospect" is someone who has taken some action to inquire, interact or meet with you. A "client" has purchased. These groups can be further sub-divided.

Worth   A, B, C, D, E.

If they bought, how much would they buy? Keep it simple and define A – E ranges. "A" is the highest worth range. "C" is average. NOTE: How much they will buy has nothing to do with <u>when</u> they might buy. Whether they may buy now or 2 years from now, their potential worth is the same. Do not mix the concepts of how much and when they might buy into one field.

Another way to use the worth field is to segment by whether they are a client, prospect or suspect. For example, different clients have varying levels of repurchase potential. You might "worth" code your clients as C1, C2, C3, C4, C5. C1 is the highest value, C3 an average value, etc.

You could do the same conceptually for your inquiries (prospects) and suspects.

This helps you with integrating other marketing or sales tools. Example: You might put your higher than average repurchase potential clients on a direct mail follow-up program.

Another example: When you are calling you might run into a higher-value suspect worth more effort and investment. If you code it a certain way that could trigger them getting a direct mail touch from you every week for 6 weeks, without you having to think about it, because you have thought ahead and coded it appropriately. They are now part of a group that is easily selected. Working with groups is far more efficient and makes things far more likely to happen than coordinating follow-ups on an individual record basis.

Date In:

When did they first inquire? If recency of inquiry correlates to purchasing you will want to be able to sort by date of inquiry. I like to code "date in" by week. If you enter my system during the 26th week of 2018 your "date in" code would be 1826. Very simple. This way touches and activities can be launched by groups. "Grouping" greatly increases efficiency and the likelihood that a follow-up or touch will happen.

Source:

What list did the record/lead come from?

SIC Code or industry:

Use SIC Codes, NAICS codes or standard industry descriptions to be able to sort by industry.

Another worth field:

Many times there is something you can find out that is a very good indicator of potential worth. It might be units per month, square footage, annual spend. So set up a field to note this number. For example, in my business, the number of salespeople at a company is a very good indicator of the potential worth of an account. So I have a field labeled "Salespeople" tucked right under my worth field. You can do something similar.

Revenue range:

What is the company's annual revenue? This data might come from your list source or be picked up by you when calling.

Employee range:

How many employees does the company have? Again, your list source may estimate this. You would verify/update during calls.

The contract, bid, or vendor review date:

When will they review their current relationship? When does a current contract expire?

Do they have a current vendor:

Yes or No.

Name of current vendor:

Whose lunch money are you trying to grab?

Product or service lines they may need:

If you sell widgets, wadgets, and donuts you might have a field for each you could check off. That would enable you to customize your sale and marketing efforts to exactly what these sub-groups might buy.

Other Helpful Fields

Refer to as: This is a field for your eyes only. If someone has a hard to pronounce name, a nickname, or Robert is going to throw a fit if you call them Bob, note it in this field.

SOR: See another record. Sometimes you may have multiple records for a contact. Maybe they have two offices. Maybe you have a company and home address, so you maintain two records in your database. But only one should be your control. So very simply, when a contact has more than one record, I label the control record as MR (main record.) This is the record where all calls and activity are noted. The other records are coded SR (secondary record.) When you see this, you know to work from the main record. Avoid having notes in multiple places.

LI location: Linkedin location. Sometimes your decision-maker may not work at headquarters, or you may not have an address. Note their LinkedIn location here.

SELL THE MEETING

LI: Are they a LinkedIn connection? You might code this as CN: Connection, IS: Invite sent, IP: Invite Pending, IR: Invite Refused.

ML: Is the address mailable? If mail is returned, put NDA in this field. Non-Deliverable Address. Update it or don't waste mail money in future mailings to them.

Needs: Did they fill in a form when they made an inquiry and describe what they needed? Have a field for this info to flow into.

TGrp: These are for "Touch Group" coding. As you have given yourself the ability to slice and dice your database, you can interact with groups of records in different ways. Set up a few fields to code these "touch groups." TGrp1. TGrp2. TGrp3. Much easier to manage and launch group interactions.

Email2: Many times it is helpful to have a field for an additional secondary email address. If you send group emails using your CRM/contact manager you might use email1 as the field for group email blasts and email2 if a contact has not given permission, opted out, or you just want a place for a secondary email address.

Step: What step of the call process are they?

I use the following coding for the step field. This field is labeled "C-Step" for calling step on the sample contact manager layout provided. See link at end of chapter.

1/ Worthless
2/ On-deck
3/ Active
4/ Inactive
5/ Special
6/ Priority
7/ Hot
8/ Meeting booked

Very simply, when I call a record and determine that it is worthless and should never be called again, I code it as a "1" in the step field. Even though a record should never be called again, don't delete it because if ever that company shows up in a new list you will know not to reach out.

"On-deck" simply means that it is waiting. It flags that there is something to do on this record before you call. Maybe research or an update. Maybe you got an inquiry from a sales rep within a company that might be worth calling. You would code this record as a "2" for "on-deck" and make a note to research the company.

"Active" and "Inactive," tells you whether you are in active prospecting mode or whether they are currently inactive. Inactive means that it is a perfectly good record that you have already called. You will call again at a time you have scheduled.

"Special," "priority," and "hot" I view as wearing a belt and suspenders. When someone indicates that they are ready to act at some time shortly, they are worth more of your time.

So if someone tells you they will book a meeting or buy 3 or 4 months from now, I code it as a "5" (special, worth more than the average record). If the time period is about 60 days that is coded as a "6." (priority). If that event occurs within 30 days, I code it a "7." (Hot, or as I like to refer to it "don't screw this up, Scott.")

So what does this do? Well, you will schedule all callbacks in your CRM of course. But let's be honest, it is normal to fall behind in your calling. For some records, just scheduling a callback date is not enough. When you fall behind, and you have a lot of stragglers in your database, suspects with callback dates that have passed, you can easily check on your 5's, 6's and 7's with a few keystrokes. Those will not slip through the cracks. Avoids the problem of dialing your fingers raw to identify a solid opportunity then forgetting to call back when agreed.

Meeting Booked: Check this field when they have agreed to a face-to-face meeting or discovery call.

Sales Stage: This is S-Stage on the sample layout. Once a record moves beyond the calling stage to the sales stage, I use these codes to note sales stage status.

Closed
IP-High (In process, high chance of closing)
IP-Low (In process, low chance of closing)
MT/Inq (Meeting or inquiry stage)
Nope

Key Info: I love this field. When you are calling a record, you do not want to have to bop around multiple pages and scroll up and down to see if there is any key info you should know before making a call. On the sample layout, you will see a larger space for "Key Info." Here is where you can put the stuff you want to hit you in the face before you make a call. It is not the place you put your call by call notes. It is reserved for the most critical info and reminders you want to hit you in the face when you open a record.

Even More Fields You Might Find Helpful

In my system, I use direct mail to touch certain classes of clients, prospects, and suspects. This is done by groups and not individual records to make it easier to get out the door. To do this, you might want to vary the frequency of the touches, and the date of the starting point for the touch sequence. In my world, I have a field "freq" for the frequency of the touches. 0=they get nothing, 1=every six weeks, 2=every quarter, 3=every six months. This makes it easy to get newsletters, special reports, and other touches out the door to those I want to mail to on an ongoing basis.

For those who are new and worth the extra effort and investment, they may receive a multi-step touch sequence by mail over 7 weeks. (I am a big believer in the "Rule of 7." I note the date the touch sequence is going to start in the "TchS" (Touches Start) field. In that field, I enter the year and week of the first touch. I am writing this on February 7, 2019, which is the 7th week or 2019 so that would be coded as 1907. Every week we select the records designated for mailing on a rolling basis. Makes it much easier to get things out the door to those I want to be on the receiving end of a consistent touch sequence to start the relationship and cement certain impressions in their mind. After that, they would get ongoing touches based upon their potential value. Simple, easy, effective. All due to a little forethought and preparation.

Recent: You will see this as "Rcnt" on the sample layout. Sometimes a record may enter your system and not respond for years. Might be a past client or previous inquiry. Their record will be coded with a "date in" that might be years ago. But if they call you again, and recency of inquiry relates to the probability of sale, you might want to note their most recent action. I use this field to note the date of recent activity.

Enable Yourself To Use More Advanced Marketing

This simple setup enables you to implement marketing initiatives to more defined sub-segments for even more response and sales conversions.

Imagine you have called 500 companies. That takes a lot of time and resources. Your calling process should uncover for you who buys what, when, and in what amounts. Wouldn't you love to be able to launch targeted marketing campaigns to the 50 biggest potential buyers among that 500? How about the 100 companies you determined buy a lot of widgets? Or the companies that will buy within the next three months, or the companies that buy from your competitor with the worst service and the highest account turnover rate?

What I want you to get from this is how much value you get from simple coding and segmentation. If you have a team, these concepts are even more valuable to you. You might think "Channell, some of your codes are dumb," but they work for me. Start thinking about how coding and segmentation would help you.

Remember, you are making the calls anyway. You might as well extract all the info you can when you do and have a place to put it so that you can use it. You are making the calls anyway and should be gathering this information. Make maximum use of that time and investment.

Think Ahead For Maximum Advantage From Your Calling Efforts

The small number of hours you spend thinking about the fields that would help and properly setting up your CRM/contact manager return that investment multiple times every single week.

Skip this step, and you doom yourself to significant calling inefficiency. You also deny yourself the opportunity to implement more advanced calling techniques or to target sub-groups for greater penetration and response.

Skip this step, and you doom yourself to long-term entry level calling. You won't be able to meaningfully allocate time to the more worthwhile targets as you won't know who they are. If you do know, but that info isn't in a searchable field, you have no way to extract them in groups for efficient action.

You doom yourself to an activity based, make more dials, short-term focused calling effort. As you have no way to reach out smarter or more efficiently, your only option will be to "make more dials." Another way to describe hell.

View My Layout

I use ACT as a contact manager/CRM and you can view a screenshot of my layout by using this link. Https://www.scottchannell.com/crm-layout

Worksheets, additional scripts, and periodic updates are available to readers of this book at ScottChannell.com/STM-book-extras

Chapter 8
Your Call Process:
The Three Cycles of Three:
Dials, Touches, and Letting Go.

Your "great scripts" do you no good if you are not talking to the right people. A great script doesn't help you if you are not talking to enough of the right people.

Whether they pick up the phone and you slay them with your script, or they respond to a voicemail or mail, you must interact with the right level of decision-maker at the right frequency to have any chance at setting appointments or discovery calls.

This chapter is about the process you follow to maximize the odds that you will interact with your targeted decision-maker, and enough of them to reach your overall goals for success.

This chapter is also about the efficiency of your calling. The process you use to "bump" into as many targeted decision-makers as you can with the time you dedicate to prospecting. The more decision-makers you interact with per hour or week of calling, the greater your chance of success.

Efficiency And Effectiveness

The efficiency of your calling is at least as important, if not more important, than the effectiveness of your calling.

Effectiveness is how good you are at converting an interaction into a meeting. What good is having the right scripts or ability to convert a conversation, voicemail or email reply into a meeting if you don't have many conversations or replies? Not much.

Being efficient with your outreach efforts gives you the chance to be effective with your outreach efforts.

Without conversations and replies you are going nowhere. Don't care how good your offering is or your ability to pitch it. Without a system to generate enough opportunities to pitch the right people, you are whistling in the wind.

In this section we answer the following questions:

How often do you call?
When do you call?
When do you engage the gatekeeper?
When do we leave a message or voicemail? Send an email?
When do you let go?
When do you start again?

We will answer those questions, but first…

Core Concepts That Drive Call Process, A Few Surprises

I set more than 2,000 C-Level sales appointments.

I never cared about the result of any one call.

I never researched a company before calling it. (That you need to "research" a company before calling is the worst advice you will hear or might act upon.)

I focused more on the efficiency of my calling than I did the effectiveness of my calling.

I never tried to "get through" the gatekeeper. Why would anyone keep banging their head against a brick wall?

All To Be Explained, Some Bonus Concepts

By far your greatest chance of scheduling a meeting or discovery call arises from a conversation with the top decision-maker or a reply from an email or voicemail. By far, a conversation or reply is your best chance to set a meeting. Nothing else comes close.

Complete the process that provides you with your best chance to set a meeting before you drop down to a less effective option.

Work your plan. Do not let those you interact with dictate your plan.

SELL THE MEETING

There is no message you can leave with a gatekeeper that can sell a meeting, so don't bother trying. All that will do is throw you off the process that gives you your best chance of scheduling a meeting. Once you have exhausted the process that gives you the best chance to interact with your top-level decision-maker you might, in some high-value instances, decide to throw a "Hail Mary" with the gatekeeper. We will discuss the timing and format of a 'Hail Mary" in a bit.

Knowing when to let go and stop calling is critical to success.

All Very Important Questions And Concepts

Just as your selection of records to call has a major impact on results, your messaging and scripts has a major impact on results, your process of calling has a major impact on results.

If you call randomly or haphazardly, results for your prospecting time invested will be low. If you stick to a winning process, the results for your time will go up. Go up a lot.

Two Marketing Principles Come into Play

You want to call/email like Goldilocks. Not too much. Not too little. Just right.

But what is just right? Well, let's start with some facts. Studies have shown that it takes 9-12 dials to get a decision-maker in a large organization to pick up the phone. Not 9 dials to 9 different decision-makers. No surprise that those numbers are steadily increasing.

Over my coaching and training career of the last 20+ years, I can also tell you that those who are most successful tend to call consistent with those numbers. Those who are less successful tend to make fewer dials and in a more haphazard manner.

So, we start with the concept that if you are not making at least 9 dials to a decision-maker with your core calling process, you are not in a zone of dialing activity where we can reasonably expect them to pick up the phone.

The "Rule of 7"

There is another marketing concept important to your call process. It is the "Rule of 7."

Very simply people need to be "touched" by you multiple times with a consistent message. It is the combination of frequency and consistency that enables people to grasp what you are communicating.

One consistent message delivered multiple times. That is the winning communication formula.

Anything Communicated Once, Is The Equivalent, Of Communicating Nothing At All.

Messages that change are less likely to be grasped.

Less frequent "touches" are harder for your prospect to recognize. Messages that are too far apart have less impact.

These are all basic marketing and communication principles that come into play when formulating your call process.

You need to dial your target 9-12 times. You need to "touch" your target with a consistent message multiple times.

The Three Cycles Of Three

Reach out to your target with 3 cycles of 3 dials 3 business days apart. At the end of every cycle leave your "touches." Your touches most commonly would be voicemail and email.

So let's outline the 3 cycles of 3 calling process. Let's assume you are prospecting 20-25 hours a week. You sit at your desk and can call 4 or 5 hours a day. That is a perfect world of calling that few dwell in, but let's start there.

Once you identify or confirm a decision-maker within a targeted company you wish to meet with that is the official launch of your call process to that target. That is day 1, action 1. With this step, your call process is "launched" as to that particular suspect.

You would then make 3 dials to that decision-maker within a very short period of time, a day or 2, not a week or 2. On the first 2 dials of the cycle, if you do not speak to your decision-maker, you do not leave a voicemail or send an email. You do not try to "get through the gate-keeper" or respond to "what is this about?" On the 3rd dial, if you have not reached your decision-maker, you leave your "touches." A voicemail and an email. You schedule the next cycle of calls for 3 business days later.

SELL THE MEETING

Three business days later, when you open your CRM that follow-up call you scheduled pops up. You again make 3 dials over a day or 2. Just as in the first cycle, on the first 2 dials, if you don't speak to your decision-maker, you do not engage or try to get through the gatekeeper. On the 3rd dial, if you do not speak to your target, you leave your touches: a voicemail and an email. You schedule your next call for three business days later.

Three business days later, that follow-up call will pop up on your contact manager/CRM activity list. You follow the same procedure. Three dials. No gatekeeper engagement. Leave your touches if you don't speak to your target with the 3rd dial.

That Is Your Core Calling Process

Over about 2 weeks, you will make a minimum of 9 dials to a specific top-level decision-maker. You will do this with 3 bursts of 3 dials. Each burst of calls is made within a very short period, a day or 2. At the end of each cycle, you leave a voicemail and send an email. At the end of this calling process, you must let go and schedule another 3 cycles of 3 calling sequence to begin in the future.

9 To 12 Dials. When More Or Less?

Work your process. When in doubt, when you are bored, when you want to convince yourself that making this call at this time is a waste of time or not worth it, work your process. Don't think. Work your process.

Studies show and common sense tell us it takes a major effort to get somebody to pick up the phone or reply. A few dials or dials spread out over a longer period have proven to be less effective. It is just basic marketing 101.

Once you have decided to call someone you have committed to complete your call process. Work your process.

Vary from your core calling process only when you uncover objective information that warrants you varying from your call process. If you call and determine, not guess, but are told or determine that a prospect's potential worth is below average, that would justify making fewer dials. If you know that your bullseye profile of a good account typically has a minimum of 50 employees and the company you are calling has 25, then you have an objective reason to stop calling or call a bit less.

On the flip side, if you uncover objective information that tells you that your targeted company has an above average worth, then you might decide to add a 4th or 5th cycle to your calling. That prospect is worth more of your time.

It Is Very Important To Let Go

To be successful at appointment setting, you need to move through a large group of records that fit a very tight profile to have success. You need to call enough to maximize the chance of achieving your business objective, but you need to stop at your point of diminishing returns. If you don't stop calling at your point of diminishing returns, that limits your ability to launch your process with new targets. By dumping new targets in your funnel, calling, and then letting go at the point of diminishing returns you call a larger pool of targets. If you don't let go, you end up working a smaller pool and calling the same companies over and over with less chance of success.

When Do You Call Back?

When you do let go, you must schedule the next action. Without exception, every time you complete a call, you must schedule the next action. When you reach the point of diminishing returns with a target, at some point you will call back and try again. By default, a good rule of thumb is that for a suspect company with an average size potential worth, relaunching the cycle of calling in 6 months seems to work. For those records that you know have an above average potential value, you might try again in 4 months. For those you determine have less than average value potential, but still acceptable, you might choose to re-launch the cycle of calling in 9 or 12 months.

Time allocation is critical to your success. Not all suspects or prospects are equal. You must consciously allocate more time to those worth more of your time and spend less time or no time with those of less or no potential value.

Two Things Gatekeepers Can Help You With

Appreciate that gatekeepers can only help you with 2 things. They can provide you worth info so that you can properly sort and allocate your time. They can also provide you information that increases the odds of you interacting with your target, direct dial, extension numbers, or email address. That is about it.

You must work your process and do the things that you know provide you the best odds, by far, of booking a meeting or discovery call. That is getting your target to pick up the phone so that you can slay them with your well-honed pitch or getting a reply to an email or voicemail.

As you call, it is perfectly OK to extract from gatekeepers worth (potential account value) and contact info. You should make every effort to determine whether a target is high, average, or below average value potential. You should stockpile all the direct dial and extension numbers you can. Grab all the email addresses you can. The scripts you would use to do that are in the script section.

But, if you try to engage the gatekeeper, answer their questions, "Who's calling and what is this regarding?" That is a guaranteed dead end. You are virtually guaranteed to be told they are "all set" or be invited to leave a message. That stops your call process in its tracks. You can't work your process, call back on schedule, or if you do respond maybe, you can't call back at all. Now you are working your gatekeeper's plan, not your plan. Don't do that.

Complete and exhaust the process that you know provides you, by far, the greatest chance to achieve your objective before you drop down to a process which provides you a far less chance to do so.

Answering their questions or, heaven forbid, leaving a message with them is a low result behavior, so don't do it.

When Do You Engage The Gatekeeper?

At the end of your call process, when you have reached your point of diminishing returns, if a target has very high potential, you might want to try a "Hail Mary." Keep in mind that any message you leave a gatekeeper over the phone cannot sell your meeting. Only you can sell your meeting. So you want to put something in the gatekeeper's hands that, if it were shared with your targeted decision-maker, would have a chance of selling your meeting.

So rather than "leave a message" you might offer to send a gatekeeper a one-page pdf or email that explains what you do, the companies that have chosen you, the problems you solve with representative results. You offer to send that (they don't have to pretend they are taking a message) and then call the gatekeeper back in a few days to see if Mr. or Ms. Big wishes to meet. That way you don't have to keep calling back.

If you put something in their hands that can sell your meeting, you have a shot at success.

Leave Your "Touches" At The End of Each Cycle

You want to leave a sufficient number of consistent touches such that your target will recognize the message and act upon it. At the same time, we know that you have to make a certain number of calls to have a chance of success. Leave your voicemail and send your email at the end of each cycle of calling.

No Researching? Are You Kidding Me?

The idea that you must know something about a company before you call them, that you must research them, I think is the most destructive, insane, worthless advice you will ever hear about prospecting to set sales appointments and discovery calls. The fact that the great unwashed seem to accept it blindly does not make it good advice. I think that anyone who seriously thinks about this for just a little while would recognize just how ridiculous this commonly accepted nugget of wisdom is.

Let me explain while I hyperventilate. If you are going to have any serious chance of success at appointment setting, you will have to call a very carefully selected group of targets. A group that fits the profile of your current and past accounts you would like to clone. If the companies or individual you call is not in that bullseye, they are darn close to it or selected for very strategic reasons. You are not calling the phonebook or records selected on whims or because they happen to be easily available and, what the heck, you never know, so let's just call and see what happens. You are calling a very carefully chosen group.

As to that carefully selected target group, you should know a lot about them. As to that <u>group</u> of records, you should know their needs and wants, problems, challenges, triggers, and more. You interact with that group prepared to relate issues and offer solutions to problems <u>common to the group</u> and to speak their language.

You research the needs thoroughly within the **group** that you can solve.

Once you start calling and interacting, it is your goal to book as many appointments you can among a group of similarly situated targets. For every 100 companies you call, within that carefully selected group, you are seeking to book 12 meetings rather than 6. For every week you call you are seeking to book on average 7 meetings a week rather than 2. It matters not which companies you book the meetings with within that group.

Your goal is to work a process so that for the same amount of effort invested you book 10 qualified appointments rather than 4. Which specific companies you book with is of less significance. They wouldn't be in the group you are calling unless there was a high probability that they would be worthwhile. You would not keep calling them unless they were worthwhile. Your goal is to book the greatest number of worthwhile appointments for the time invested, not to book meetings with company X, company Y, or company Z.

The First Reason Researching Individual Companies Is Dumb: Math

If you interact with a very carefully selected **group** of targets using a consistent process at some point, you will realize that on average you book X number of meetings per week. That is your baseline. X.

Then you think, well if I researched each company before I called them, so I knew something about them, that would improve my results. So you spend half of your time researching (at least) and half your time calling. For that "researching" to be worthwhile, you would have to <u>double call productivity</u> just to break even.

That never happens.

The Second Reason Researching Individual Companies Is Dumb: Your "Research" Is Unlikely To Uncover Buying Motivations.

I would be willing to bet that if you thought about your best accounts, why they hired you, and what was going on within the company that motivated them to change vendors or launch a new initiative, that those reasons were not publicly available. Those reasons, the buying motivations, the problems you could solve that are blowing their hair back were not to be found on their website, Linkedin, or in a press release.

Let's say you did find something with your "research." How are you weaving it into your pitch? How do you use it to increase the odds that you will achieve your business objectives? When I ask reps who want to research to give me some examples of how they use it in their pitch the usual response is a Fred Flintstone imitation "Yubba, Yubba, Yubba..." This "critical" research that takes away from call time is rarely used, so why bother?

On top of the fact that what you find with your "research" will not uncover the real buying motivation, or even be used in your pitch, it has to make a big enough difference in results to justify the research time, which I have never seen.

You Are Highly Credible, Have Great Experience, Have Great Examples Of Solving Problems They Have, And You Are Going To Talk About What?

If you are a highly experienced provider, with a long list of satisfied clients with recognizable names you could mention, you have many specific project results and achievements you could mention that would be meaningful to your suspects. Instead of talking about those things, which would enable someone who has problems you could solve and would be willing to spend time with someone with expertise and experience who seems better than what they might find with a google search, you are going to talk about what? "I notice you are moving; I see you won an award, hiring some people?" You are asking a top-level person to give you 30-60 minutes of their time. The fact that you pulled something off the web or read a newspaper article or press release is not going to impress someone of that level to give you that time.

> Worksheets, additional scripts, and periodic updates
> are available to readers of this book at
> ScottChannell.com/STM-book-extras

Chapter 9
Your "Pile of Words."

Preparation For "Great Scripts" and Verbiage That Wins.

If you have a sales team that generates leads using the telephone or email and don't have a solid and complete "pile of words" to work from, it is a given that your sales reps are leaking value with every conversation.

To think that your team will be as effective marching toward their sales quota when they are guessing, assuming, saying what pops into their minds at the moment or working with whatever they can remember or feel comfortable with is delusional.

At every step, your team must be aware of the verbiage that is most likely to accomplish their business objective and move to the next step. A prospecting call is calculated to earn the first meeting. A first meeting is calculated to earn the 2nd interaction. (Reality for multi-step sales: no 2nd meeting, no sale.)

Being aware of best verbiage and being prepared to deliver it is just preparation

Common sense tells us that in any situation there are words, facts, phrases, statistics, and quotes that when used tend to achieve the result sought more than other words. If you are aware of that verbiage and use it, the odds of success go way up. Preparing to use the best verbiage calculated to achieve your business objective at any particular step is called scripting. In some stages of the prospecting or sales process it will be a word-for-word preparation. In others, you will work from a game plan and mini-scripts you work in as appropriate.

The preparation for good core scripting pays big dividends at all stages of your sales process.

To write great scripts and mini-scripts you need a "pile of words."

There may be five ways to describe what you do; you need to pick the best one. You will probably use 3 benefits at most in a prospecting script, but sales teams (not individual sales reps) will often come up with 30, 50, or more benefits delivered by your offering.

There may be multiple ways to communicate your credibility — multiple ways to describe what prospects will get at a meeting with you. You need to brainstorm all the things you might say, then prioritize. You pick the best and most impactful to use in your prospecting scripts and the rest you weave in as appropriate deeper into the sales process. If you don't create a pile of words, your sales team isn't aware of the best verbiage to use.

Script Preparation Enables You To Convey Authority And Knowledge.

People buy from peers. People buy from those they think are prepared. People spend time with those they feel are authorities and knowledgeable. When you have invested some conscious thought and written down the words to use when seconds count, your odds of sales prospecting success go up.

If you don't start from a place of preparation, every hem and haw, pause, and wasted word, and watered down phrasing, can't think of what to say so I will say something anyway blather diminishes your credibility and potential worth in the minds of your prospect.

You had plenty of things of meaningful value you could have said to your prospect, yet you chose to fill those precious seconds with spur of the moment blather rather than use verbiage that would have more impact on your prospects.

Your value bucket is leaking, and you are creating more holes.

Which Appointment Setter Is More Likely To Be Successful?

The one limited to saying what pops into their head at any moment, what they are comfortable with or the 5 or 6 things they can remember? Or the one who has brainstormed and written down all the most powerful impactful words and phrases they could use in a script in an organized manner?

Who is more likely to achieve their business objective with a call or email? The wing it person who is making it up as they go because "every situation is different, you never know" or they "don't want to sound salesy." (These phrases are code for "I am unprepared and clueless.") Or, the person who has thought through the verbiage most likely to achieve the business objective and delivers those words in a clear, confident manner? I wonder.

When given the opportunity to talk to a prospect your sales team is going to say something. Even if that something is half-prepared, unprepared, weak or nonsense, they are going to say something. Teams that are prepared to effectively communicate value and worth when the time is short have the equivalent of a "pile of words" available to them.

The top themes, benefits, credibility statements, stats, stories, talking points, and yada yada are always top of mind. If your team does not have that, then the words they choose are going to be weaker. Much weaker.

Identify Top Verbiage

Some words and phrases have more impact on your suspect than others. Identify all possibilities and use the strongest.

Organize by parts.

Think of your prospecting pitch in terms of parts. There is your name, your company name, what you do, why you are credible, benefits clients/accounts get from working with you, what they will get or learn at a first meeting/discovery call, how you ask for the meeting, then you have proofs and ear candy. These are the parts. Make each component part as strong and clear as you can.

Write down anything you might use in a script or might lead to something you would use in a script. This is where you brainstorm. It is okay if your phrase or thought is too long or not in perfect form for use in a script. Sometimes when crafting a client script, I come up with a great concept of something to use in a script but can't even describe it in less than 12-15 words. Write it down. Throw it on the pile.

Specifics, Specifics, Specifics.

Numbers and percentages win big over generalities. Brainstorm specifics you can weave into your scripts. Specifics convey a more powerful message and have more impact on your suspect.

Your Name
"Pile of Words" Component #1.

This component is fairly straightforward.

They will not remember your full name.

You want to get to words that matter asap.

The first few seconds are critical to their initial perception. You must eliminate anything that doesn't matter. Your last name doesn't matter.

Unless your full name is Bill Gates, instantly recognizable or is synonymous with status, authority, or expertise you will want to use your first name alone.

Studies show that the first 3 seconds and 30 seconds of an interaction are most critical in forming initial impressions. You want to fit as much good stuff in those initial seconds as you can. That means eliminating every unnecessary word — buh-bye last name.

Examples

Scott Sylvester Channell

Scott Channell

Scott

Your Company Name
"Pile of Words" Component #2.

Fact. People think 10x faster than you can talk. That means while you are yapping they have time to think, ponder, evaluate, doubt, disagree, and form judgments about what you are saying.

If you give them things to think about or question, their minds will be thinking and questioning and not focusing on what you say.

At this stage, you don't want your suspect to be "thinking." All you want is for them to know what company you represent.

Simple short verbiage that does not activate preconceptions, bias or previous negative experiences is what you want.

If your company name is too long, you are wasting valuable ocean front real estate. Shorten it up so you can get to the good stuff.

Sometimes a company name can lump you in with idiots or lead them to conclude that they "know all about" what you offer and can say "no" without listening any further.

If your offering is viewed as a commodity, you probably don't want to signal that up front.

In the examples below "IBM" and "Bombast" would be the winners.

Examples:

Intergalactic Big Machines Incorporated

Intergalactic Machines

IBM

Bombast Merchant Processing

Bombast Company

Bombast

What You Do
"Pile of words" Component #3.

You are looking for buyers. You want to enable buyers to grasp that you may help them with a need. A crisp and succinct statement describing "what you do" enables buyers to conclude you may be able to improve their condition. They continue to listen.

Here you start to give buyers "cause for pause." You want them to choke on the words "we are all set."

Your description should be plain, simple, and direct. We do X. No fluff words. Do not use words such as "best" or "superior" or any hype words that seek to connote a perception of being exceptional or above the rest. The problem with fluff words at this point is that you are asking them to make a judgment they are unprepared to make.

Subconsciously they think "I don't know if that is true or if I agree with that." They are thinking. You don't want them to think at this point. If you hype, they start discounting what you say. All you want is for them to clearly understand what you do. That's it. Use a simple statement with no embellishment.

The goal is to enable buyers, those who recognize a need on some level, to think "whoa. They do X. I want to improve that or make a change. I'll listen for a moment." That's it.

Examples:

We are business management consultants.

We are copper mining productivity specialists.

Cleaning systems

Commercial cleaning

Commercial cleaning company

Building maintenance company

Your Credibility Statement "Pile of Words" Part #4

The biggest hole I commonly see in scripts that are not working is the lack of a credibility statement.

Many of those who do not communicate credibility have tons of credibility yet say nothing. They are sitting on a key differentiator yet not using it.

In the old days, buyers had to meet with salespeople to get information not otherwise easily accessible to them.

Now, they have easy access to info with a few keystrokes and are less dependent on salespeople for info. Also, they can now select their potential vendors with a Google search. Why take a shot wasting time on a company or sales rep of unknown quality or reputation when you can easily select your own?

You must signal that you are top tier and worth their time.

You must signal that you have experiences, knowledge, and a history that would be valuable to them. You want them to think "hey, they sound first class. Maybe I wouldn't find someone as good with a Google search. I'll listen," your suspect thinks.

SELL THE MEETING

Assuming you are talking to a buyer, they must understand that you are worth their time and better than the rest who contact them. They will not unless you tell them.

You want them to choke on the words "I'm all set." I'm not kidding. They are dying to find a scintilla of a reason to cast you off. You want those words to get stuck in their throat. You do that by communicating sufficient credibility so that a buyer concludes "whoa, they may have something that could help me and seem worthwhile. I'll listen a bit longer."

Why should a serious buyer invest even a few moments on the phone with a stranger of unknown qualifications and experience when they can choose among a pool of qualified vendors and experts they deem worthwhile with just a few keystrokes?

Numbers matter here. Has your company worked with 3,000 businesses? How many in your local metro area have chosen you? What percentage of customers buy again? All of these numbers connote credibility. "They must be good if all those companies worked with them. I'll listen."

Think of the number of companies/people who you have worked with. The number your company has worked with.

Think Local, Region, State, Nationally, Globally.

Name drops are very powerful. Combine name drops with specific numbers of those who have selected you, and you have a powerful combination.

You might mention two names recognized nationally in a vertical and one that is local. You are trying to enable them to conclude "hey, they must be good if they were selected by those companies."

Don't approach it from "we have worked with companies A, B, and C…." That emphasizes you. Approach it like this: "companies such as A, B and C have selected us…"

Specific results can also serve as credibility statements. But they look very much like benefit statements so be careful.

Examples:

4,000 businesses have selected us

500 Boston metro businesses work with us as they get

425 Louisville area families rely on us to

98.5% of customers purchase again

IB Sorry, Microsquish and Billy's Burgers work with us as

7 of the top 10 hospitals in Texas work with us as

#1 in the Tri-State area

3 recent projects resulted in cost savings of $50,000 or more

1,100 Dallas area companies work with us including Megatron, Nasty Burger and Lonestar U

Your Benefit Statements
"Pile of Words" Part # 5

Benefits are the Holy Grail of script writing that sells. Benefits.

You must quickly, clearly, and concisely communicate 3 benefits they want.

VALUE knocks down doors. Remember that.

2 X 4 Impact

When you relate benefits that connote value desired by a buyer along with credibility, you have what I call "2 x 4" impact. What is that?

When I called, I used to imagine the phone being 3D and when a decision-maker said "hello" I would reach through the phone and start smashing them with a 2 x 4. My 2 x 4 were the words used and my delivery style. You want your words to have a 2 x 4 impact.

Do not confuse IMPACT on the buyer and being direct, with being rude, loud, unprofessional, pushy, or salesy (whatever that is.) Remember, you are fighting gravity here. They are predisposed to reject you. You must jolt them out of their automatic knee-jerk responses. You must project an impact greater than those forces.

The best appointment setters speak softly and relaxed, yet their words have a great impact on buyers.

When crafting your benefits (or your whole script for that matter) do not give 1 second of thought to pleasing non-buyers. Many water down their impact so that they can have more comfortable conversations with those who will never buy. Do not do that. Craft words and relate benefits directly that will have an impact on buyers. Throw the non-buyers down the stairs with no regrets. Do not give one second of thought to non-buyers.

Craft bottom-line benefits. Those who can authorize the biggest checks think differently than lower-level decision-makers. Details and the day to day don't appeal to them as much as issues that impact the big picture and bottom line.

Bottom line benefits are things like productivity, competitive advantage, time to market, and margins.

Two Super Words You Should Include. Options. Strategies.

Decision-makers love to hear about them, and the idea that there may be a selection lets them have a sense of control. Decision-makers want to choose and be in control. Use those words.

Special note. What words do you not see on the list? Cost. Lowest cost. Inexpensive. Cheap. Save you money. Never use those words as part of a script. They devalue you, they attract the wrong type of client, they make it easy to lump you in with all the other prospecting knuckleheads who can't think of anything substantive to say, so they say, "I can save you money."

Never lead with saving money as a benefit. If you feel compelled to mention cost savings at all, it should be the last benefit you mention. Even then, never say "lowest price" or anything similar, say "competitive pricing."

Something like… "… 1,500 New England manufacturers selected us as they get monster benefit A, colossal benefit B, and competitive pricing."

If you or your team really think buyers only care about the price, I feel sorry for you. You are doomed to low margins and high client churn. Even commodity type products have considerations other than price that matter to decision-makers.

Examples:

Decrease cost of X by Y%

Reduce cycle time by 31%

Increase revenue by X%

Increase revenue by X% within 6 months

Decrease prep time by 1/3

Competitive advantage

Reduce X usage by 45%

Customized solution

Reliable and consistent

Single point of contact

Productivity gains

Cost certainty

Avoid business interruption

Less down time

Faster restore time

**Value Delivered At The Meeting
"Pile of Words" Part # 6**

Remember, you set a meeting or discovery call by offering an exchange. Their time for information or knowledge that would be helpful to them, to be delivered <u>at the meeting</u>. Not down the road. Not if they hire you, you do good work, and they are satisfied, but at the meeting.

You want them thinking "hey, I probably won't work with them, but it sounds like they have a ton of experience and I can learn some things worth the time." The meeting or discovery call should be worth their time, even if they don't hire you. To achieve that you need to describe what they will get at the meeting worth their time.

Examples:

Samples

Case histories

Customized analysis

Proprietary analytics

A customized report

A competitive analysis

Ask For The Meeting
"Pile of Words" Part #7

You must ask for the meeting.
How you ask is strategically important.

You must end your 30-second initial "set the appointment" pitch with "would you have some time in the next week or two?" Why? You need to know whether the suspect has agreed with your substance and concluded that you are worth their time. If they say "sure," you know they have concluded you are worth their time, and now all you have to do is park them into a mutually agreeable date and time. Boom. Perfect!

But what if you ask like many? "would you have time on Tuesday at 10 or Wednesday at 2?" If they say "no," you don't know whether they are rejecting your request or merely objecting to the time. (Plus every newbie time-waster seems to use that approach, so you make it easy for them to lump you in with the idiots.) So you get into this awkward dance trying to figure out what the real issue is.

If you ask "would you have some time in the next week or 2?" and they say "we are all set," you know they are rejecting your substance and you have a calculated response ready for that. If they say "sure," you can focus solely on date and time.

So you have just finished your "what they get at the meeting" statement." You continue.

"You will learn a few things, and we hope you think of us in the future. Would you have some time in the next week or 2?"

Proofs
"Pile of Words" Component # 8.

We now review the first of 2 supporting categories necessary to a great pile of words. Keep this in mind. Your pile of words will not only enable you to craft the most impactful scripts, it will be a great resource for you in conducting "first meetings" and writing emails, presentations, and proposals. You want all your key "go to" info you might use during the sales process in one place.

You want to list out what I call "proofs." This is simply anything that proves or validates what you say:

Industry statistics

Quotes from experts

Quotes from studies or industry journals

Stories of companies you have worked with

Before and after stories or statistics

Statements of previous clients

Reference statements

Regulatory or government regulations

3rd party rankings or endorsements

Awards or recognitions

Anything that proves or supports what you say should be written down. You may use it in a script, to respond to an objection, at a first meeting, or some other way in the sales cycle. If the good stuff is not written down, it will not be accessible or used. Write all your good stuff down.

Ear Candy
"Pile of words" Part # 10.

"Ear candy" is the miscellaneous section. When I am researching and preparing to assist a client with scripts, sometimes I see something. It might be a concept; it might be a phrase, something that I could see being used somewhere in the sales process, but don't know where to put it.

So I park it into the ear candy miscellaneous catch-all section.

Remember the goal here is to create a "pile of words" document that is your go-to place for all the most powerful words, phrases, examples, statistics, yada yada that could be used in a script or might lead to something you would use in a script. Your "pile" is used not only for scripting but a resource you reach for when crafting emails, objections, preparing for meetings, or crafting proposals. All your impact words and stats should be in here.

Chapter 10
Crafting Your Scripts

Fact. People think 10X faster than you can talk.

That means while you are yapping, they have time to think, ponder, evaluate, doubt, disagree, and form judgments about what you are saying.

If you give them things to think about or doubt, guess what? Their minds will be thinking or doubting and not focusing on what you say.

"Thinking" Is A Bad Thing.

Simple short verbiage that does not activate preconceptions, bias, or previous negative experiences is what you want.

Stay away from hype words or obvious puffery.

When you use words like best, superior, top rated, you are asking them to make a judgment. Are they going to accept what you say or not? As they don't have the information to agree or disagree with your hype words, they immediately discount what you say.

As soon as they start wondering whether they can believe what you say, you are doomed.

Stick to solid, straightforward statements of fact.

Your goal is to say things they can grasp, process, and then say "yes" or "no."

If you say things that get them thinking, they cannot say "yes." Why? Because they are thinking.

The First 3 Seconds

The first 3 seconds are key as to whether they will continue to listen or not. You cannot botch the first three seconds and expect to win. Not happening.

Once you hear "hello" you must activate something within that enables a buyer (someone who recognizes a need you can fill and if they heard the right things would agree to participate in a reasonable next step with you) to determine that you are worth listening to a bit longer. That is it.

What Are The Important Issues In The First 3 Seconds?

First, your presence. Do you sound like a peer? Do you sound like someone capable of helping them? Are you perceived to be cool and confident? Or, has just the slightest hesitation, lack of confidence, or touch of confusion crept into the first few seconds of your interaction?

If so, you are toast right from the beginning.

If you don't sound confident about what you are saying, why would a top decision-maker feel confident about spending some time with you?

If they cannot immediately grasp what you do, they will not invest time trying to figure out if you are worth their time. Buh Bye.

You must pass this initial 3-second test.

The 30-Second Test.

All right, they are listening to you. Now what?

You must communicate the proper foundation for them to conclude that you are worth spending more time with. You must touch all the necessary bases to enable them to conclude that within 30 seconds.

SELL THE MEETING

For them to meet with you in-person, over the phone, via skype or string phones, you need to cement all the bricks in place necessary for a strong foundation. You are not working from strength if your foundation has holes in it, or worse, you are building on sand.

These are the building blocks you must communicate within 30 seconds to maximize your shot at selling the next step.

Who you are and where are you calling from.

What you do.

That you are credible.

3 benefits clients/accounts get from working with you.

What they will get at the first meeting with you.
(Worth their time even if they don't buy.)

Ask to meet.

Be Professional

Your goal is to earn the next step: To sell a meeting.

That is your sole objective, and you must stay locked onto it.

Be professional and respect the person you are talking to.

That means being prepared and quickly communicating a message they can grasp and say "yes" or "no" to.

In my opinion, you show respect for those you are purposely interrupting when you are prepared and take the least amount of their time possible. Say what you need to say, then let them respond "yes" or "no." Done.

Many seem to think that they first must communicate that they are kind, considerate, and nice — not the kind of person who would rudely interrupt someone when they are busy. But the fact is, you are interrupting them. When you call you have decided to interrupt them. That is the point. To interrupt them and get them to focus on you. So, the insecure feel compelled to start with "how are you, is this a good time?" or "I know you are busy so I will be quick." Or other such drivel. This has never made any sense to me. It is contrary to the core beliefs we started with.

You are interrupting them. Nothing you say can change that.

Once you decide to call you have decided that interrupting busy people is acceptable. That being the case, why not make that interruption worthwhile for those you can help. For those who have needs you can fill, who would love to speak to a top-shelf credible, experienced provider. Make the interruption worthwhile for them.

Nice is not the issue. Enabling those you can help to conclude that you are worth more of their time is the issue.

Busy people in positions of authority say "no" to nice people all the time.

Think of it another way. The people you are communicating with get dozens of calls a day. Most of those calls are quickly perceived to be a waste of time, and the callers are thrown down the stairs. Many of those who find themselves at the bottom of the stairs are nice, kind, considerate callers who started out apologizing for the interruption, promising to be quick and acknowledging that the suspect is undoubtedly a busy person. They still find themselves at the bottom of the stairs.

Do you really think you are separating yourself from the rest by somehow being nicer or more considerate than the rest?

Don't Confuse Being Prepared, Concise And Direct With "Salesy."

How often do you hear "I don't want to sound "salesy."

After 20+ years of sales training, I have concluded that "salesy" is anything that a sales rep doesn't want to do or feels uncomfortable with.

SELL THE MEETING

"Salesy" is your issue. Not the issue of those you speak to.

You earn the next step by saying things that enable buyers to conclude that you are worth more of their time — nothing else.

Communicating what you do, your credibility, benefits, what they will get if they spend more time with you and exactly what you want, have a chance of earning you that next step.

Anything else does not.

The Fence Balancing Vision

Let me share a thought that was always in my head when I was crafting scripts.

Reality is that our calls are rarely slam dunks. It would be lottery ticket luck to hear "wow, am I glad you called. You sound just right. Come on down." Not happening.

It is far more likely that the decision to meet, speak, or communicate again teeters between "Ahhhhhh, well…. Ummmm… I think we are all set" and "Ahhhhh, well….. ummmm…. Okay."

That is the space where success or failure on the phone is determined.

I always envisioned my suspect balancing on a fence.

On one side was "Ahhhh, well, I think we are all set" and on the other was "Ahhhh, well….. Okay." They were balancing on that fence, and a slight breeze would move them to one side or the other.

You only have two things to work with on the phone: your brain and the words you use. I envisioned the words I chose to use as the breeze. If my words had enough impact, they would be moved onto the "Ahhhhh, well…. Okay" side. If not, they landed on the "we are all set" side.

So the first 3 seconds and the first 30 seconds are crucial to whether your words have an impact. No impact and you don't last 30 seconds, never mind get the next step.

Every word matters in those crucial first seconds.

Choose words with enough impact so that if you were speaking to someone who had a need you could fill, you would enable them to conclude that you were worth speaking to a bit longer. That is your sole objective.

Speaking Of Impact

You want to speak softly, yet have a "2 x 4" impact.

Many confuse having an impact on the phone with being pushy or "too much." Not the case.

The most skilled and successful lead generators speak softly and have understated laid back phone personas.

You want to be understated yet have a "2 x 4" impact.

Here is another vision of mine. I imagined the phone was 3D and when a decision-maker uttered "hello," I would reach through the phone and start clubbing them with a 2 x 4. I'm not kidding.

My "club" were words I had carefully chosen and delivered. The impact necessary for prospecting success was to knock them out of their knee-jerk patterns of rejection. The words delivered and the manner of delivery were powerful enough to enable buyers (those with a recognized need, who, if they heard the right things, would agree to a solid next step) to conclude that I was worth spending more time with.

If you tiptoe up to your suspect while lightly tapping them on the shoulder and whispering "excuse me," that does not have sufficient impact to overcome the environmental and gravitational forces conspiring to thwart your success on the phone.

You need a "2 x 4" impact.

SELL THE MEETING

Always professional. Always softly communicated. But every word is calculated to have an impact and enable buyers to conclude that you are worth more of their time.

Seconds Cost You Opportunities And Closes.

If it takes you 50 seconds to say things you could say in 30 seconds, you will lose opportunities. Buyers, those who have needs you could fill and will end up writing checks to another provider within 3-15 months, will tune you out. They will say "all set" or "we don't need that," but they are thinking "this person is not worthy and is wasting my time."

You will lose great opportunities if your opening is not good enough. If you haven't given them enough reason to listen a bit longer in the first 3 seconds, If you don't touch all the bases necessary for your suspect to conclude you are worth more time within 30 seconds, you will lose out on qualified opportunities.

Even when they desperately need what you are offering, even when they plan to buy within the next few months, if your opening 30 seconds is weak, if you don't sound credible enough or heaven forbid you should sound just like most of the other knuckleheads who call them you will hear " we are all set" or "not interested."

Because you sounded like all the rest and said nothing sufficient for them to conclude you were worth listening to.

Phone Time Condenses By 10

On the phone, everything is compressed by a factor of 10. When you sit down face to face, they will indulge you a few minutes of idle chit-chat before they expect you to get to the point. Face to face they will listen and give you 7 - 40 minutes before deciding whether you are worthwhile or a total waste of time.

But on the phone, that decision takes mere moments.

If you are not prepared to make maximum use of every precious second to state your case and get where you want to go, you will lose opportunities.

You will lose *great* opportunities. Not because you were not the best option. Not because you lacked the experience or know-how. But because you didn't say the things in the first 3 and 30 seconds of your prospecting call to enable a buyer to conclude that you were worth more time.

Assume There Is A Buyer Behind Every "Hello."

Very important.

When crafting your scripts, you must assume that every person you speak to has a need you can fill. Every syllable that comes out of your mouth must be structured to reach your business objective with buyers.

Ya, I know. Most of the people you speak to will not be buyers. Meaning that they don't have needs you can fill. They won't be writing checks to your competitors within the next 3-15 months. So what? Forget about them.

Focus solely on those who have needs you can fill. Pretend that the person behind that "hello" will be writing a check to you or one of your competitors. Disregard everyone else.

Real world – Most You Interact With Will Have No Needs You Can Help With.

Sad but fact.

Most of the people we choose to prospect and will have conversations with do not have needs we can fill. They will not be buying. They could not care less about anything you say. They are going to say "no," "we are all set." They may even call your mother names. Nothing we do or say will change that.

If you water down the words you choose to say in the first 3 and 30 seconds of your conversation so that you can have more comfortable conversations with those that will never buy, your words will have much less impact on the buyers, when you happen to bump into them.

SELL THE MEETING

When You Hear "Hello," Are They A Buyer Or A Non-buyer?

This was my nightmare, and it should be yours.

You work your fingertips (or automatic dialer) to the bone to get suspects who fit your profile to pick up the phone. When you hear "hello," is it someone who recognizes a need you could fill and will end up writing a check to you or a competitor or not.

Well, most of the time, the answer is .... not. The numbers will vary by industry and your offering, but the reality is that somewhere between 3 out of 4, or 9 out of 10 of decision-makers you will speak to have ZERO chance of agreeing to your offer. Zero. And that is before you even say anything.

If you water down your words to have more comfortable conversations with those who will never buy, you will be less effective when you hear "hello" from a top-quality prospect who has a need you could fill, who would love to meet with top-shelf providers.

At the moment they say "hello," you don't know if they are a buyer. They don't know that you can help them and just how capable and credible you are.

Within a few seconds, that future buyer will decide if you are worth listening to for a few more moments.

If you use up those precious seconds with "hi, this is Harry from Mega Corp. Did I catch you at a bad time? Do you have a few moments? I know you are busy, so I'll be quick..."

What in those opening words has been said that would signal to a buyer, someone who is going to write a check to one of your competitors shortly if they don't give it to you, to conclude that you might be worth more of their time?

Nothing. Nada. Zilch.

No information as to your value or credibility has been communicated.

Most calls from prospective vendors waste the time of the recipient. The decision to stop listening or terminate the call will be made within a few seconds.

What are you going to do to avoid the possibility that a great future account for you, someone who wants and needs what you provide, will choke on the words "we are all set." They choke on their automatic reject blow off words because you communicated credibility and value that may help them.

Assume that everyone you speak to is a buyer.

Stay locked on communicating what buyers need to hear to trade you 30-60 minutes of their time — waste not one syllable on anything other than that objective.

Stop worrying about the clear majority of people you will contact who have no needs you can fill. Worry only about communicating effectively with those who do have a need.

Those who have no need and will not be writing a check to you or one of your competitors, or are displeased with the interruption, will still have no need and be displeased after they know what you might do for them. They are no worse off.

Give "Buyers" Cause For Pause.

However, if you structure your script carefully to have an impact on buyers, within the first seconds, you will give them "cause for pause." 100% of those who have needs and will be writing a check to you or one of your competitors shortly, who could be a great future account, will continue to listen to what you have to say.

Because your words had an impact, you didn't sound like or say the things that those who waste their time say. You didn't make it easy for them to lump you in with the time-wasters. You just clearly communicated what you do, your benefits, your credibility, what they will get and what you want in a crystal clear professional manner. Those who have needs will "get it" and listen more. Those who do not have needs will also "get it" and cast you off. So what? Next.

SELL THE MEETING

So long as you say the things that buyers must hear to conclude you are worth more of their time, do not worry at all about those who do not need your offering.

You Are Not Trying To Implant Something; You Are Seeking To Activate Something.

A lot of callers stress themselves out suffering from the illusion that they are trying to convince people of something. You are not trying to do that.

Buyers are out there and with your calls you are searching for them. Buyers are those that on some level already recognize a need and are likely to write a check to you or one of your competitors within 3-15 months if you are not there. You are seeking to activate a thought that on some level is already within them. It is not your job to implant a thought that is not there. It is your job to activate and leverage a thought that is already inside them.

If you think of it that way, it takes a lot of pressure off you. So long as you know that your verbiage is powerful enough to intrigue those who already have issues, a problem or an itch, you can stop pressing.

As a practical matter, your scripting must appeal to someone who is in the early stages of a buying process or at least thinking about it.

So the scripts you craft are calculated to compel action among those who already recognize they have an issue. You are activating something; you are not implanting it.

I like to say that appointment setting is working a process such that you bump into as many active buyers as possible, and then don't screw it up when you do.

The bumping into the most buyers possible part has to do with your list, your setup, your call process, and how efficiently you work. The not screwing it up part is about your scripting.

You Will Need Four Core Scripts.

You are going to need four basic scripts and an email to start your call process.

>An identify the decision-maker script

>A set the meeting script

>Your voicemail script

>Responses to resistance (3 variations)

>An email touch

2 things to keep in mind as you approach writing these scripts.

Don't even think about crafting these scripts until you have fully brainstormed your "pile of words."

Great scripting arises from solid preparation. If you have not fully explored all your wording and phrase options for each component part of your scripts, stop now. Go to the "pile of words" section and complete your preparation. If you do not do this, any scripts you create will be weak and superficial.

It will take 6 major rewrites before you conclude that you have scripts that work.

Those major rewrites occur after you start calling. If we could predict human response, we would not have to work. Start by creating the best script you can using your pile of words. It won't be perfect, and you will feel uncomfortable with it. Start using it anyway. As you engage your suspects, you will smooth things out and punch up the wording to improve results. Expect to work through 6 major rewrites after you start calling, before you have comfort and confidence with your scripts.

>Worksheets, additional scripts, and periodic updates
>are available to readers of this book at
>ScottChannell.com/STM-book-extras

Chapter 11
Your "Identify The Decision-Maker" Script

Once you identify a company that fits your high-probability profile (hopefully an "A" or "A+" record), you will have to identify or confirm the decision-maker within that company to call.

As a practical matter, today, with tools such as LinkedIn and various databases available, this step has been largely eliminated. For a very high percentage of your initial calls, you will start with a high degree of confidence that you know who you need to contact.

In instances where you have a name, you start by asking for that person. If they are not there, then you will use a variation of the identify the decision-maker script that follows.

In some cases, you may not have a name. In some industries or with some offerings it may not be so clear-cut who the "decision-maker" is. So then you have to go old school. You have to ask.

If You Don't Know Who The Decision-Maker Is

Let's set up the scene. You are calling into Mega Corporation. You will encounter the main receptionist or corporate voicemail tree hell. If you encounter the phone tree, you will need to pick the most appropriate department.

Your objective with this call is threefold. 1. Get the name. 2. Get some nugget of "worth" or qualifying information. 3. Get contact information. That is it.

If you do not have a name, it is not your intent with this first call to identify them *and* speak to them. Your objective is to get the name, pick up some recon info that helps you to qualify or increase the odds that you will speak to them with future calls, then get off the phone.

Do not try to speak to them on this call.

Step 1: Get The Name.

You call and an overwhelmed person picks up the phone.

Receptionist: "It's a bright sunny day here at Mega Corp, how can I help you?"

Lead Generator: "I'd like to send some information to whomever handles your marketing and advertising. Can you tell me who to direct it to?"

Or "I'd like to send some information to whomever handles the purchase of your computers or technology equipment. Can you tell me who to direct it to?"

Or "Hi, I'd like to send some information to your Vice President of Sales. Could you tell me who to direct it to?"

Or "I'd like to send some information to whoever handles employee relocations. Can you tell me who to direct that to?"

Now, let's ponder this a moment.

Most sales reps call companies to speak to the decision-maker. It is the receptionist's responsibility to protect those decision-makers from time-wasters. But you are not asking to speak to them. You merely want to send them some information.

This is something the overwhelmed receptionist does not get very often. They are thinking… "all this person wants to do is send some information that will probably be thrown away… no problem."

As you have not acted like the typical aggressive faux happy and fake smiling salesperson, you will get the name you want with the first call 19 out of 20 times.

So, if you don't have a name, the sequence is like this:

Receptionist: "hello, life is happy and sunny at Mega Corp. How may I help you?"

Lead generator: "hi, I was hoping to send some information to your MIS director. Could you tell me who to send it to?"

The script is very direct and tells receptionists exactly what it is that you want. Clear. Concise. Not one extra word. As there is no doubt whatsoever as to what you want, they can give you what you want.

SELL THE MEETING

It is also helpful if you come across as bored or nonchalant. You are less of a threat. They may even take pity on you.

It's Easy To Sabotage This Simple Step

How can you screw this up? Many ways. Use 33 words rather than 21. Throw in a few pauses. Ask how they are. Comment on the weather, a local sports team, or other irrelevancies, give them multiple opportunities to conclude that you are like all the rest. Be less clear so that they have to think a bit about you want. That should do it.

Usually, they will say… "Send it to Joanna Bent."

You immediately act to obtain a few more nuggets of info. What info? Info that will help you to determine worth and info to increase the chance you will get them to pick up the phone at a later date.

So here is how you might follow up once you get the name.

Lead generator: "Oh, great thanks. Just so I know what to send do you happen to know _____ ?"

Receptionist responds: "About a million."

Lead generator: "That is helpful. Would it be ok if I emailed this?"

Receptionist: "I can't give that out."

Lead generator: "Sure, is there an extension or direct dial I should ask for when I follow up?"

Receptionist: " 8675309."

Lead generator: "Thank you very much. Appreciate it. Have a great day." Click.

As a practical matter, you will only be able to rattle off 2 or maybe 3 of these questions if you are lucky.

So once you get the name here is what you can try to pick up.

1. Info as to potential worth.

2. Direct dial or extension number.

3. Email address.

You might also seek to:

4. Confirm the title

5. Confirm the mailing address

If you are prepared, and practice, with the first call to the company you can get a name, some info to help you determine the potential worth of the suspect, and some info to increase the odds that you will interact with them.

You will be calling this suspect a minimum of 9 times, so whatever "recon" info you don't pick up on the first call, you try to pick up on future calls.

About The Worth Info

This is very important. After you get the name, the first thing you should try to do is extract some info as to the potential worth of the target company.

I'm in the sales training business. Companies with more salespeople are higher-value targets than companies with fewer salespeople. So my potential worth question is:

"Just so I know what to send, do you have a rough idea how many salespeople work at the company?"

If the number of employees on site provides a clue as to potential worth the question might be:

"Just so I know what to send, do you have a rough idea of how many employees are at that location?"

If knowing the square footage of the facility or a certain technology they use or how many times a week the rubbish is picked up would give you a clue to separate the potential high-value, from the potential medium-value from the potential low-value, try to get that information.

When I started 24 years ago, I did a lot of calling in the employee relocation industry. That industry is all about moving executives from one location to another. A company that made 250+ moves a year had a much higher potential worth than a company that moved 5. The potential worth question was, "Just so I know what to send, any ballpark idea as to how many moves the company does a year?" BOOM.

You may be thinking "Oh, great idea. I can find out right away who the most valuable targets are." That may be true, but that is not the most important strategic reason why it is important to ask the potential worth question upfront and with every interaction in the future until you get the answer.

In The Beginning, It Is Far More Important To Identify The Time-Wasters <u>And Not Call Them Again</u>, Than It Is To Identify Those Most Worthy Of Your Time.

A counter intuitive truth: In the beginning, it is far more important to identify the low-value and no-value targets and not call them again than it is to speak to qualified decision-makers. In the beginning, during your "first pass" through a new group of records, dig in hard to determine the potential worth of every record. Not to find the most valuable, but to identify the low-value and no-value and not spend anymore time on them. Be very aggressive upfront in determining those that are not worth more time.

Think of it this way. Once you lock onto a decision-maker, you will work a process that has you making 9-12 dials to that decision-maker. If you can determine on call #1 that the potential worth is too low to be a good client, you won't be making those follow-up calls. You just saved yourself from making 8-11 future calls to a low-value or no-value prospect.

If every day you are aggressively seeking to ID the low and no- value and stop calling them, guess what happens? You end up making more dials to higher value prospects.

There is an old saying. "Those best at finding gold are best at determining what is not gold." Get good at determining what is not gold as soon as possible.

But Wait a Minute, I Have Some Great Accounts…

Here is a common act of self-sabotage you can avoid.

Callers start to think, "hey, we have some great accounts that are on the small side. I don't want to miss out on them, so I will call them, also."

People who think that way eventually buy Ramen noodles by the case and wonder why they fell so short of quota and lost their job. "But I was making a ton of dials."

The answer has to do with math. Take a pencil and the back of an envelope and calculate how many appointments/discovery calls need to be set, realistic closing ratios, various average account sizes, and margin generated. There is a potential account size below, which is economic suicide for you to call given realistic closing ratios and the cost of getting those meetings. If it doesn't work on the back of that envelope, it won't get better when you call.

I have had some great accounts with 1 or 2-person sales teams. I liked them a lot and they were great to work with. But I wouldn't think of investing in prospecting to companies with 1 or 2-person sales teams. That would be delusional and economic suicide.

Don't start rationalizing here. Stick with the numbers.

What's Missing

Notice that we did not identify ourselves or our company in our "Identify the decision-maker scripts."

Why not? Three reasons. 1) You can get the same result without the extra verbiage. 2) Less is more. The less information you give them, the less info they have to conclude they should screen you out. 3) Most who identify themselves and their company immediately wave a red flag that identifies them as exactly the type of person to be screened out.

"Hi, this is Scott Channell from Finding Business. How are you today? That's great. Weather treating you right down there? Super. Say, I was looking to speak to your vice president of sales. Can you tell me who that is?"

Can't you hear the click right now?

Don't red flag yourself. Be simple. Be direct. Be nonchalant. Get your info. Hang up. Next.

Worksheets, additional scripts, and periodic updates are available to readers of this book at ScottChannell.com/STM-book-extras

SELL THE MEETING

Chapter 12
Your "Set The Meeting" Script

You launch your call process with many decision-makers by making the first call to get the name or, if you are confident you know the name, making the first call to try to get them to pick up.

Your objective is to obtain a commitment for that person to spend more time with you or a representative of your company. That time could be face to face, a discovery call by phone, webinar, or attendance at an event — same concept. You are seeking to enable them to conclude that more time spent with you would be worthwhile. That the risk of you wasting their time is pretty low.

Let's review two variations of a "set the meeting" script.

Script Number One:

Suspect: "Hello, Busy Bobby here."

Lead generator: "Hi, this is Paula from Super Service Group, specializing in widgets, wadgets, and custom services. More than 600 companies such as Mega Corp, Brito and I. B. Sorry have worked with us to reduce production cycles by 12%, downtime, and unplanned expense. If you are open to reviewing options regarding widget production and customization, we would like to introduce ourselves and share case histories, strategies, and some things we do differently that companies appreciate. No clue if we might be a fit some time, but willing to share our experiences. Would you have any time in the next week or two?"

BOOM. Read that script again and think about all the bases that are covered.

Script Number Two: Slight Variation.

Suspect: "Hi, Distracted Dan here."

Lead generator: "Hi, this is Scott from Super Services. We specialize in employee relocations. Companies like L. L. Beanstock, Microsquishy, and 500 others selected us to manage the move process for 30,000 employees last year, as they get a single point of contact, 98% transferee satisfaction and competitive pricing. No idea if you might be open to reviewing options to improve your employee move process. If so, would like to share some examples of strategies used to improve satisfaction and cost efficiencies. If you hear something you like and think of us in the future that would be great. Do you have any time in the next week or two?"

BOOM. This verbiage covers the same bases in a slightly different way.

Your Mindset

When you approach these calls and these scripts, I would recommend you adopt the following mindset.

1. The buyers are out there. There are people right now who understand they have problems to solve, that certain things could be better, and they have an itch. A good number of these people will write checks to one of your competitors within the next 3-15 months. Or maybe you, if you are there.

2. You have a worthy offering. You or your company are superior, dependable, top shelf, and do a great job for your accounts and clients.

3. It is the most normal and natural thing in the world for you to be calling those who are most likely to benefit from your offering.

4. It would be the most normal and natural thing in the world for them to conclude that you are worth their time.

5. You are doing buyers a favor, performing a service for them, and helping them by contacting them and enabling them to become aware of a quality provider who could be of great service to them.

6. On this call, you are a peer. You may not be a CEO, VP of Sales, or Exec VP of HR, but on this call and at this stage you have information that is valuable to them. Communicate with them at their level.

7. Be professional and direct so that the buyers can grasp that you may be able to help them.

8. Resist the temptation to water down your upfront verbiage to have more comfortable conversations with non-buyers. Non-buyers will make up most of those you speak with. You do a disservice to those you <u>can help</u> <u>and would welcome interaction</u> with a provider of your caliber when you water down your verbiage. It is less likely they will conclude you are worthwhile. They lose a great provider option. You just shrunk your paycheck.

Worth Repeating: You Do A Disservice To Those You <u>Can Help And Would Welcome Interaction</u> With A Provider Of Your Caliber When You Water Down Your Verbiage.

To gain a commitment for the next step, you must convey confidence that your prospect would agree to invest more time with you.

Within the first 3-5 seconds after saying hello, your target is going to make a decision. "Is this a person worth listening to or not? Is this a waste of time or someone who may have something beneficial to me?" Within the first 3-5 seconds after hello, assuming you are talking to a buyer, you must enable them to conclude that you would be worth listening to just a bit longer.

Again, assuming you are talking to a buyer, if you don't give them "cause for pause" within seconds of hello, what you say after that doesn't matter. They have concluded you are not worthwhile; they cast you off; they are not listening anymore. **You lost them at hello.**

If they are not buyers, if they do not recognize a need you can fill, or they would not be willing to act, fuhgeddaboutem. What they think is irrelevant. Focus on making an initial connect with buyers (those that recognize a need you can fill) within seconds.

So, Let's Dissect The Script And Use The Second Script As An Example.

The opening is: "hi, this is Scott from Super Services. We specialize in employee relocations."

Analysis: Notice the use of the first name only. Get into the habit of eliminating every syllable that does not communicate value. Your last name is irrelevant right now so don't use it. You relate the company name and clearly describe what you do. It is crystal clear. No extra words, no pauses, no confusion. BOOM.

You then communicate credibility: "Companies like L. L. Beanstock,

Microsquishy, and 500 others selected us to …"

Analysis: By using name drops and a specific number of client companies you establish your credibility. Your suspect is thinking "hmm, those companies mentioned select vendors very carefully. That's a lot of business they have. They sound like they are better than most. Maybe I would not find a company as good as them with a Google search. I'll listen a bit more." That is what you are going for. When a buyer says hello, within moments you want them to have absolute clarity as to who you are and where you are calling from, what you do and how credible you are.

If that person has a need, you must give them "cause for pause" ASAP. Insert not one extra word between hello and giving them "cause for pause." Every unnecessary syllable and split-second pause enables them to click into an automatic rejection mode. Even if they know they need someone like you, you lose out, as you didn't get to the point.

You must plant the thought "hey, maybe I should listen a moment longer. We need to improve in that area. Hmmm, our current provider is a bit shaky, service hasn't been great lately. They must know what they are doing, or they wouldn't have customers like that and so many. I'll listen a bit more."

That is all you are going for in the first few seconds.

Benefits And Outcomes

You then move on to relating benefits or outcomes: "…manage the move process for 30,000 employees last year, as they get a single point of contact, 98% transferee satisfaction, and competitive pricing."

In this part of the script, we move on to describing bottom-line benefits. You want to relate 3 buckets of benefits that would have an impact on buyers.

You want to relate benefits with impact. Use words that hit the bullseye of something they want and need, which is powerful. Try not to use generalities. Don't say things that you could easily imagine your competitors saying. Don't say things that are common and ordinary, to be expected. "Oh really?" Yawn.

Try to work in specifics. Numbers. Percentages. Specifics matter. Specifics carry more weight. They have more impact on your buyers.

What has more impact? "Your employees will love our service." Or "You will achieve 98% employee satisfaction."?

Three Buckets Of Benefits

Touch upon 3 different "buckets" of benefits. In the above script, we touch upon administrative ease, employee satisfaction, and pricing. By mentioning 3 buckets of benefits, you increase the odds of hitting something that matters to your suspects. Also, you are communicating a breadth of expertise. Even if your 3 benefits mentioned don't hit something that itches them right now, along with your name drops and credibility you are communicating a wide range of expertise and value. If they have other needs, they will recognize your worth, listen, and engage you in further discussion.

Competitive Pricing

Let me say something very politically incorrect.

Only the incompetent would prospect someone and use these words "We can save you money." In your opening script.

Only those who are working for lousy sales managers would say that.

Only the lazy and those who do no preparation and create no original thoughts whatsoever would say that.

Saying those words or something very similar is for those who find themselves in the dungeons of sales hell. Those words are usually uttered by those practicing activity based selling, dialing faster and faster hoping to bump into someone who will give them a check, any check, right now. If you say that, even if you make a sale, it is probably to a low-profit client — someone who will abandon a quality dependable provider to save a nickel maybe. And oh, by the way, those who buy strictly on price (not cost, which is another story) are also those who cause you the most headaches. You rarely generate margin on low-price buyers.

Now I suppose if you are taking boxes of stuff off a shelf and your box of stuff is the same as boxes of stuff sold by others, you could say, "we can deliver boxes of stuff for $XX." But if you are talking a major sale or service delivery that entails quality assurance, dependability, knowledge, judgment, customization, delivery, transition issues, troubleshooting, compatibility, and myriad other considerations of satisfaction, the price is only one piece of the equation. For many, it is a small chunk, and the lowest price is not close to the determining factor.

Assume You Are Talking to A Buyer With A Brain

If you are talking to a buyer with a brain, they know that "lowest price" often increases costs in other areas and usually isn't worth it. It is my opinion that if you are talking to a top decision-maker in a complex sales environment with many moving parts that must work to reach business objectives and your main message is "we can save you money" that you immediately flag yourself as an idiot not worthy of their time.

If you think that is what matters most to them, you have immediately disqualified yourself.

Lower price does not mean lower cost. Not by a long shot. If you are going to prospect in a major sales environment, you must understand the difference between price and cost.

End of rant.

Back to the analysis of the script.

Price is on the minds of buyers. So a reference to it is sort of obligatory. My strong recommendation is that rather than say something like "we can save you money," which immediately lumps you in with all the other idiot time-wasters who call and will earn you an immediate rejection, use a phrase like "competitive pricing."

And when you use that phrase, make it the third of your 3 buckets of benefits. Don't lead with it, end with it.

What Happens Within Seconds Of Hello?

Fact: People think 10X faster than we can speak. While we are talking, there is an avalanche of thoughts moving through their heads. We want them to be positive.

You cannot give buyers time to think on their own. The natural tendency of those we prospect is to jump to the conclusion that you are an idiot, wasting their time, don't have what they need, and they must get back to what they were doing before you interrupted them (you are interrupting them, get over it.)

SELL THE MEETING

First Few Seconds Script No No's

Don't ask them how they are or if this is a good time.

They know you don't care about how they are doing so such drivel wastes precious seconds.

Most people feel more comfortable opening get the meeting calls with social chit-chat. Plus, it fits people's desired image of being non-salesy, whatever that is.

I certainly wish that what we were comfortable with and what we wish would work mattered. But it doesn't. What works, works.

I wish that "hi, how are you… is this a bad time… have you got a few minutes… I'll be quick, you are busy…" type banter helped to achieve the call objective. It doesn't.

The individuals you are targeting are top executives making fairly large economic decisions. Large in the monetary sense or large in the impact on the organization sense.

Footballs Are Not Square; The Sun Will Rise In The Morning And Executives That Can Authorize Big Checks Are Busy.

You can assume that the person who can authorize or influence a check that can make you a lot of money is busy. They are difficult to reach. They don't know you. Many will buy from someone shortly. So **why give them the opportunity to say they are busy and terminate the call before they know what you can do for them and just how credible and valuable you are?**

If they have problems you can help them with, how do they know it if you don't tell them? You won't be able to inform buyers who would welcome your message if their minds shut down or they blow you off.

You Are Interrupting Them. Get Over It.

We must interrupt the train of thought of active buyers when we speak to them. We need them to focus on us for a moment rather than what they were doing when they picked up the phone. Yes, it is an interruption to launch into your spiel when they pick up the phone but strategically, logically, and practically -- you have no choice.

Now The Pace Of The Script Changes

Once you have clearly and succinctly communicated who you are, where you are calling from, what you do, why you are credible and three different buckets of benefits, my personal preference is to change the pace and tone of the script.

In the first few seconds, I am very direct and straightforward. Buyers need to know those things to conclude I am worth more of their time. If they don't know those things, the odds of someone who will write a check to a competitor shortly, blowing me off, is pretty high. They will not know those things if I don't tell them.

So being direct and to the point is in the best interest of those we can help and will soon be looking for help. Your being direct and straightforward is in the best interest of prospects and is consistent with your business objectives on this call.

But once you break through the mental barriers of your prospects, I adopt a different tone.

"No idea if you might be open to reviewing options to improve your move process. If so, would like to share some examples of strategies used to improve satisfaction and cost efficiencies. If you hear something you like and think of us in the future that would be great. Do you have any time in the next week or two?"

BOOM. End of script.

Now You Must Do The Hardest Thing In The World For A Salesperson.
You Must Shut Up And Listen.

Let's dissect it.

"No idea if you might be open to reviewing options to improve your move process."

Now the tone has changed from boom, boom, boom to something softer. Saying "no idea if" or my phrase was "no clue if" is more laid back and softer. Using the words "might be open" "reviewing" and "options" are all soft easy to swallow words. These words are not pushing so much as they are inviting.

Stay away from harder words like "buy," "meet," "proposal."

Options And Strategies

You don't know anything about the needs of those who just said "hello" so you use very broad general terms like "review," "information," "options," or "strategies." I have discovered that people love "options," I think because they love to have a sense of control. "Options" connotes choices they can make. The other magic word I would recommend you plop into your verbiage here is "strategies." Decision-makers love strategies to ponder. Try to work those words into your scripts.

You also again remind them what you do so there is no doubt in their minds. "…reviewing options to improve your move process."

As you move into the middle of the script, you have changed the tone and admitted the obvious. You have no idea if they are "open to reviewing." You have phrased things in a very broad open manner and spoken of "options" and "strategies." You haven't eliminated much from their minds. And you have reminded them of what you do with the phrase *"your move process."*

With the last statement of the script, you tell them specifically, clearly, unequivocally exactly what it is you want them to do. No guessing. "If so, would like to introduce ourselves and share some examples of strategies used to improve satisfaction and cost efficiencies. If you hear something you like and think of us in the future, that would be great. Do you have any time in the next week or two?"

BOOM.

Analysis. We ask to "introduce ourselves" and "share." That is a lot softer than saying you want to meet to try to sell them something. It is a softer language. It is inviting language. That language does not activate any resistance from our suspect.

What are you conveying? That you are a highly credible organization that has been selected by many companies and have mentioned several well-known companies that are not in the habit of hiring bozos. You are going to share information that other companies have found valuable. You are communicating an exchange.

The exchange is your information delivered at the meeting in exchange for their time. If they perceive your info to be more valuable than their time, you have the next step. If they don't, you don't.

Ultimately everything you do with the script has to do with this moment. If they have a need and grasp that you may be able to help them, that you are a top-notch provider, that you deliver benefits that they want, and have information worth their time, then the value exchange is in your favor and you earn a meeting.

But if your script is weaker, you are unclear, if doubt creeps into their mind, your benefits seem ordinary, your credibility is lacking, if what they will get at the meeting is unknown, if you let any of those situations exist, you have created a risk. A risk that time with you will waste their time or that you might pressure them.

With your script, you are seeking to punch up the value exchange so, at the ultimate moment of decision, your info is worth their time and the downside risk is minimal.

Remember, they can easily select potential vendors with a Google search. Why waste time with you if they have the slightest doubt you are worth their time?

You want them thinking "well, we will probably never do business with them. But it seems they have a lot of experience, are reputable, and have done a lot of projects. I'll hear what they have and maybe pick up a tidbit or two. That would be worth my time even if we don't hire them." That is what you need them to be thinking. Your objective is to earn a next step, meeting, or discovery call with clones of your best accounts. That's it. Communicate that and deliver on that and you will launch your sales process with more qualified prospects.

The final 2 lines in the script are strategically very important.

"If you hear something you like and think of us in the future, that would be great."

I always used this line — 3 reasons.

1. Our objective is to convey value and enable people to feel comfortable meeting or speaking to us again. By using softer language again "think of us" and referencing the future, I am taking the pressure off. I

am not using language like "see what we can do for you" or anything that connotes that I expect anything to happen quickly. No pressure.

2. It is the truth anyway, so why not say it. Remember, the odds are that only 1 in 6 of those you speak to are "in-play" at the moment. Meaning, that they will change vendors or buy within 3-15 months. **So the real world is that you are more likely to bump into a great buyer during a non-buying period.** So getting them to meet you and maybe think of you in the future is realistic.

3. It sets you up perfectly for a very common objection. "We are all set." "We have a vendor we love." Or something similar. Those words may be true. More likely they are a knee-jerk blow-off. But your words connote that you don't expect anything to happen quickly. If they do run the "we are all set" objection on you, you will have a great response that can convert that into a meeting now.

If You Hear Something You Like And Think Of Us In The Future, That Would Be Great.

Of all the script stuff I preach, the phrase "if you hear something you like and think of us in the future that would be great," gets the most push-back. "I don't want to say that. I don't want them to think of us in the future; I want them to think of us now." This is what I hear all the time.

Strategically I think it is very important to take the pressure off them and make them more comfortable with the idea of investing more time with you. You also want to reduce the risk in their mind, that you may try to push or hard sell them. And, since you are going to hear "we are all set" a lot, this phrase helps you to overcome that.

Interesting to me is that trainees who give me the most grief over saying "If you hear something you like and think of us in the future that would be great," because they want the person to buy now, not in the future. These tend to be the same students who want to start with "hi, how are you? Have a got a minute" I know you are busy so I will be quick." Why? Because they tell me they don't want to appear pushy or "salesy." I don't get it.

Do You Have Any Time?

The wording of the final line is also strategically very important. "Do you have any time in the next week or two?" Not, "do you have time Wednesday at 2 or Thursday at 11? But, "Do you have any time in the next week or two?"

If someone says "no" to you after you finish your pitch, are they saying "no" to your value proposition? Or, are they saying "no" to the time you suggest?

If their issue is substantive, you will respond differently than if their issue is the timing of the meeting.

If they respond "yes" to "do you have some time in the next week or two?" you know they understand your value and are willing to meet or schedule a discovery call. You can focus 100% on scheduling a mutually agreeable time for that next step.

However, if their issue is substantive, if they have a hesitation or objection, you need to know what that is so you can respond properly.

If you end by asking them for a specific time and they say "no," you don't know if the issue is the date and time, or if the issue is substantive. You end up in an awkward word dance trying to figure out what the issue is. Substance or timing? You have lost control.

If they have a hesitation or doubt, you must know what it is to overcome it.

Ending your "set the meeting" pitch with this line separates those issues so that you can respond appropriately and increase the odds that you get a meeting.

Additional "Set The Meeting" Script Models

Note: At the end of this chapter there is a link to a fairly extensive report with additional script samples, a list of sample bottom line benefits that would provide you some ammo for your scripts, and an expanded "phrases of shame. It is free to readers of this book and updated periodically.

Script Model #1

Hi, I'm Billy, from Shrinking Securities, specializing in estate planning and wealth management for households with a minimum of $2 million to invest. Over 210 individuals have selected our firm to minimize estate taxes, investment risk and make sure they do not out live their assets.

Would like to introduce you to our capabilities and if you wish, provide some options for you to consider. You could review a complimentary analysis which takes your family situation today and projects future courses of action in various scenarios. There is no obligation and worse case is you confirm that you are in good shape.

Would that be worth some time in the next week or two?

Script Model #2

Hi, this is Lauren from Meatball Marketing, more than 496 dental service providers, including 24 in the Boston metro area have selected us to generate more new patient calls with improved local online visibility. These practices have realized more than $75 million in increased local business.

If you are open to reviewing methods (strategies, processes, options), other dentists use to gain competitive advantage we would be happy to introduce ourselves, share specific tactics and if you wish, provide you with a visibility ranking report that compares you to competing offices.

You would learn a few things and we hope you think of us in the future. Would you have some time in the next week or two?

Script Model #3

This is Sadie from Big Bucks Consulting, we are _____ productivity specialists. More than 60% of the global _____ companies including Mega Corp, Idiots International and AGD have selected us for more than 340 engagements over the last 7 years.

They chose us to, on average, increase throughput by 22%, reduce unit cost by 13% and eliminate capital project overruns.

Have no idea if you wish to review options and strategies used by other _____ companies to achieve these results. If so, would be happy to introduce myself and discuss specifics of various strategies. You would pick up some good ideas and food for thought and we hope you think of us down the road. Would you have some time in the next week or two?

Script Model #4

This is Scott from OnlineU, a skills solution provider offering upskilling and reskilling. More than 1200 corporate partners work with us to improve communication, productivity and employee retention. 25% gains in skills are common and many are able to reduce recruiting dollars per employee by 50%.

If you are open to reviewing upskilling and employee retention options would be happy to introduce myself and share specifics of how other companies are meeting these challenges.

You will definitely learn a few things and I hope you think of us in the future.
Are you available for a phone discussion within the next week or two?

Worksheets, additional scripts, and periodic updates are available to readers of this book at ScottChannell.com/STM-book-extras

Chapter 13
A Message About Voicemails

Bulletin: Very few people who listen to a voicemail will return the call. How insightful. Some will and we want every word we select to encourage that. However, an immediate response is not the only purpose of a voicemail.

The voicemail works as part of your total system of interaction to ultimately achieve your business purpose. Gain a commitment for a solid next step from a highly-qualified decision-maker.

The other purpose of the voicemail, just as important as generating an immediate response, is to increase name recognition and build familiarity with your message.

People respond to things they are comfortable with. You want to keep your message consistent among your phone scripts, voicemails, and emails so that your suspects can absorb the message and be comfortable with it. If they can absorb it and understand it, you have a greater shot of them saying "yes." If they cannot grasp it, they cannot say "yes." So, you get a non-response or something else.

It's common for newbies to think they must write multiple voicemails to mix things up. That is not what you should do — two reasons. First of all, it's difficult enough to write one good voicemail that works for you. Trying to write three good ones is mission impossible stuff.

You want to keep your messaging consistent so that people can absorb it, understand it, then act on it. If you send them mixed messages, it is less likely they will absorb it, it will be harder for them to understand it and the odds that they will act on it plummet.

The consistency of messaging builds credibility and recognition.

Your voicemail is a touch. The more touches you deliver to your carefully chosen suspects with consistent messaging, the more likely it is that they recognize your name and grasp what you might do for them.

If that happens, it increases the odds that they will respond, call you if they have a need or be more receptive to your phone call. That is why we leave voicemail messages. It is part of a total strategy to penetrate the minds of our suspects.

Let's Review A Voicemail Script

Beep. "If you are looking to improve your employee relocation process, companies like L. L. Beanstock, Microsquishy, and 500 others use us to simplify administration and achieve 98% employee satisfaction. Would be happy to share case histories and strategies that worked for others. This is Charlie Chatty. Super Service Group. 1-800-123-45XX. Charlie. 800-123-45xx." Click.

A slightly different version.

Beep. "Dan… regarding your employee relocations, 500 companies selected us to move 30,000 employees last year as they get improved transferee satisfaction and cost efficiencies? Would be happy to share examples and strategies as to how they improved their programs. This is Charlie Chatty from Super Group. 800-123-45xx. Charlie 800-123-45xx." Click.

The Hovering Finger Problem

Decision-makers listen to their voicemails with their fingers hovering over the delete button. The task of your voicemail script is to keep it hovering — just one split second of say nothingness, or no value being communicated and DELETE.

Voicemails should be 20-seconds long. Look at all that you do within 20-seconds.

"… regarding your employee relocations…"

BOOM. Within 2 seconds you have told them what you do. If they have a need in this area, you have given them a nugget of info to help them decide to listen a few moments longer.

SELL THE MEETING

Then you continue.

"… 500 companies selected us to move 30,000 employees last year …"

You just slayed them with a credibility statement. If they have needs with their employee relocation program, they know you might help them as you have been crystal clear as to what you do. Not only that, they know you must be a top-notch provider as 500 companies work with you and you moved 30,000 employees last year. *BOOM.*

If they are open to making improvements in this area, they now know within seconds, you might help them and that you are a top-shelf provider. Those likely to write checks to a competitor soon are still listening. The rest? Who cares? Buh-bye.

You then continue to drop a few benefit bombs "… improved transferee satisfaction and cost efficiencies… " offer to deliver something at a meeting worth their time even if they don't buy from you "…examples and strategies as to how they improved their programs…" and leave your name and contact info at the end "This is Charlie Chatty from Super Group. 800-123-45xx. Charlie 800-123-45xx."

You covered a lot of bases in about 20 seconds.

This voicemail structure is part of an overall plan that will earn you next steps.

Water it down, beat around the bush, and add extra words and your voicemails will earn you silence.

Another Voicemail Challenge. Technology.

In addition to the fact that most people you leave messages for have no needs and are guaranteed to ignore you no matter what you say, you have another modern-day challenge.

Most people don't listen to their voicemails.

Most are reading transcriptions of them.

So your great delivery and confident voice have no impact on the majority who are reading your message, not listening to it.

Worse still. Most of those viewing transcriptions of your voicemails are reading them on mobile phones. So, the first 2 or 3 lines will determine your success or failure. Fill that space up with blah blah blah, and you get zip. Fill that space up with info that signals to a buyer that you might be able to help them and are super credible, you have a shot.

The modern-day human attention span is your enemy. It is now 8 seconds. Goldfish have longer attention spans than those you prospect. Not kidding.

Worksheets, additional scripts, and periodic updates are available to readers of this book at ScottChannell.com/STM-book-extras

Chapter 14
Emails: Strategies & Samples

Emails are an integral component of your overall touch system.

The goal is to increase the odds that you earn the attention of someone likely to write a check to either you or a competitor within the next 3-15 months.

Once you earn that moment of fleeting attention, you must communicate what you do, how you might help and your credibility so clearly, succinctly and powerfully, that when they get to your "ask," they feel comfortable responding "yes."

That's it.

You are not trying to sell your product or services. You are not trying to convince a buyer that you are superior to all others. You are simply facilitating a mindset such that a buyer will feel that the risk of communicating with you is outweighed by the benefits speaking to you may bring. If the risk that you might be a fraud, liar, misrepresenting your experience, exaggerating your credentials or results, or are mean to animals is greater than the value to be received at the first meeting, you are out.

If the odds of meaningful rewards outweigh the risks and time involved, you get a reply and probably a meeting. If they perceive that what you do may assist them in improving their business condition or meeting a need they recognize they have, you get a reply, so long as they perceive you to be credible.

Your perceived credibility is key. How many times have you passed on communicating with someone, when you have strong doubts as to whether they can do what they say they can do? All of us have been burned so many times by reps and marketing messages that lure us in with promises of results we wish for, but once we meet, jump on the phone or spend time exploring further, we find out that the results were exaggerated or experience/dependability is lacking. Without a strong credibility component, many who need what you have to offer will pass because the perceived risk that you are a fraud or incompetent is so great they will not invest the time.

Just as with your scripts and voicemails, absolute crystal clear clarity as to what you do and why you are credible are paramount. If you are wishy-washy or your suspect has to stop to think, even momentarily, about what you do you are out of the game. Buh-bye. You did all the hard work to get a buyer's attention and then you blew it. You failed to deliver a message sufficient so that a buyer could perceive you as being worth some time -- even if they did not eventually do business with you.

There is a trend away from phone conversations toward emails.

In some industries I work in, with some projects, it is fair to say that almost all the results arise from email replies. This is a growing trend.

Email was always an important component of an effective appointment setting system, but in some situations today it has outsized importance.

It is important to note that even within industries where it seems nobody picks up the phone and most of the meetings set arise from email replies, successful appointment setters feel strongly that the calls and voicemails work to lift the number of email replies that turn into discovery calls and appointments. Working the total system is what brings results.

Only An Idiot Would Say "Nobody Picks Up The Phone Anymore, Everything Is Email."

It is about using the right tactics in the right places. If you are a knucklehead calling a lousy list with an ineffective process and very inefficiently to boot, you may feel that "nobody picks up the phone," but that does not make it true.

You must match the tactics you use to segments of your list where they will do the most good. The process of calling, leaving voicemail, and email touches will only generate a response and make economic sense when used within a portion of your overall target market. Match the tactics you use to each subset of your target market.

Let's review and dissect an email

What follows is my control email. Have used it for years, it outpulls every other email I have tried and tested. Take a look, then let's break it into pieces.

Subject Line: B2B Phone Scripts & Appointment Setting

Firstname, I set 2,000+ C-Level meetings before authoring three books on the topic and working with sales teams. (Search "Scott Channell" on Amazon.)

A different process was used that was neither comfortable nor popular.

Saw your position, insert title, mention of B2B lead generation in your Linkedin profile, and thought it worth a shot that someone at CompanyName may be open to reviewing some ideas to improve the pipeline.

The process or timing may not be a fit but willing to find out.

Is this worth a chat,
or, could you refer me to someone?

Thank you for your time,
Scott Channell
ScottChannell.com

PS: Contact me directly at 978-296-2700 if you have any questions

Scott Channell
Finding Business
39 Dodge St. #288
Beverly MA 01915

Subject line: A direct "what you do" statement. Do not use any hype words or promises of super results. Enable someone who has a need you can fulfill, at a glance, to read that and think "I need that" and continue to read.

First name: Better if you can include it. Have had success with and without.

Credibility statement: Put it right up front. Make it powerful. If you are not perceived as credible, no statement or promise you make will be deemed worthwhile to act upon.

Hint at a "difference": You must arouse a bit of curiosity or suggest a variation from the norm that may help them. "Difference" is not superiority. If you promise superior results, you run a major risk of being discounted and dismissed immediately. Merely hint at a difference worth finding out about.

Incorporate some customization: In this example, my list came from multiple advanced Linkedin Sales Navigator searches. No big surprise that my target market is CEO's or VP's of Sales within companies of a certain size range, selling B2B, with lead generation responsibilities. If you are set up correctly and think ahead a bit as to how you will leverage your lists, you can automate this with the use of templates, particularly if you can incorporate specific words found within their Linkedin profile, that is very specific and personal to them and will lift response.

Note the light "ask": Note the very light "ask" here. "May be open to reviewing some ideas." You are not asking for a meeting where someone might be pressured to buy, nor are you asking them to accept that you are "superior" or deliver exceptional results. Your "ask" is low-level and low-risk. You are suggesting that maybe someone would wish to review some ideas. That is it.

Acknowledge that you may not be a fit: reality is that you may not be a match. Take away the pressure and risk of meeting or having a discussion by acknowledging the obvious. You may have a discussion and one of you might decide that you are not a match or timing may not be right. In fact, it is probable that if you have a discussion that one of you will decide not to proceed. Acknowledge the obvious and put that out there as a way of reducing the risk of having a discussion.

Note: of all the advice I give, the idea that you might in any way hint that you would not be a match, the timing might be wrong or that you hope they might think of you in the future, gets the most pushback. "But I don't want them to think of us in the future; I want now."

Of course, you do but the goal is to have more first sales conversations, face-to-face meetings, or discovery calls with top decision-makers within companies that fit your best client profile. The more they are comfortable with the idea of talking to you, the more first meetings with qualified targets you get. More meetings mean more opportunities to sell. No meeting, no opportunity to sell. Remember, you are not trying to sell your product or service; you are trying to sell a meeting. That's all — big difference.

SELL THE MEETING

Your "ask": Is this worth a chat? It is the only question you ask in your email and the only question they must focus on and answer. Your "ask" is also pretty light and non-threatening. Rather than suggest you meet so that you can interrogate them, ask them to endure a presentation or put them into a potentially uncomfortable situation, all you are suggesting as a first step is that you have a "chat."

If you have clearly communicated what you do, your credibility and a difference or experience worth hearing about you have a shot at a meeting. If the benefit to be gained during that "chat" is perceived to be greater than the risk that you are a time-waster, liar or, an idiot then you have a meeting.

Ask to be referred as an option: If you have laid the proper foundation, someone who is not the most appropriate contact within a company will hopefully think of this without being prompted, but a reminder helps. Again, if you have not laid the proper foundation, you have no shot at this. A big part of getting a maximum response is having your email forwarded to a more appropriate person.

Three Additional Points About Emails

Make sure you comply with all applicable laws, the CAN-SPAM Act, and that you provide an opt-out or unsubscribe method.

Should you include live links in your emails? My preference is to not include live links in a "get the meeting" email. The goal is to sell a meeting, and the most direct route to that is a response to the email.

By providing a live link to your website or a download, you are inviting your very highly qualified target to go exploring. If they explore, you give them things to think about (if they are thinking they cannot say "yes,") confuse them, give them something to hang their hat on to conclude that you are a waste of time.

Roll out your big guns in your email. Communicate a value worth more than any perceived risk to a discussion. Let them say "yes" or "no."

Do not follow up on "opens." Refer to discussion elsewhere in this book about always working in a high-probability zone. Well, following up on email opens is an extreme low-probability activity. You are far better off investing that time in high-probability areas.

That someone opened an email is not a probable indication that they have a need or are (the word that never should be uttered) interested. If you or your team go down this rat hole, you are chasing a mere possibility, not a probability. Even worse, you are not even chasing a possibility, you are chasing a smidgen of a possibility.

Some Additional Email Samples

Here are some additional examples of emails taken from my client files. Understand that clients get a little hesitant about publicizing such things, so company names, benefits, and offerings have been changed.

What you really should focus on is the structure of these emails.

#1

Subject line: Better Corporate _____ – Less injury

{{first_name}}, 2,000 SoWazoo companies work with us to save lives and limit injuries among more than 100,000 employees with the best _____ supplies in Wazoo. Motorcycle delivered & restocked.

Why do so many select us over mega national companies?
Multiple program options, single invoice, top quality, personal attention, beat national company pricing by 50%.
Local and trusted for 20 years.

Saw your position, {{title}} and mention of _____ responsibilities in your Linkedin profile and thought it worth a shot that you or someone at {{company_name}} may be open to reviewing ideas to improve your widget and wadget ordering & refill process.

We may not be able to offer enough to justify a change right now, but willing to find out.

Is this worth a chat?
Or, could you refer me to someone?

Thank you in advance,
Name
Company / domain.com

PS: Contact me directly at 8675309 if you wish.

SELL THE MEETING

#2

Subject line: Widget Industry Payment Systems

Firstname, Companies such as CE, Stardimes, tens of thousands of emerging and micro businesses (including 876 in Wazoo) have selected us for widget processing technology after reviewing all their options.

If you are open to reviewing options, we could share specific case histories as to how others with similar _____ volumes have seamlessly integrated the latest technologies to upgrade safety, cost-efficiencies, and ease of use to their widget payment systems.

When you process $10.7 zillion per year for widget companies in 57 countries with 8,000 transactions per milli-second, you have a lot of expertise to share, and we would be happy to do so.

Saw your position, Title, and thought it worth a shot that you or someone in your company might be open to upgrading your widget technology.

If you wish, we could discuss a cost and system assessment to pinpoint areas you may wish to focus upon at some time.

An assessment may not uncover anything worth changing but willing to find out.

Is this worth a chat?
Or, could you refer me to anyone?

Thank you for your time,
E. Fudd
Wabbit Data
DomainName.com

Worksheets, additional scripts, and periodic updates are available to readers of this book at ScottChannell.com/STM-book-extras

Chapter 15
Objection Response Concepts

You must understand 10 concepts before crafting your responses to resistance.

1. They Expect To Say "No."

Every speck of DNA in your suspect's body is aching to say "no."

They have no need, no time, or have had too much time wasted by others that sound just like you. So they say "no." Not an informed "oh, I know what they do and how credible they are, but we don't need that" kind of "no."

But an "oh God, another one, what do they do? Not going to hang in and try to figure it out" type "no."

Your targets immediate knee-jerk response when they realize they are being interrupted, prospected, about to be asked for something is to say "no" in some form. 'I'm busy' "we are all set" "call me back" "we love our vendor and would never change" is what you often hear. They are telling you "no."

They are on the receiving end of a lot of calls that start and sound just like this one and know the drill. "Sounds like another time-waster." Buh-bye. For them, it is a normal, natural pattern that makes sense. Why spend time with someone, even a few moments, with someone of unknown value and credibility?

If they have a need, they can choose among providers they feel are worthwhile with a few keystrokes.

How long do you expect someone to listen to you when you sound like all the rest? Especially when "all the rest" waste their time.

To succeed with the business objective, you must get them out of familiar territory. Your first objective is to get them to choke on "no," "we are all set," "don't need it" and myriad other euphemisms for the words "get lost."

If you want to add to your paycheck, the first job when speaking to a highly-qualified buyer (of course, when this person says 'hello" you don't know they are a highly qualified buyer likely to write a check to your competition within 3-15 months) is to enable them to understand that you are not like all the rest.

Act and sound like most of the callers who preceded you and guess what the result will be.

The result will be the same "no thanks." Bye. Click.

You must choose words, especially up front, that are more powerful than their normal, natural knee-jerk "no" reaction.

2. Initially, You Don't Hear "Objections."

You must overcome objections. That is what we are told all the time. But, do you really think it is accurate to think of what we hear on a prospecting call as "objections."

I set more than 2,000 C-level appointments and feel strongly that what we hear on these calls are not "objections." It is "resistance." They are very different, and your response to them has to be very different in the "get the meeting" stage, or you will self-sabotage your efforts.

For something to be accurately labeled an "objection," it has to be based upon some knowledge, some modicum of understanding and appreciation of what is being presented before it can be truly "objected" to. It is a strategic mistake to think of what they say at this stage as "objections" and respond in kind -- big mistake.

Their words sound like objections, but they are substantively different, and your response to them must be different to achieve the purpose of your call.

It Sounds Like An "Objection," But It Isn't.

When you go out to meet a prospect you have more time to present, go deeper, ask and answer questions. If there is a potential match, you will typically meet with a prospect several times. At some point in the process, the prospect starts discussing hesitations and doubts about whether your company will get the order. **These are "Objections!"**

The prospect has been meaningfully informed about what you can do but still expresses reservations or rejects going forward.

Those are objections in the truest sense of the word. You must overcome them to close the deal. If you don't fully respond to the prospects satisfaction, bye bye deal, new account, all the revenue, and commission.

At the prospecting stage, you are not trying to close a deal. It is to schedule a substantive next step, in-person or by phone, with a top decision-maker who recognizes a need and is likely to write a check to a competitor in the near future. That is it.

3. Sell The Meeting Only, Not Your Offering.

You are selling the meeting. Not your offering. Big difference.

Once you move beyond selling the meeting to trying to sell your service, you will sell fewer meetings. You will lose opportunities for great accounts simply because you strayed from selling the meeting to trying to sell your offering. Knucklehead.

When seeking to sell a meeting, every word you utter must stay focused on _your_ business objective, _your_ call plan. The person you are speaking to does not have a plan to meet with you. If they have a plan or inclination at all, it is to _not_ meet with you. Let the conversation wander into places where your prospect wants to go, and you will end up somewhere, but it won't be where you want to go.

When setting a meeting, you must resist the urge to respond to resistance as if it were an objection.

If you give them information to overcome their objection you are now working on their agenda (which does not result in a meeting), not your agenda (book a meeting.)

If you swing into "super smart rep" land and think "oh, I know a lot about that. Let me provide info to overcome that," you commit a fatal strategic mistake. What is it? You are giving them information they have to think about and process.

When They Are Thinking They Can't Say "Yes."

Why not? Because they are thinking. If you give them things to think about they cannot say "yes."

Plus, If you fully answer the prospect's questions and give them the information they request, there is no longer a reason for them to meet with you. By your actions and choices, you have knocked yourself out of the setting sales appointment game.

4. Promise Benefits At The first Meeting.

What is the #1 reason why prospects don't agree to meet with you? Simple. You don't give them enough reason to meet with you. Those reasons must be delivered at the first meeting.

At any stage of the sell the meeting call, every stage of the conversation is an opportunity for you to reinforce the benefits they will receive at the first meeting or discovery call.

Think about the foundational bricks that must be laid to build a winning sell-the-meeting script. Who you are, where you are calling from, what you do, why you are credible, the benefits accounts get by working with you, what you want to share at the meeting, asking for the meeting.

Will What They Get At The Meeting Be Worth Their Time If They Don't Do Business With You?

You are going to share information, case studies, reports, and options that have worked for others, a specialized report, a competitor analysis, an analysis of how they rank for XXXX; you need to communicate something that you will deliver at the meeting that is worth their time. Something worth their time even if you don't meet again.

A lot of callers use scripts that essentially say "we are great, we care, let's get together, see what we might do for you, if you hire us, we will do a great job and at some point in the future you will be glad you did. Got any time?" Well something like that is very nebulous for the suspect. There are a lot of if's and but's that must be satisfied before the suspect gets anything.

You must stay focused on describing what they will get *at the meeting* that is worth their time. They can say "yes," they can say "no," or they can offer some resistance you can respond to.

When they do offer resistance, this is an opportunity for you to repeat and reinforce the value they will get at the meeting, and once again, ask for the meeting.

No matter where your suspects want to go with the conversation, you'll always want to steer it back to your purpose by restating the benefits they will get by spending more time with you, and again, ask for the meeting.

5. Never Lose Control.

You must always maintain control over the conversation.

If you lose control over the conversation and go where the suspect wants you to go, you will end up in "Maybe Land."

Remember, your suspect is not working a plan to meet with you. They plan to latch upon something that verifies their strong inclination to get rid of you ASAP. You lose.

Once you lose control, you at best will be thrust into "send me some information, call me back, "hey, why don't you spend time doing work putting together info or quotes while I do nothing." That, my fellow appointment setters, is a very low productivity place to work.

6. Think In Terms Of "Groups."

We have previously touched upon the necessity of thinking in terms of **groups**. Rather than caring about what happens on any individual call or whether you penetrate any specific account, worry much more about how effective you are obtaining a result within a similarly situated group of suspects.

My recommendation is not to worry about getting a meeting with company X, company Y or company Z. But to care a lot about whether you book 2 meetings, 10 meetings, or 20 meetings when you call a similarly situated group of suspects.

Group Think And Common Scenarios

Think of everyone who says "send me some info" as a member of a group. Those who say "call me back" or "we are all set" are also members of groups.

There is the most effective way to respond to those scenarios, which results in helping you to achieve your call objective, book a meeting.

There are many other ways to respond that decrease the odds of you achieving your call objective.

If you think of those who say "send me some info" as a group, what is the response most likely to help you in booking a meeting? Use that response. Practice it, polish it, refine it. Get good at keeping things focused on the result you seek and increasing the odds you will book a meeting with every common scenario you face.

In the "send some info" scenario we know that 9 times out of 10 that is a blow-off. Maybe 10% of the time this is a legitimate request from someone with a need who, if they heard the right things, would book a meeting with you. When you hear "send some info" you want to relate a prepared response strategically calculated to identify the 10% so that you can continue with your objective, booking a meeting now, and waste no more time on the 90% tire-kickers.

Do not try to deliver an individualized response to the person you are speaking to when encountering common scenarios. Rather, concentrate on delivering the response you know from trial, error, and experience is most effective overall, when you hear "send me some info" or "call me back."

7. Don't Try To Prove How Smart You Are Or What You Know.

If you focus on the individuals, once they start talking about their standards, their issues, their challenges, or whatever else they bring up, your natural tendency will be to think "well, this is important to them. I'm a super smart person and know a lot about that. I'll show them how knowledgeable I am and tell them the most important things right now."

If you do that, you make a couple of strategic errors. First, remember that gravity is working against you. Your suspects expect to say "no" or blow you off. The more you talk, the more likely it is that you give them something to hang their hat on to conclude you are not worth their time. Second, if you answer their questions, they don't need you anymore. So why meet? And third, when you respond in detail to what they say, you are now working on their agenda. You have abandoned your agenda.

If any of those 3 things happen: you talk too much, you give out too much information, or you let them determine the course of the conversation, you can only lose.

SELL THE MEETING

Say good-bye to meetings with buyers who will write checks to competitors shortly. Bye-bye. You lost an opportunity, not because you were not capable and qualified. Far from it. If the suspect had gotten to know you, they would have welcomed the opportunity to work with your company. But that won't happen. Why? Because you lost control over the conversation and were unable to sell the meeting.

No meeting, no future account.

More meetings, more accounts.

When you lose control over the conversation the result is "no" or to be cast into the dungeons of "Maybe Land" where few escape. By your word choices and decisions, and your actions, you have slotted those records into a group in which there is a low probability of success.

You want to slot them into a group in which there is a much higher probability of success. That group is the group that has agreed to meet with you. Now. If you maintain control over the conversation, you maximize the odds for scheduling a meeting. Always come back to your agenda no matter where your suspect wants to go.

8. Get A "Yes" Or "No" Within 4 Minutes.

Most successful conversations last about 4 minutes. If the conversation lasts longer than that the odds decrease that someone will book a meeting with you. Probably because that longer conversation has given them things to think about and when they are thinking, they can't say "yes."

Remember, every molecule in their body is expecting to conclude that it is not worth their time to meet with you. Speak too long and you make it a lot easier for them to reach that conclusion.

Every word counts.

You must ruthlessly eliminate unnecessary or wishy-washy words. Any word that is not directly reinforcing why suspects should meet with you and what they will get from that meeting should be eliminated.

What are they? Statements like "we want to see what we can do for you" or "we want to tell you about the services we offer." Any word you say that is non-specific and not related to communicating a benefit they will get at that first meeting must be eliminated.

9. They Can Think 10 Times Faster Than You Can Talk.

Moments matter here. While you are blathering and searching for a point, your suspects are thinking 10X faster than you can speak. Their thoughts are not in your favor.

Once you have given it your best shot, you are better off to be silent than to fill space with wishy-washy, meaningless words.

This is one of the reasons why you prepare and use scripts -- so that you can write them down and eliminate all the meaningless time filling words that don't contribute to achieving your call objective.

Tip: Tape record your end of the conversation. You will hear all the unnecessary words and pauses that slip into your conversation. Eliminate them. You will also hear what you sound like to your suspects. You can alter your words, tone, and delivery to maximize results.

Be relaxed and confident

When in doubt speak in a clear firm voice.
Most will assume you know what you are talking about.

It's not only what you say but how you say it that counts.

Project a relaxed and confident demeanor.

10. You Are Doing Buyers A Favor By Calling Them.

You are calling from a great company that provides superior service and has a long list of satisfied clients. You provide high-quality products and services and stand behind them. If someone needs what you offer, you are doing them a favor by calling. If not for your call, they may not know about you or just how good you are. If not for your call, they would choose a provider less satisfactory to them than you.

It is the most natural and normal thing in the world for you to be calling companies and seeking a meeting.

And, it would be the most normal, natural thing in the world for them to agree to meet.

Think and plan out in advance what words are best used to achieve your call objective. Practice delivering those words naturally and confidently, without hemming or hawing, without hesitations or awkward pauses, without throwing in needless and meaningless words. You will greatly increase the odds that people will conclude that it would be worth spending time with you.

When you seem to be searching for words or hesitating and not quite sure of yourself on the phone, what do you think is going through your suspect's mind? " Well, if this person isn't quite sure of what to say over the phone, how worthwhile would it be to have a meeting with them?"

People Buy From Peers

Remember this. Suspects relate to, trust, and buy from peers.

On these calls, you may not be a CEO or an Executive VP of Worldwide Widgets, but you are their peer on this call. On this call, you are absolutely prepared and more knowledgeable than they are on the topic of whether it makes sense to meet. On the issue of whether they should meet with your company, you are their peer.

Believe it. Project it.

Worksheets, additional scripts, and periodic updates are available to readers of this book at ScottChannell.com/STM-book-extras

Chapter 16
Objection Response Scripts

**You Hear The Same Objections Repeatedly.
There Is No Excuse For Not Handling Them Well.**

Now you must prepare your responses to common expressions of resistance you will encounter.

This is important for 2 reasons.

First, 25% to 33% of the next steps you schedule will be booked after you hear the word "no" in some form

When your first request for a meeting is denied, you are now at the moment of truth. These are the skills that separate effective lead generators (and quota busting sales reps) from those left muttering excuses.

You will lose well-qualified opportunities at this stage if you are not prepared. Your hard work in selecting the list, setting up your system, and implementing your call process consistently so that you can bump into a buyer at the right time will be wasted if you are not prepared for this moment.

This is the moment when your back needs to stiffen. Your preparation for these moments determines success and failure for many.

You must leverage your target's response, re-state the benefits they get *at the meeting*, remind them of your credibility, then *again ask for the meeting*.

Preparation and practice to deliver appropriate responses when encountering these common forms of resistance moments will lift your results significantly without making more dials.

Strategic Reality Of Your Responses To Resistance

Your purpose is to book the meeting right now, on this conversation.

Yet, we know because we have brains that the odds of us bumping into a buyer at exactly the right time for a meeting is slim. The odds are much greater that we will speak to a buyer before they are willing to meet. These "buyers" recognize a need, know they must take action at some time, but before your call felt that it was "too early" to meet with someone.

Many buyers we speak to who do not agree to meet now, will buy from a competitor within 3 to 15 months. Your goal is not only to book meetings with buyers now but to identify future buyers and obtain permission for future action.

Understand this. The greatest revenue and profit is found among the group that does not immediately agree to meet with you, but shares a need and gives permission for future action.

How many times have you spoken to someone who is a perfect fit for your offering only to hear them say "no, no, no" and call your mother names? You wimpily say "okay, sorry to bother you, have a good day." Click. You dutifully follow your system and schedule them for a routine follow-up in 6 months. What do you hear this time? "Oh, we just signed a mega-contract with one of your competitors, too late." Happens all the time.

You need to follow a script path that enables you to identify those who won't meet now but do have a sparkle in their eye and are likely to buy from someone shortly.

My point here is that when responding to resistance you have a dual purpose. It is not just to overcome the objection and book the meeting now. It is to deliver the most effective response to common forms of resistance and if they still say no, to ID those who are likely to buy in the future.

You use the magic question script after they have said "no" to your attempt to overcome their objection. Those who respond to the magic question in the affirmative will book a meeting with you in the future 50% of the time. These are lay-ups.

In fact, within 2-4 months 25% of the meetings you book will be scheduled with people who told you when to follow up with them and gave their permission and encouragement to do so.

SELL THE MEETING

Both objectives are critical.

Your prepared responses to resistance will bump your immediate results and your longer term results.

You are already making the calls. Why not make the most of them.

Common Scenarios

There a lot of common forms of resistance you will hear on the phone. "I'm all set," "send me some info," "call me back," "what do you do?" " we have no budget," " we have a vendor we love," "I get 20 calls a day like this," "we have a signed 20-year contract that can't be broken," "I'll meet but call me back" are among the most common. There is no need to try to master a response to each of 20 different objections.

All anticipated forms of resistance break down into 3 standard paths of response.

I'm all set.

Send some info.

Call me back.

Before I review how you best respond to these 3 scenarios, let me remind you of a few things.

When you are seeking to generate leads, the bigger picture is that you are trying to re-shuffle the deck in order of priorities. You identify your best opportunities and schedule appointments with them. With better than average value suspects that say "no" to meeting now, you ID those who are likely to buy shortly and obtain their direction and permission to call back. You identify your no-opportunity and low-probability targets and cast them into the dungeon, never to be seen again. If your suspect lies in a gray area, you seek to obtain the information you need to prioritize them properly.

The information you need to sort suspects properly is obtained when you maintain control, *work your plan* and effectively respond to initial resistance.

Responding To "We Are All Set"

This is sometimes expressed as "we have a vendor we love," "we have 5 vendors already," or even "we have a contract with 12 years left to run, which is unbreakable."

You have two choices for how to reply:

"That's fine. Does that mean you will never look at new options or could you suggest a better time for me to call in the future?"

Or

"That's fine. Look, wouldn't expect anything to happen quickly if we met anyway. Not the way it happens in this business. We made 30,000 moves last year for companies like Mega Corp and 500 others. They looked at their options and selected us. Just looking to introduce ourselves and share info as to how other companies have achieved high transferee satisfaction ratings and greater cost efficiencies. If at some point in time you seek to improve your program, review your providers or need extra help, you will have someone familiar with your program you can reach out to. If you feel that is worth about 30 minutes of your time, I'm happy to share specifics that may help. Any chance you are available next Wednesday or Thursday, the 18th or 19th?"

A slight variation of this script…

"Not an issue. Even if we get together would not expect anything to happen quickly. That is not the way it works in this business. We do a lot of business with companies like Mega Corp and 50 companies in your area. There are good reasons why they picked us — just looking to introduce ourselves and provide you with some info and strategies to make your process a bit easier. If in the future you are looking for options or need special help, we hope you think of us. Would that be worth 30 minutes of your time on Tuesday or Wednesday the week of the 22nd?"

Now with the first response, "That's fine. Does that mean you will never look at new options or could you suggest a better time for me to call in the future?" What you are doing is giving your prospect the opportunity to reconfirm that they are truly "all set" and give you permission as well as direction as to when to call again.

You have no chance of getting a meeting with this response as you have not provided any additional reasons why they should meet with you and you haven't asked for the meeting again.

This response is probably best when you encounter someone who is gruff or appears rushed and you don't feel you can deliver a longer response.

It is very important that you ask them when to call back. It never ceases to amaze me how people in one breath emphatically tell you they are "all set" then in the next breath tell you they will meet in 30 days to discuss an upcoming purchase. **Happens all the time,** *if you create the opportunity for it to happen*. Ask the follow-up question. Reap the rewards.

If you wimpily accept the "no," you won't identify those great opportunities that are lurking just below the surface of that answer. You have done all the hard work, now make that little extra effort that generates disproportionate results.

Another option to use:

"That's fine, don't want to be on your back, but we do an awful lot of this. Could you suggest a time I should call in the future?"

If they truly have no need, they will reconfirm that. But if they are open to listening to options at some point, you have said something calculated to elicit that fact.

My opinion is that you should try some variation of the longer response.

"That's fine. Wouldn't expect anything to happen quickly anyway. Not the way it happens in this business. We do a lot of business with companies like Acme United, Brito International and 50 companies in your Atlanta metro area. They chose us to get mega-benefit A and monster benefit B. Just looking to introduce ourselves and share specific examples and strategies other companies have used to improve their move process and be more cost efficient. If you review options in the future, we hope you think of us. Is that worth 30 minutes next Wednesday or Thursday, the 19th or 20th?"

What you are doing with this script is lowering their expectations, assuring them that they will not be pressured and giving them reasons to meet even if they are in fact "all set."

Side Note: Don't Assume That What They Say Is Literally True.

Remember this when responding to resistance. What they say to you is probably not literally true.

When they say "we are all set" they may really be thinking, "ahhh, we are going to change vendors or buy this soon but don't know whether I should tell them or meet with them yet," or, "this group doesn't sound good enough to be worth my time."

They might be thinking, "they don't sound so special. I'll check out others first."

When you hear "all set" or any form of resistance for that matter, it is probably literally true a small percentage of the time. Your response, by repeating and reinforcing your value and credibility, providing additional reasons to meet, and giving them more time to process what you are saying enables those who linger just below the surface of "yes" to come forward and agree to meet.

Notice the name drops and "other companies have chosen us." The reference to "including 50 companies in your Atlanta metro area" is a way to reinforce your credibility in a slightly different way than again saying "500 companies." You are reinforcing your credibility and benefits, which enables them to conclude that it would be worth their time to meet with you. Then you end up by telling them what they will get *at the meeting* that is worth their time, even though they are "all set."

"... you will get some specific examples and strategies as to how others have achieved these results."

Add Other Reasons They Might Meet Even If All Set

You then go for the close by saying "if in the future you are looking for options, or need to source a hard-to-find item, we hope you think of us. Would that be worth 30 minutes of your time next Wednesday or Thursday?"

You are only asking your suspects to answer one question either "yes" or "no."

You have kept control of the conversation, reinforced your credibility, given them additional reasons to meet with you and asked for the meeting again. If they say "no," you then ask them to suggest a good time for you to call back.

Responding To "Send Me Some Information." Are You A Wimp Or An Appointment Setter?

"Send me some information" is one of the most common things you will hear. Let me be blunt. If your response to "send me some information" is to mindlessly mutter "um, okay," then send something and then follow up, follow up and follow up on the mere possibility that a sweet nothing whispered in your ear will lead to something, you are a certified wimp and dooming yourself to lead generation frustration. By this choice, you waste your time and company resources.

"Send me some info" is typically code for "get lost." It's almost always a blow-off. You know that. It's easy for those you call to get rid of you. They play to your emotional need to please, not to offend and the mental gymnastics people do to avoid hearing the word "no" and buh-bye to you. But for you the call is not over. By your choice and behavior, you have committed to spend time and maybe money to send something. You are now working their plan, not yours.

If allowing them to knock you off your plan isn't bad enough, you are also going to follow up, follow up, and follow up. As most of these (90%+) are blow-offs and worthless, all the time following up on them is wasted. You could have chosen to find out if they were real and worth more time, but you didn't.

You are a wimp.

Your "okay" to the send-more-information blow-off provides you with no information of value to your prospecting efforts. You turned control of your actions over to the caller. You did absolutely nothing to determine if they were among the less than 1 in 10 who are real and worth more time. You chose to invest time in a scenario where at least 90% of your effort is totally wasted. You chose a path of guaranteed bang-your-head-against-the-wall frustration. Even if after many failed attempts you do get them back on the phone they at best vaguely remember you or don't remember or haven't reviewed what you sent.

With very few exceptions, the end of that road is a dead-end. You chose a low-probability path rather than a high-probability path. If you get on this treadmill to nowhere, it is your fault, not the fault of those you call. You made the choice. You are a wimp.

The Greater Sin Of Being A Wimp

The fact that you will waste gobs of time that could have been put to better use is bad enough. But the bigger sin is that you had the opportunity in your hand to identify legitimate high-potential high-value prospects, and you let it slip right through your fingers. You did all the hard, monotonous, torturous work to get a qualified prospect to pick up the phone and then you choked.

You must have a scripted strategy for this common scenario that enables you to separate legitimate pad-your-paycheck opportunities from the time-wasting shrink-your-paycheck opportunities.

Once you do identify someone as worth your time, do you send the information? Oh no, no, no as you will soon learn.

When you expose the time-wasters what do you do? Simply state the truth and ask them if there is a time they would like you to be back in touch. (You never suggest a callback time. They must tell you.)

"Ethel, it doesn't seem that investing time right now would be mutually beneficial, but we do an awful lot of this. Is there a time you would like me to be back in touch?"

The next time you hear "send me some info, schmo," consider saying something like this.

"You know, I don't send out generic information. The standard corporate marketing stuff is just going to tell you what I just told you. We are a $90 million company that supplies widgets to companies like I.B. Sorry, Ray's Burgers and 1,200 others. If there is some specific information that would be helpful to you, I would be happy to put something together that would be of some real help. Do you have anything specific in mind I might help you with?"

Now you do the most difficult thing a sales rep has to do. Say nothing. Be silent.

If your suspect cannot come up with something specific, recognize that with your set-the-appointment pitch and your response to resistance that you have delivered a clear, succinct benefit-laden credibility-building message. You have offered something specific that could help them if they have a need. You have rolled out the big guns and fired.

If they don't respond to that with a specific request, you can be confident that they do not currently have a need you can help them with. You can slide right into "Ethel, it doesn't seem that investing time right now would be mutually beneficial, but we do an awful lot of this. Is there a time you would like me to be back in touch?"

If they give you a callback time that meets your requirements, schedule a callback at that time. Otherwise, assuming they still are a member of your high-probability group (industry, company size, number of employees, etc.) you just call them back in accordance with your standard follow-up schedule. About 6 months seems to be the norm.

But what if something out of the ordinary happens? What if they respond to your question about whether they have something specific they need with something specific? They say something like "well, we are going to buy $500,000 worth of widgets in a month… " or "well, we think we could be a lot more efficient with our widget packaging…" or "well, we have had some quality and delivery concerns with our current supplier…" followed by "can you send me some info on X, Y and Z?"

Whoa. Now you know you have a live one.

What do you do? Do you send them the specific information they have requested? What, are you an idiot? Your job is to book meetings now. After tremendous effort, you have a live one on the phone. Stick to your plan and try to book the meeting now.

You must do 3 things. Not one of them has anything to do with you sending them information.

First, you must listen intently. Listen. Let them spill their beans. Don't interrupt. When they are done, ask a couple of open-ended questions that require just a short answer to clarify their request and spur them to tell you more about their needs and situation. Then, you go back to your agenda. Work your plan.

You never let your target's agenda become your agenda. They are requesting information, but your objective is to book a substantive next step on the path to a closed account. Your agenda is to sell the meeting. Now.

When your suspect tells you they have needs, have doubts about their sources of supply, or will be reviewing providers, it is even more important that you work your plan and stick to your agenda, which is to book a meeting. Now.

Remember, the biggest reason people don't meet with you is that you don't give them enough reason to meet with you. And you must **ask** for the meeting.

So, after (1) listening to their request and then (2) clarifying it with a couple of open-ended questions, you then (3) swing the conversation back to your agenda and say something like the following.

"You know, I could put together a lot of info that would be helpful to you… right off the top of my head, I can think of 3 companies in your industry we have helped with those issues. Don't know much about your company, but you do have a few options to consider, and there are a few common landmines you want to avoid. Dapper Danielle is our rep in your area, and she has experience with this. If she had the opportunity to learn more specifics about your situation, she could give you a lot of information that is tailored specifically to your needs. It may or may not lead to a next step. Either is fine. Would that be worth 30 minutes of your time?"

Let's look at what you will have done. You will have given those companies that do have a specific need the opportunity to inform you of that need. You have leveraged that information into a tremendous benefit they will receive if they meet with you. They will get specific information on their particular needs from someone very knowledgeable. That is usually a pretty good reason for people to meet with you.

If they say "yes," book it. If they say "no," say something like this.

"Understand. It doesn't appear we are a match at this time. But obviously, we do a lot of this. Is there a time you would like me to be back in touch with you?"

So let's look at what you have done here with the send-me-some-info objection.

First and most importantly, you have refused to be sucked into time-wasting frustration with follow-ups just because some knucklehead of unknown qualification and needs asked you to. We know that 90%+ of these requests are veiled "no's" and are going nowhere. By responding in a structured way, you were able to identify the few that were legitimate. Of those that were real you leveraged information gained into a very good reason to meet, and you asked for the meeting. If they don't meet, you learned from them the best time to be back in touch. (They suggested the time, not you.)

So you stuck to your agenda. You eliminated the future wasted follow-up time from the 90% that was blowing you off — picked up more meetings from those who had legitimate needs. Got callback dates from high-probability prospects that are well informed about what you do, your credibility, and the benefits you deliver.

All because you had a plan.

But what if you were an appointment setting wimp?

What if, when they said "send me some info" you said "um, okay" and sent some info?

This would be the result.

You would spend time and money emailing or mailing stuff that would be ignored by more than 90% of the recipients.

You would call, call and callback repeatedly to these faux information seekers only to have them ignore you, blow you off again, or many times not remember you at all.

All that time invested in follow-ups to the 90% that were blowing you off could have been invested in follow-ups to higher-probability prospects or working a group that would lead to you speaking to high-probability prospects.

You will get frustrated and less enthusiastic about calling. All predictable, all avoidable.

All because you chose a low-probability path, rather than a high-probability path.

A Bit More About The "Send-Me-Some Information" Response

Before I get off the, "send-some info" objection, I would like you to keep 2 other points in mind. First, remember that sometimes your greatest strength can be your greatest weakness. It is very difficult for someone who has a lot of knowledge in a particular area to withhold information when talking to a suspect. It is normal human behavior to want to be liked every second and recognized as being smart and knowledgeable.

But what you withhold is as important as what you decide to say. If you spill your beans too early, if you provide too much information too early, you give great suspects the opportunity to become uncomfortable and conclude that they should not meet with you. Not because they don't have needs you can help with, not because you are not capable, but because you went too far showing off your knowledge and it was too much for them to process. They became uncomfortable with too much to process in too little time, so they reject the meeting.

When you share too much, you are crossing the line between selling the meeting and selling your offering.

When you cross that line, your chances of selling the meeting plummet. Stay focused on selling the meeting only. That will get you more opportunities to sell your offering. Try to sell your offering too early and you will book fewer meetings.

Every bone in their body is looking for a reason to not meet with you at this point. When you ramble on, when the conversation lasts more than 3 or 4 minutes, you will probably give them something to hang their hat on as a justification for blowing you off.

Also, if you talk too much, you are working on their agenda, not your agenda, and you can only lose in that arena.

Responding To "Call Me Back."

The majority of the time "call me back" is a road to nowhere. If you just say "okay" you are now working your suspect's agenda. You lose.

When you hear "call me back" you need some information to properly slot them so that *you* can decide whether you will call back.

I would recommend you proceed as follows:

"Sure. When would you suggest I call you?"

Once they give you a time period, say:

"That works. Happy to do that. Is there a specific reason why that's a good time to call?"

Their reply will generally fall into 1 of 2 buckets. They will give you a general "I'm really busy right now" or "this isn't a good time" type response. A general non-specific response gives you no clue as to whether they have a need or situation to improve. You have no information that indicates they have an issue or a vision (however foggy) that may include you helping them: no vision = bundles of guaranteed wasted prospecting time for you.

Now if you are going to prospect in the land of mere possibilities, maybe's and you never know, you have chosen to dwell in a smaller paycheck space. The more time you allocate to low-probability smaller paycheck activities, the less successful you will be.

If they respond to your "why is that a good time to call you?" question with a generic non-specific answer do not let them cast you into time-wasting, go-nowhere follow-up hell.

Do not let them do this. Find out now whether they have legitimate needs or are blowing you off and dooming you to follow-up frustration.

Respond to a non-specific answer with something like this:

"Hmmm. Well, I'm certainly happy to be back in touch if it is worthwhile for both of us. I'm not hearing an issue and wondering if a call is worth our time. Feel free to tell me it is not and I won't be on your back."

Those who are real will typically respond with:

"Oh, no, no, no. Please call. This is happening _____, and it is a good time to call because _____ "

If they are real and sense you are credible and worth spending some time with, they will share more information with you.

Now if they are blowing you off, they will respond with something like "I'm not sure what's going on. Just call back when you want and feel free to keep in touch." Or something similar.

You say "thanks, I'll keep in touch" and schedule for a routine generic follow-up in about 6 months.

Congratulations. You worked on your plan and did not get sucked into go-nowhere land.

But What If They Say Something Specific?

The other option is that they give you a more specific response. They provide some tidbit that indicates that they have a need and some form of vision that could lead to closing a sale.

Their more specific response might be something like this: "Well, we are planning on buying a billion dollars worth of widgets next quarter, and I will have the specs then." Or, "we have had some service issues and plan on reviewing our vendors when our fiscal year closes, so that is a good time to reach out." Or, "we are hiring, firing, moving, merging, installing, back from vacation, getting a new VP up to steam, sweeping the floors, so won't have time to focus on this till then."

Once you have a valid, ballpark legitimate reason and know your suspect is viable, you can end up saying:

"Thank you very much. I will contact you then. One quick question… (Ask a worth question here.) "Roughly, how many employees work for the company?" Or, "how many sales people do you have?" "what XXX technology are you using now?"

They reply. You end with:

"Talk to you then, thanks." Click.

Eliminate The Tire Kickers Before You Call Them Back 10 Times.

Remember those core concepts discussed earlier? That your behaviors must stay consistent with certain beliefs and practices to set more discovery calls and sales appointments? Well, here is one of them in action.

You are not trying to keep records alive; you are trying to kill them.

If a suspect does not meet your minimum standards for follow-up, you discard them for now.

Those who cannot articulate a minimally acceptable reason for follow-up are part of a group that is a lower-productivity lower-paycheck space. The more members of that group you let slip into your calls, less and less of your time is devoted to higher-productivity higher-paycheck calls. More and more of your time, by your choices and actions, is being allocated to lower-productivity lower-paycheck activities.

SELL THE MEETING

So, are you going to be a wimp and a choker at the moment of truth?

If they give you an "I have no clue why you should call me back" type response, could you bring yourself to say something like this:

"Happy to call you back…but keep in mind that 600 companies including Mega Corp and Ray's Burgers selected us from all their options, and there are very good reasons for that. Don't want to be on your back. If you are not open to a new source of supply just tell me and I won't bother you. Let's save both of us some time."

Or,

"I'd be happy to call you back. We have done projects for companies like A, B and Z… (Or, you might say… "achieved results like 1, 2, 3 within your industry.) I don't want to be on your back. If you don't think it would be worthwhile for us to meet (have a discovery call) at some time, it is perfectly okay to say that."

Or,

"Jane, happy to call you back, but let me save both of us some time. We do a lot of work in your industry. If you don't think it would be worthwhile for us to meet at some point, just tell me. The word "no" doesn't bother me."

There is nothing wrong with being direct.

In any group of 100 send-me-some-info, we-are-all-set, call-me-back responses, 90 or more of them are blow-offs, time-wasters, and guaranteed to suck your time away from legitimate higher-probability opportunities.

Let me repeat: out of 100, 90 or more of them are a total waste of follow-up time.

It's a lot easier to just step up to the plate and ask a few direct questions so that you can decide whether this suspect is currently in a fatter paycheck or a thinner paycheck group.

You have a choice. Execute a strategy that identifies the time-wasters before you call them back 10 times. Or, find out who they are after you make all those calls — your choice.

Responding To The Rest

If you prepare and practice responses to those 3 most common scenarios, you will be in good shape to respond to pretty much every objection you will hear.

Keep the following in mind:

You must reinforce your credibility and the benefits you deliver with your response.

You must respond. You don't need to answer.

You must ignore their agenda and stay focused on your agenda.

You must seek a clear "yes" or "no."

Even if they say "no" or they don't meet your minimum standards for follow-up, you can still pick up some worth or qualifying information to properly allocate your time for future calls.

You are actively trying to disqualify people here. You should only allocate time to those who give you specific answers so that you can objectively decide they are worth your time.

If you allow too many low-probability, lower-paycheck prospects into your call schedule, you take time away from higher-probability, bigger-paycheck suspects.

Worksheets, additional scripts, and periodic updates are available to readers of this book at ScottChannell.com/STM-book-extras

Chapter 17
Introduction To Managing Your Day

There comes the point where all the big thoughts have been thunk, and now you have to do something.

You have your list prioritized, and you know you are calling the highest-probability / highest-worth group you could with the time you have. You have set yourself up to prospect very efficiently with the setup and coding options within your contact manager/CRM. You created a kick butt pile of words and from that arose very powerful impactful messaging that would give "cause for pause," to a buyer (someone who recognizes a need on some level and is likely to write a check to someone within the next 15 months.) You have planned out your call process. You have thought about all the repetitive scenarios you will encounter, and you are ready for them.

Now you have to call.

Yikes.

Every day you will have dozens of records to deal with in various stages of your call process. Dozens. To juggle them effectively you want to have a game plan in your head as to how you are going to manage each day for maximum productivity.

Also, you should have a game plan as to how you will prospect each individual record from start to finish.

You must manage your day effectively juggling dozens of targets in various stages of your prospecting process.

You must manage each record from the first call to last.

Once you grab your coffee and power up your CRM I would recommend that your behaviors maximize results in three distinct areas.

How you manage your day.

How effective you are with individuals you call.

How effective you are interacting with distinct groups of contacts and handling common scenarios.

Managing Your Day

My suggestion is that you break up your day into three parts.

Part A: Launches

Part B: Follow-ups

Part C: Investing more time with those worth more time.

So let's take a perfect world. You are prospecting full time and sitting at your station all day with no other responsibilities than to book meetings: over the phone/web discovery calls or first sales appointments face-to-face.

To have a successful day, you must "launch" your process with a reasonable number of new targets. You must follow through and take the next scheduled action on those in the middle of your call process. And, you should leave time to make additional calls, emails or make some extra effort above and beyond your usual call process to those who are worth more time and extra effort.

Launches.
Follow-ups.
Extra effort.

You don't have to do them in the same order I did, but I do recommend that you be consistent.

Calling A Suspect From Start To Finish

In addition to managing your day, you must have clarity about how to call a record from start to finish over about two weeks.

Hopefully, you are not just "dialing" the phone and suffering from the belief that "it is a numbers game" and the more times you dial the phone, the more likely you are to book a meeting. Only the "unconsciously incompetent" as Zig Ziglar used to say, think that. If you are an unconscious incompetent, you have no clue as to what you don't know.

SELL THE MEETING

When you launch your process with a suspect, in addition to dialing the phone you have made sure that you are calling the very highest-probability and value records with the time you have to prospect. Not records that are OK or good enough and "you never know" so let's just start calling. You have made sure that you are calling the very best records from all your choices. You are calling "A+" and "A" records before you call your "B" records and all the rest, and you know the difference.

As you call you are making a major effort, in the beginning, to weed out the worthless so that you don't waste your time with them. You are consciously doing everything you can to determine worth and pick up contact information such as direct dial, extension numbers and email addresses. You are well aware of all the common scenarios you are likely to encounter, and you have prepared, prepared again and written down (it is called scripting) the very best words to use in these common scenarios to achieve your business objective.

You also know that the odds of bumping into a buyer at the very best time to meet is unlikely. Knowing that it is crucial to identify those who won't meet now but are likely to write a check to a competitor in the next 3-15 months, you have a strategy to identify them and get them to tell you how to start selling them.

Yikes. Guess there is a lot more to this than just dialing the phone.

Remember, the very best and most productive sales appointment and discovery call setters do not make the most dials. They make a reasonable amount of dials, are prepared, and work very smart. You can too.

If you manage your day well, are effective with individuals and handle common scenarios consistently, you are well on your way to setting discovery call success.

Let's review how to manage your day and work an individual record from start to finish.

> Worksheets, additional scripts, and periodic updates
> are available to readers of this book at
> ScottChannell.com/STM-book-extras

Chapter 18
Managing Your Day Part One: Launches

Start with your "launches."

Understand this. The best correlation with the number of meetings you set will be the number of "launches" you make — not the number of times you dial the phone. I find the number of dials made to be virtually useless in determining success or diagnosing why a program is not working. Chew on that.

FACT: Those who are consistently successful at booking meetings with decision-makers do not make the most dials.

FACT: If you are calling the wrong people with a lousy process and your scripts and emails are poor and watered down, making more dials will not save you.

It is certainly true that you have to make a reasonable number of dials. But once you are in a certain zone of activity and find it is not working cranking up the activity or dials will not transform a dumpster fire into a barbeque.

The most direct correlation to your success is the number of contacts that you initiate your call process with: these are "launches."

Your Launch "Assumptions"

There are a couple of assumptions here. We assume that you are launching your call process with the highest-probability/highest-potential value records you can.

We also assume that once you launch, you are implementing and sticking to your call process.

If your process is the 3 cycles of 3, you have committed to making 3 bursts of calls ending with touches. Each burst should be 3 business days apart. Your targets will receive a minimum of 9 dials from you, 3 voicemails and if you have an email address, they will also get 3 emails. In some circumstances, direct mail, Linkedin In-mail or dropping off a lumpy package might be part of your interaction process.

You do not short-circuit your process except for specific objective reasons. You do not lengthen your call process unless you have objectively determined that a target is worth more time.

How Many Launches Are Enough?

For people prospecting full-time, a reasonable number of launches would be 10-15 a day. 50-75 a week. 15 a day or 75 a week would be a stretch. 10-12 a day or 50-60 a week is a more typical ballpark.

So let's assume that most of you will have to launch your call process with 10-15 records a day to have even a chance of managing a process that consistently spits out enough qualified discovery calls and sales appointments.

You take a record that you have not called before. You have a company name and most of the time you will have a contact name. Today, given the quality of the databases available and Linkedin, a very high percentage of time you can be very confident that your contact name is the decision-maker or very close to them.

Tip: You can save a lot of time and greatly increase efficiency by having someone else at a lower pay grade and skillset level look up decision-makers within targeted companies. I'm a big believer in having data ninjas identify the most likely top decision-makers. This saves appointment setters a lot of time that could be spent reaching out to people. Also, it eliminates a great deal of monotony and boredom from a very repetitious job.

If you feel confident that the name on your list is the decision-maker, you make your first call and confirm that they are still with the company by asking to speak to them. On this first call, you might also pick up additional information as to potential worth, direct dial or extension number, email address, confirm the title or mailing address.

Once you confirm that they are still with the company, you then schedule your next call in your well-thought-out pre-planned most-likely-to-get-you-a-conversation and a meeting call process.

That record is "launched."

Summary Of What A Launch Is

We assume that you have chosen a record that belongs to the very best group you could call given time available to you. You have profiled and evaluated your total potential call universe and based upon research you have prioritized your call universe into groups based upon potential worth and probability of buying.

You have chosen a record within that group, and in most cases you will have the name of whom you believe to be the decision maker. You make your first call.

The purpose of your first call is to:

1) confirm that your target is still with the company. If not, to obtain another name.
2) pick up some worth info to gain insight into the potential value and properly prioritize.
3) get the direct dial, extension number, and email to increase the odds of speaking to them or getting a response.
4) pick up any other info if possible, that helps you to prioritize the call and properly allocate your time or improve the quality of your information.

On the first call, I don't recommend even trying to speak to the decision-maker. On the first call, if you can confirm your target, get some worth info, and most importantly of all, identify low-value and no-value targets and never waste any more time on them. Those objectives are far more important.

Don't Even Try To Speak To The Decision-maker? Are You Kidding? Nope.

Think of it this way. You will speak to far more decision-makers worth speaking to if you can make fewer calls to those not worth your time. Every call not made to a non-qualified target means more time to call higher-value qualified targets. If you are serious about booking meetings, you must get good at identifying those not worth your time. In the beginning, it is far more important to identify the higher value targets and knock out the non-qualified and those worth too little to be worth your time than it is to try to speak to the decision-maker.

You may end up speaking to your target on this call, but that is not typical. Your purpose is to confirm the decision-maker and while you are on the phone to pick up whatever recon info you can.

Once you confirm that the name on your list is, in fact, the decision-maker, you schedule that record for the first call in your well-thought-out call process.

That record is launched.

But What If You Don't Have A Name Or Are Not Very Confident That The Name You Have Is The Decision-Maker?

Sometimes despite all the data resources available to us, you might not know who the decision-maker is within a company. In that case, you have to go old school. You have to ask.

I cover this first "identify the decision-maker" call in more detail in the script section. It would go something like this, "hi, I would like to send some information to whoever handles X. Could you tell me who to direct it to?" They respond with a name. You ask additional questions as to title, potential worth, direct dial or extension number, how many times they have watched "The Shawshank Redemption," and at some point say "good-bye." You hang up and schedule the next call consistent with your call process.

That record is now "launched."

What Happens If You Can't Confirm A Decision-Maker Or Obtain A Name?

Sometimes the name you have is no longer with the company, has the wrong title, or is not the decision-maker. In that case, you have to get a new name. That record is not "launched" until you do.

So To Summarize, Again

You must "launch" your call process with a certain number of records per day and week.

Those records you choose to launch must be the ones that most closely fit your profile, are of the greatest potential value to you, and be most probable to buy of all your choices.

A full-time appointment setter would "launch" 10-15 records a day, 50-75 a week. A reasonable pace would be 10-12 "launches" in an hour. If it takes you much longer than this, you are either calling the wrong list or doing it wrong.

Before We Leave The Topic Of "Launches"

Please excuse this rant before I leave the topic of launches.

The #1 cause of failure with appointment setting or set-the-discovery-call programs is that the wrong people are called. If you call targets within your bullseye profile of those with high-potential worth most likely to buy, if you call *them*, you can make a lot of mistakes with your call process and scripting, and you can still make money.

But if you call the wrong group of people, those too far removed from your bullseye profile of most likely great potential accounts, you will not be successful no matter how great your call process or your scripting is, how much you know or the quality of your witty phone banter and repartee. None of that will matter.

If you do not allocate your time to the highest-value/highest-probability group, no matter what else you do well, you will fail or generate measly results at best — no doubt about it.

I Never Let Clients Tell Me Who To Call.

In my calling days, I booked a lot of meetings. C-Level or executive suite decision-makers. Typically for larger value transactions. I was very good and got results.

One of the reasons why was that I never let a client tell me who to call. Never. No exceptions.

Do Not Cast Your Net Too Wide.

Clients and companies make a very common mistake of casting their prospecting net too wide. They have FOMO big time. Their fear of missing out, leads to them dooming their chances of prospecting success before the first call is made.

Let me give you a very common example. I have a large national brand client that is heavily dependent upon setting sales appointments and discovery calls for new business. We know from research and prior history that 50% of "great" new accounts are found within a very tightly defined 3% of the potential account universe. The other 50% of the "great" new accounts are found sprinkled throughout the other 97% of the potential account universe.

Hmmm. 50% of great new business is found within 3% of the total potential prospect pool. The other 50% comes from all the rest. Who do you think should be called first?

So Let's Assume A Potential Client Pool Of 10,000 Suspects

3% (300) of the pool are "A" quality highest-potential value most probable to buy suspects.

5% (500) of the pool are "B" above-average value and probability suspects.

12% (1,200) targets are average "C" value suspects.

20% (2,000) are less than the average value "D" suspects.

60% (6,000) are "E" suspects, deemed unqualified by potential value or probability of buying.

If You Are Prospecting Smart

Common sense would tell you that you should call the best before all the rest.

In this very common prospecting scenario, the "A's" should be launched before the B's and C's. No time should ever be spent researching or reaching out to D's or E's.

If you could expect to "launch" 50 records a week, it would take 6 weeks for 1 person to launch all the A's. You should do that first.

Then you would call out and "launch" all your B's. At 50 launches a week that would take another 10 weeks.

Then you start launching your C's.

Let's Take Another Example, Based Upon Company Size.

Here is another common scenario. Very commonly, company size within a certain range of SIC or NAICS codes can be a reliable indicator of potential worth and the probability of buying.

Let's consider a company that sells something potentially "any business' could buy. (Let me add that if you sell something that potentially "any business" could buy, you are in a very precarious slippery slope situation when it comes to prospecting.)

In this example although "any business" might buy, 75% of the good solid, decent accounts are businesses with sales revenue of between $2.5-50 million. There are a handful of solid, decent accounts to be found in the $1-2.5 million range, a handful in the $50+ million range, and less than a handful found in the smaller than $1 million range.

Old Marketing Saying

There is an old marketing rule of thumb that says that those most likely to buy tend to look like those who have already bought.

So if you knew that 75% of the clients you would like to clone had revenue of between $2.5-50 million, that is where you would start.

A typical distribution for this example would look like this.

75% of good accounts found within businesses with between $2.5-50 million in revenue. 6,345 records fit this profile -- 10% of all businesses.

A handful of good accounts are to be found within businesses with between $1-2.5 million in revenue. There are 9,965 records that fit this profile — 16 % of all businesses.

Another handful of good accounts are found within businesses with revenue ranges of more than $50 million. There are 375 records that fit this profile -- 2% of all businesses.

And less than a handful of good clients are to be found among business that have less than $1 million in revenue. There are 43,855 business that fit this profile — 72 % of the total.

If You Don't Know What You Are Doing

If you don't know how to properly create a profile of your best-prospecting targets or, if you don't know how to separate the A's from the C's from the E's, or maybe the concept of spending your time where it will do the most good, is foreign to you then you would just jump in and start calling. And you would be doomed.

You would be doomed because if you "just start calling" you would be spending a very high percentage of your time with "D" and "E" quality records. In the example above, the D and E below average and unqualified records represent 74% of the pool. So if you "just start calling," 74% of your time investment and expense will be directed toward records that are virtually worthless. That is dumb.

This is why I am not a fan of Chamber of Commerce lists, top company type lists published in business journals, or generic lists of businesses. I also wince when I hear of companies that require salespeople to turn in a certain number of leads per week. Those lists and names are convenient, and many think "there are some good ones in here," which is a very poor and, I might add, a dumb reason to call a list. But the reality is that only a very small percentage of names on those lists are within your bullseye. Most of the names on those lists are way outside of your bullseye and if any business results it is more because of lottery ticket luck or randomness than because you are working a solid plan with high-probability suspects.

You Have A Choice To Launch Your Call Process With High-Probability Suspects Or Lower-probability Suspects.

If you don't prioritize or don't know how to prioritize and "just start calling," you doom yourself and your team to spending a very high percentage of time in low-probability land.

When you "launch" records to call, if you know that 50% of your good accounts are found within just 3% of your list, call all of that 3% before you start calling all the rest.

If you know that three-quarters of your good accounts are found within certain SIC code ranges and have revenue between $2.5-$50 million and companies with that profile comprise 10.5% of your list, call them before you call all the rest.

Launch your process with the highest-potential value highest-probability records available to you. No exceptions. No rationalizations. No excuses.

End of rant.

Worksheets, additional scripts, and periodic updates are available to readers of this book at ScottChannell.com/STM-book-extras

Chapter 19
Managing Your Day Part 2: Follow-ups

Once you complete your launches for the day, the second part of the day is to complete calls scheduled to be made that day — your follow-ups.

You have a plan.
You must work your plan.
Every time you complete a step, you must schedule the next.
No exceptions.

You must complete all calls scheduled to be made. You need to work your call process on the largest high-value / high-probability group you can handle. To achieve the goals, you have set up your CRM / contact manager to maximize the efficiency with which you can execute your process with the largest high-probability group possible.

Maximize Efficiency And Prospecting Velocity.

Every dial, email sent, and voicemail left is done in accordance with the process that you have decided will give you and your team the best shot at achieving your business goals.

Earlier, I outlined for you a call process of interaction I call the "3 cycles of 3." Very simply, once you have confirmed or identified your decision-maker within a bullseye high-probability target company, you will make 3 bursts of calls.

Each burst of calls, made within a day or 2, will consist of 3 dials. The first 2 dials of the sequence will be an attempt to connect with the decision-maker. If they are not available, you should try to extract more worth information to better allocate your time. If you don't have a direct dial or extension number, you should try to get it. But on these first 2 dials, you do not leave a message with the gatekeeper or try to "get through" the gatekeeper.

On these first 2 dials of the cycle your purpose is to speak to the decision-maker, pick up worth information so that you can decide if this record is worth your time, or pick up information such as direct dial, extension number, or email address to increase the odds of communicating with your decision-maker in the future. Nothing else. If the gatekeeper tries to suck you into a "what is this about" conversation you do not participate. Your response is "not a big deal. I'll give a callback. Thank you very much." Click.

On the third dial of each cycle, if you do not speak to your decision-maker, you leave "touches." A touch will be a voicemail, email, and at times a touch could be a snail mail letter, a Linkedin in inmail, or a lumpy mail dropoff.

Once you complete a burst of calls, you schedule your next call 3 business days later and complete another cycle. You do this 3 times.

If you complete 3 cycles, that means you have made a minimum of 9 phone dials to try to reach them. Nine dials is on the lower end of a reasonable range of dial activity. Remember, it takes on average 9-12 dials to a decision-maker to get them to pick up the phone. You have left 3 voicemail messages, 3 emails, and on top of that may have sent letters, texts, ravens, Linkedin messages, or dropped off lumpy mail.

But the bottom line is that you have a plan and you are working your plan. So with every action, you know what you are doing on that call, what you are trying to achieve with that call, and you know what your plan calls for as a next step when each call is completed. You must schedule that next step. And oh yeah, you have to take the action called for by your plan.

An Absolute Must-Do, Every Time, No Exception

Every time you complete a step, you must schedule the next step.

When you complete a launch, you schedule the first call of your follow-up sequence.

When you complete your first call, you will record the result of that call and then schedule the second call.

When you get to the third call if you don't speak to your decision-maker, you leave your "touches" and then schedule the next burst of calls to start 3 business days later.

You are working a plan. Every time you take action or complete a step, you schedule the next action or step in your sequence — every time. No exceptions.

Even when you are not sure exactly when to call next, you schedule the next call. Don't know whether you want to call that knucklehead back in 1 month or 2? No problem, schedule a call for one month. When it comes up on your activity list, you can either call it or reschedule it. But the bottom line is that you don't have to think about it or try to remember when to call.

What Happens When You Reach The End Of Your Outreach Process?

Once you have completed your call process, you need to let go for a while. A record can fit your profile and be a high-probability record; you may have identified the decision-maker; they are a perfectly good record to call. But at some point, you need to let go and pick it up another day. Once you have completed your process and reached what we refer to as the "point of diminishing returns," you need to follow the rule that you must never break. Schedule the next action. You might reach out to that record in 6 months, 4 months or 12 months, but you must schedule that action in your CRM so that it pops up on your activity list automatically.

As long as a record is worth calling, there must be a next action scheduled. Always.

Violate This Rule At Your Peril.

The reason for always scheduling the next action is simple. To increase your efficiency and cut down on the amount of thinking you have to do.

If you are a top-producing discovery-call setter, you must have a certain size pool to work with. Big enough so that your odds of bumping into active buyers with your outreach process is good. But not so big that you are hitting targets infrequently or include lower-value/probability targets.

You need to launch fresh meat into your process consistently. Once launched you must work your plan and as you complete each step, schedule the next.

As you work your plan, you must constantly seek to upgrade the quality of the records you are calling. That means 1) obtaining "worth data" so that you can identify a record as A, B, C, D or E value potential and better allocate your time, 2) increasing the odds of speaking to your target by doing everything you can to add direct dial and extension numbers, and 3) being ruthless about identifying and discarding low-value, no-value, low-probability or no-probability records. Every time you decide to stop calling a low-value record, you create more time to call high-value records or to identify more high-value records.

When you reach the end of your calling process and the point of diminishing returns, you must let go. When you do let go, schedule that record for follow-up at some point in the future to start your outreach process anew.

Launch, Work The Plan, Let Go.
Do It Again At A Later Date.
Over And Over.

If your pool is too small, you end up calling them more frequently, but due to the size of the group the odds of any one of them being "in play" and looking to change vendors or buy are few and far between. You are fishing in a pond with very few fish.

You Need To Work A Group Large Enough So That It Is
Realistic That You Bump Into Someone Ready
Or Is Thinking About Buying.

If appointment setting or setting discovery calls is part of your sales process you are probably selling something that is not purchased frequently or where vendors are changed on average every 3-5 years. My rule of thumb is that in any pool being targeted only about 1 in 6 is in play, which means that in any group of really high-value decent-probability records only about 15% to 18% of them are thinking about changing vendors or buying your service.

If your pool is too small, you have self-sabotaged yourself from the beginning because no matter how hard you work or how good a job you do at prospecting, there will not be enough active buyers in your call pool to win. You are defeated before you make your first call.

If your pool is too big, your impact will be watered down. You won't have the time to solidly work your process on individual targets. You end up cutting corners and surfing your database, calling targets less frequently, more randomly, and with far less impact.

So you want to work a pool that is big enough to contain enough prospects realistically "in play" so that you can be successful. You must decide upon a process of interaction that you feel provides you the best chance of success, *and then you must work that process, and work it well.*

Efficiency Wins The Day.

This is where planning your outreach process and properly setting up your CRM pays big dividends

For you to work a large enough group that contains enough records "in play" so that you can meet your business goals, you must work very efficiently. Working efficiently is a huge factor in calling success.

Why do you spend time profiling the best records to call, creating a call process to follow, and setting up your CRM? So that when the rubber hits the road and you pick up the phone, you can feel confident that you are calling the best records with the time available to you. You are calling with a plan that provides you the best chance to connect with a buyer, and that you are working through that group very efficiently so that you can reach the highest number of potential buyers with the time you spend on prospecting.

Your Contact Manager/CRM Layout Is Important.

As you work your call process, as you complete every action and schedule the next action in your process, you will then click over to your activity list for the next record due for a call.

Prospecting Velocity: At A Glance, Instantly, You Must Know What To Do.

When you open the record at the top of your activity list, you want to know at a glance what the status of that record is, what step you are on, and know what you need to do at this step.

At a glance, instantly, when that record pops up, you should be able to know what to do. You do not want to be scrolling down or clicking around to open up multiple pages to get a sense of what has happened previously, and what you need to do on this call. At a glance, you want to know the potential worth of the record and what information is missing. If you know that, you can try to pick up missing information if you don't speak to your decision-maker. Plus, you will know whether you will be leaving a voicemail, sending an email, or hanging up if you don't reach your decision-maker.

You need to know all that at a glance when you open a record, with a minimum of clicking open pages and scrolling down, to get a sense of where you are, and what you need to do at this step.

Appointment Setting Is Repetitive and Boring.

Calling to set appointments and discovery calls is very repetitive. Once you figure out what works, you have to do it again and again. That gets boring quick. What makes it even worse is to add a giant dose of inefficiency to your challenge. And guess what? If every time you open a record you have to bop around 3-5 pages and scroll around to figure out what to do, you have decreased your efficiency by 25% or more.

If you are not set up properly, you decrease your prospecting efficiency, and therefore your results, by 25% or more. I'm not kidding. As you are wasting so much time bopping around trying to get a handle on the status of each record, you are making fewer calls and getting fewer results. Working hard at a repetitive task with not enough results is a recipe for disaster.

This is why it is so important to set yourself up for efficiency and to set your team up for efficiency. What good does it do to hire great people and write great scripts if your team cannot move fast enough to reach business goals? It's nuts.

**You Don't Go Swimming With Weights On.
Don't Try To Set Discovery Calls With A Poorly Set Up CRM.**

If you neglect proper setup, you will drastically reduce efficiency. For the time and money invested, you will make fewer calls, interact with fewer high-value higher-probability targets, and see fewer results. If you are set up structurally so that you are working very inefficiently, you make a tough job much harder. (A word to management: setting higher quotas for dials made and activities completed in a structurally inefficient call environment. You are not helping. You are a major cause of the decline.)

SELL THE MEETING

You wouldn't go for a swim with weights on your waist, wrists, and ankles. Don't try to set appointments or discovery calls with an improper setup and therefore inefficient system. You won't get very far in either circumstance.

Set your CRM up with the result in mind.

Readers of this book can review how I have set up my CRM at ScottChannell.com/crm-layout.

> Worksheets, additional scripts, and periodic updates are available to readers of this book at ScottChannell.com/STM-book-extras

SCOTT CHANNELL

Chapter 20
Managing Your Day Part 3: Spending More Time With Those Worth More Time

You have completed your launches for the day. Follow-up calls scheduled to be made are done. Now What?

With the third part of your day, you make an extra effort on those records worth more of your time. What do I mean by that?

Someone promised you a meeting if you called back. They are worth more dials.

You have a record that looks just like three other companies that are clients you got great results with. Those records are worth more dials and a slight altering of your script to include those specifics.

Gatekeeper lets slip that Ms. Big is traveling and in the office on Thursday and Friday. You might add more dials on those days.

You have some high value "A" and "B" records and have the direct dial or extension number of the top decision-makers within each. You have a much higher probability of speaking to someone when you have their direct dial and you know they have a higher than average potential value. Those records are worth more of your time, so you spend more time with them

Power Calling

Think it might be tough to get a CEO or Executive Level VP of a company with 1,000 or more employees to pick up the phone? When they do, how easy do you think it is to say things that enable them to conclude that meeting with you or a representative of your company is worth their time? Well, that is the environment where I learned to set appointments.

One of my most successful techniques was "power calling." Three or 4 times a week I would call before or after business hours. I would only use this technique with records that had above average worth, the A or B value records. Never the average value "C" records or below the average value "D" or "E" value records.

With a few keystrokes I would create a filter of decision-makers that were of A or B value and that I had direct dial or extension numbers for. (Again, if you can't do this with your CRM or contact manager I pity you. Good luck with calling, you will need it.) Then I would dial the phone. If a decision-maker picked up, I would slay them with my set-the-appointment pitch. If I hit voicemail, I would immediately hang up. If an assistant picked up the phone, I would get off asap. No messages. No explanations. No apologies. "Oh, Jane isn't in? It wasn't a big deal anyway. I will call back later. Thanks. Bye." Click — next call.

The purpose of this was to increase the number of conversations with decision-makers by allocating a certain amount of call time to the subset of the database who was more likely to pick up the phone — those with direct dial or extension numbers.

In an hour, it was not unusual to make 60 or 70 dials and to have 2 or 3 conversations with decision-makers that I would not have otherwise. If it takes 4 or 5 conversations to get a meeting, do the math.

Worksheets, additional scripts, and periodic updates
are available to readers of this book at
ScottChannell.com/STM-book-extras

Chapter 21
Calling A Suspect From Start To Finish

In the previous chapters, we approached calling from a "how to organize" a day perspective. In any calling day, you will be launching your process with new targets; it might be your 3rd call or 9th call with other targets. With some records, you will reach the point of diminishing returns and stop actively calling them for some time. With other records, you might feel that they are worth more dials than usual. On any given day you will work with records found in various stages of your process.

Now, let's approach calling from a "how do I call a suspect from start to finish" perspective. What should your mindset and priorities be from the perspective of working your call process from start to finish with individual records?

You Start With A Record From Your Highest-Probability Group.

First, you would not be calling a record unless you are confident that they belong to the group of records that provide you with the highest probability of success. If you have time to launch your process with 50 records a week, those 50 records are the best records you could call, given all your options. If there are 1,000 records or 10,000 records that might be worth calling, it is not good enough that the records you call are merely part of this larger group. The records you call must belong to the subset of those records that have the highest potential value and be most likely to buy.

You are calling your "A" records before you are calling your "B" or lower-value records and you know the difference.

You know that if you just jump in and start calling a non-prioritized group to see what happens, that easily 50%, 70%, or more of your time (I'm not exaggerating) would be allocated to lower-probability lower-value records and the odds are stacked against you before you even make your first dial.

So you start with confidence, knowing that you are calling a record from the group of records that is the very best group of records you could be calling that week.

Making Your First Call

Once you pick that record from the group, you need to make your first call.

Most of the time you will have a contact name on that record. Given the quality of databases today and with Linkedin access, you can be fairly confident that the name on the record is your decision-maker. With your first call, your top priority is to confirm that the name on the record is, in fact, the decision-maker. If not, get the name of the decision-maker. And, get some potential worth info so that you can start your sorting process.

Right up front one of your most important goals is to extract info that gives you some insight into the potential worth of the target if they were to become an account. Not necessarily when they might buy, as the "when" is a different issue. On these initial dials, it is a top priority to try to gauge potential worth so that you can start separating the highest value, from the average value and the below average value.

Kicking Out The Low-Value And No-Value Is Top Priority.

It is counterintuitive, but by far the most important thing you can do on the first call and the first few calls is to identify those not worth your time, code them as such, and never call them again.

You might think that with your first call and first few dials that you are trying to keep a record alive, but the opposite is true. You should make a concerted effort to try to kill it.

The reason is simple and a key to your overall success as an appointment setter. Remember, everything you choose to do is done at the expense of something else. You are working a process that entails a minimum of 9 dials. If you can knock out the low-value or unqualified on the first call rather than the 7th, those dials can go to a higher-value higher-probability group.

SELL THE MEETING

You want the highest possible percentage of your efforts to be directed at those worth calling. Up front, you must dig in and identify the dregs and those not worth your time so that you stop calling them. You are going to be much more successful if you only make 1 or 2 calls to a low/no value record, rather than 8 calls.

Initial Call Script Structure

So on your first call, you might start with just asking for your decision-maker. "Jane Adams please." The gatekeeper might transfer you, the phone tree might direct you, but the most important thing on the first call is that you confirmed that Jane Adams still works for the company. The first step is done; the name is confirmed.

Now, on the same call, you want to try to obtain some worth info. Why worth info? Because it is critically important to your overall success to identify and stop calling those not worth your time as soon as possible.

So you would call right back, and you might say something like this to the gatekeeper or receptionist. "Hi, I just called for Jane Adams, and you were kind enough to transfer me. I'm sending out some information and just so that I know what to send, do you happen to know…. How many employees work at the company, do you have a vendor for X, about how many salespeople work for the company, do you use Y?"

Once you have a name you must make some effort, ask some questions, do whatever you can to try to get some worth info.

The response you hear might be…

About 200 employees.
Yes, we have a cleaning vendor.
There are 20 salespeople in the department.
Yes, we use XYZ software.

Once you get some worth info, assuming that the answer indicates that the record is worth more effort, you would then try to extract other information that would help. You might seek to confirm the title, get the spelling of difficult names, get the direct dial or extension number, confirm the address, find out whether they are on the left side or the right side of the street, whatever. The point is that you have an extremely short period, seconds, to extract info from a distracted gatekeeper so you must be prepared to ask the questions to get the info you need with the precision of a surgeon.

A first call might go something like this:

"Hi, I was looking to send info to whoever handles your pencil purchases. Can you tell me who to direct it to?"

    That would be Jane Adams

"Thanks. Just so I know what to send, do you have a rough idea as to how many employees are at that location?"

    About 25.

"Super. When I check back is there a direct dial or extension I should use?"

    978-123-4567

"Would it be OK if I emailed the info to her?

    Sure. Her email is Jane@happyindustries.com.

"I have Jane's title as Chief Pencil Purchaser, is that correct"

    Yes.

"ThankYouVeryMuchYouHaveBeenVeryHelpful." Click

The Order Of Your Questions Is Very Important.

It is critical on the first call to get as much information as you can. You seek to confirm or obtain a name, get some worth info, then try to get the direct dial, extension and email address. Anything above that is gravy.

The order in which you extract information on this first call is very important.

This is what you would _not_ do:

"Hi, I was looking to send some information to whoever handles your pencil purchases. Can you tell me who to direct it to?"

    Jane Abromski

"How do you spell that?

SELL THE MEETING

    A-B-R-O-M-S-K-I

"Thanks. Can I confirm her title? Chief Pencil Officer."

    Yes, that is correct.

Then the direct dial or extension question.

Then the get the email question.

Then whether they are on the right side or the left side of the street.

Then the how many employees question.

"ThankYouVeryMuchYouHaveBeenVeryHelpful." Click

No, no, no, no.

That would not be the order in which you ask the questions. Why?

Once you have the name, what is by far the most valuable information you can get at this point? Some bit of worth info that would indicate whether they deserve more of your time.

Let's assume that a pretty good indicator of potential worth is the number of employees at a business location. Let's assume further that your typical good account is with companies that have 50 to 500 employees at a business location. You want to get as many 50+ employee companies in your process as possible. Between 20 and 49 employees could be acceptable to call, but accounts from that group tend to be on the lower range of an acceptable sales volume.

As you call companies, you identify those in the 50-500 employee range and it is full steam ahead. Go get em. Companies in the 20-49 employee range can deliver acceptable business volumes, but you would want to be careful not to overload your call pipeline with 20-49 employee companies as those tend to deliver less valuable clients. When you identify a company with less than 20 employees? See ya. Buh-Bye. You would waste not one more dial on those records.

In our example, a record with 20 or more employees may get additional calls. So once you confirm that, you can move on to your other questions — the title, direct dial, email, astrological sign.

Even A Great List Will Include Some Not-Qualified

On your first call and subsequent calls if you don't get it on your first call, your top priority after identifying or confirming your decision-maker is to get worth info.

Even with very good lists and assuming you did a top-notch job in profiling the best groups to call, even the best group of records to call is going to include some records that don't belong. There will be some stinkers.

Let's assume that you have prioritized your potential prospect pool into A, B, C, D, and E groups by potential worth and probability. Your "A" group, even though it is by far the best GROUP of records for you to call, may include some B or C records. Your "A" group may even contain, aghast, some D and E records. That is typical and to be expected.

If your "A" target pool profile is of companies with between 50 and 500 employees within certain industries or SIC code ranges, guess what? There will be some records with less than 50 employees. Some will be way off the mark, maybe less than 10 employees. There will be some records in industries you don't want to call. Some will be out of business. Oh well.

Working Through A List For The First Time

When you are calling a new list, a top priority on the first few calls is to do everything you can to weed out the stinkers. With a new calling program, this can seem like a hassle and a waste of time but you should think longer term. If you do a good job weeding out the stinkers during the first pass through, and hopefully with the first few dials, what is left is 100% solid gold to call.

By emphasizing weeding out the stinkers with your early calls, you have greatly increased your productivity longer term. If you or your team don't "dig in" to ask those worth questions up front, you doom yourselves to placing vast amounts of guaranteed to go nowhere calls.

Think of a series of calls you make to a Mr. Jones, head of wastebaskets at Mega Industries. You call and confirm that Mr. Jones is indeed head of wastebaskets and call, call, call to finally get Mr. Jones on the phone. Your pitch is magical and he agrees to a meeting. While confirming the meeting you ask the worth questions. "Mr. Jones, so that I can be better prepared for our meeting, how many employees are there at your location?" The answer? "Five." Yikes.

A company with 5 employees is far below the minimum acceptable size of 20 employees. If you had asked that question up front, think of all the dials you would not have wasted on that target. Even more importantly, think of all those calls you make and never speak to the decision-maker. At some point, you will reach the point of diminishing returns and start the call cycle all over again in the future. Many of those will be "totally not qualified," and because your call process does not include asking questions to determine worth, you are making a ton of calls that will never get you anything.

A Worse Example

In the above example, you can see how unqualified targets can be called over and over without knowing they are unqualified because your call process does not place proper emphasis on identifying them and you are not prepared to ask the right questions. So the unqualified are called over and over at the expense of targets that are highly qualified and likely to buy.

But let me give you a worse example, and I see this way too often: The calling of unqualified targets over and over, even when the appointment setter knows they are unqualified.

I have a vendor who remarked to me once, "I know a company that could really use your service." This vendor is a home-based consultant. Every single month she gets a call from a particular cleaning company seeking to send a rep out to her office to bid on cleaning services. Every single time she explains to the rep that she is a home-based business and would never need a cleaning service. Yet, they call back every single month.

There are a couple of problems illustrated here. Common sense tells us that single person companies, particularly those working from home, are not good prospects for commercial cleaning services. With the right process, the right questions, with a CRM set up so that this info can be captured and be immediately visible when the record opens up, that complete waste of time call to that home-based business would not be made over and over again. And certainly not at the expense of calling more highly qualified targets, thousands of them, that were not being called at all. (I know as that company later hired me.)

It is Critically Important That You Weed Out The Unqualified ASAP.

When you start to call an individual record, you can see how important it is to determine on the first dial, or first few dials, whether that record is worth calling at all. If not, code it as not qualified and do not schedule another call for it.

What if you are having trouble qualifying a record?

It is easy to disqualify and stop calling a record when you can confirm that they fall far outside your target profile. If you find out that they have 5 employees when your minimally acceptable is 20, it is easy to disqualify that record. Same with the cleaning company that determines they are calling a solopreneur working from home, good-bye, nice knowing you.

But what if you call and call and for whatever reason can't confirm their potential worth and don't have enough information to determine whether they are worth calling or not? To be successful overall, you need at some point to treat these records as unqualified and stop calling them. Now many would say, "hey wait a minute, there might be some good ones in that group. I don't want to miss out on them." Thinking like that places you on the slippery slope to disaster.

Even when you are calling an individual record, you should be making decisions as to what to do based upon what is most likely to get you results among a group of similarly situated records.

You do not know for sure what will happen on a specific record you call. Nor can you predict the result on what happens on any individual call. But, very importantly, you should have a sense of what tends to happen when you work a group of similarly situated calls.

So you pick an individual record to call because it belongs to the highest value and probability group you could be calling with your time. As you call, you will confirm that hopefully most of the records are minimally qualified and worthy of your time and attention. For many, you will be able to go beyond that and determine which have the highest value, above average value, average value, and below average but still an acceptable value. You will code them as such and call them.

As I have noted, even in high-value high-probability groups there will be some that don't belong. As you call, you make a concerted effort to identify those that belong to this non-qualified group and spend as little time as possible with them.

But what about the records that for whatever reason, after a reasonable effort and multiple calls you can't determine whether they are qualified and worth your time. Do you continue to call them? Too many would conclude "you never know. There are some good ones in there, don't want to miss out" and would continue to call records that belong to a group of records that you have no clue if they are qualified or not qualified.

The answer is that although there may be a few "good ones" in that group of records, most of them are not qualified, not worth more of your time, and you need to be proactive and aggressive in deciding not to call them anymore.

When you call individual records, there is a tendency not to let go as it is only one record. People think "I have made 3 calls already, have tried to determine potential worth but still have no idea if this a qualified prospect. Hey, you never know. I will keep calling." This is not the way you should think.

You Are Not Trying To Keep It Alive.
You Are Trying Hard To Find The Slightest Excuse To Kill It.

Once you have determined that a record fits into a GROUP of records that provides little or no payback for the time invested, you need to stop calling. Yes, it is true that as to any particular record it is possible that they might be qualified and agree to a meeting, but as they belong to a GROUP of records that is very low ROI for resources invested, you need to stop calling.

Stay In The High-Probability Zone, Not The Mere-Possibilities Zone.

I urge you to step back and think of the big picture of what you are doing. You want to be confident that an extremely high percentage of your time is spent in a high-probability of success zone. In this zone you are calling records that fit your bullseye profile, your call process is solid, your scripts are spot on and impactful, you call enough to get results but not so much that you are wasting your time. When you reach the point of diminishing returns with a record, you schedule a round of calls for another day, typically 6 months in the future. That is high-probability of success call behavior.

You want to feel confident that 85% or more of your activity is invested in a high-probability call zone. I think that we can agree that if 85% percent of your efforts is spent in a high-probability of success zone, you will schedule far more meetings than if only 50% or 30% of your efforts are being spent in a high-probability of success zone.

If You Don't Know The Difference Between High-Probability And Low-Probability Zones, You Are In Big Trouble.

You need to avoid slippage in the percentage of your time being spent calling in a high-probability of success zone. When you continue to call records that belong to a group of low-probability records, the percentage of time spent in the high-probability zone slips, and you will work hard with less to show for it.

Calling Too Often

Let's go back to our example where the cleaning company was calling the home-based solopreneur every 30 days. That was nuts for two reasons. The first was that the record was unqualified and they continued to call it again and again. But there is another reason why that calling behavior was nuts.

If You Are Calling Companies Back Too Often, You Are Not Calling Many Companies

If you are calling records back every 30 days you cannot be calling many companies. As you call individual records you need them to be qualified, but you also need to call a large enough pool of qualified companies or you have no chance of success.

If you are calling to set sales appointments or discovery calls, you are probably offering something that is not purchased frequently, or vendors are changed every 3-5 years on average. In any given pool of highly qualified prospects you call, only a small percentage of them are going to be in-play. Meaning they plan on or are open to buying or switching vendors and are likely to do so within the next 3-15 months.

Even when you are calling a high-qualified pool of targets, only 15%-18% of them are in-play at any given time. To book sufficient discovery calls to meet a quota or your business goals you must be calling a qualified pool large enough, so that it likely contains enough active buyers or companies in-play so that you can be successful.

If there are few fish in the lake, you are not going to catch much fish. If there are too few active buyers or companies in-play within the group you are calling, you are not going to book many worthwhile appointments that convert to sales.

So the caller who was calling back every 30 days is doomed to fail. If you are calling people back too frequently, you are calling a smaller pool and have drastically cut your chances of success. You can dial like a maniac all you want, but if you are calling a pool that is too small, there is no way you can be successful.

Qualification And Efficiency Wins The Game.

So as you start to call, you win by making sure you are calling qualified records by aggressively knocking out those that are not qualified and those that after a reasonable effort you can't tell if they are qualified. Buh-bye.

On top of that, you need to be working with a large enough group so that you know there are enough fish to catch. That is where call efficiency comes into play. It is not enough to call qualified records. You must call efficiently enough so that you can work a large enough pool to be successful.

What Calling Interval is Right?

Once you complete your call process with a record the default callback date is 6 months. Meaning that once you pick a record to call, along the way confirm that it is qualified, and you work your "3 cycles of 3" call process on that record, if you don't speak to your decision-maker at some point you have to let go. There is a point where more and more calls to the same record is the equivalent of beating a dead horse. You reach the point of diminishing returns and need to stop.

Once you stop, that does not mean you never call that record again. It just means that you have worked your process, made enough calls but not too many, left your voicemails and sent your emails and received no response, so at some point, you need to let go. You need to let go as you have reached the point of diminishing returns with that record and need to call another.

When you reach the point of diminishing returns and let go, you must schedule that record for a future round of calls. It is a qualified record. It fits your profile. You didn't get a response from this round of calls, but things change and tomorrow is another day. So you must schedule that next round of calls.

For an average value record, that default callback date would be 6 months. If the record has a higher than average value, you might call back in 4 months. If the record has a less than average value, you would want to allocate less time to it so the callback date might be 9 or 12 months.

You Seek To Balance The Frequency Of Your Call Cycles With The Size Of The Pool Called.

A common strategic mistake made by callers is that they decide to call back records too frequently, thinking that it is better to make more effort and call more often. The problem with that thinking is that it also shrinks the size of the pool you can call, and there are only so many active buyers in any qualified pool.

Calling more frequently is not going to save you if you are working a small pool and there simply are not that many fish to catch.

Dealing With Gatekeepers. Aye-Yie-Yie.

As you call your suspects, you will face fire breathing dragons, aka "gatekeepers."

Understand this, gatekeepers, personal assistants, or anyone that stands between you and your decision-maker can help you in three ways.
1) Provide information as to the potential worth of your target. 2) Provide you with information that greatly increases the odds that you will speak to or interact with your decision-maker. If you can obtain a direct dial number, extension, or email the odds of you having a conversation or getting a response from your decision-maker goes way up. 3) The third way they can help you, which is very unlikely, a true "exception to the rules," a lottery ticket win, rarity, miracle, and serendipity. That would be the gatekeeper "putting you through" to the person you wish to speak with.

Keep In Mind, You Must Work Probabilities, Not Possibilities.

It is a very bad prospecting strategy to try to get the gatekeeper to connect you. Why? Well, the whole point of your effort is to book qualified discovery calls or sales appointments. By far, your greatest chance of making that happen is when you speak to your decision-maker, or they respond to an email or voicemail. That is, by far, your highest-probability path to your goal.

It takes on average, 9 to 12 dials or more, and multiple touches made to a specific decision-maker to get that decision-maker to pick up the phone or respond. If you are not in that zone of activity, you are not working a process with a probability of success.

So let's go back to our gatekeeper issue. If on the first, second, or an early dial you interact with a gatekeeper who asks you "what is this regarding?" What is virtually guaranteed to happen? The gatekeeper is NOT going to assist you in connecting with your target. You are very likely to be stopped in your tracks with "we are all set" or "we have a vendor we love." Or, you will be asked to leave your name, number, and message for Ms. Big, which is the equivalent of saying "get lost."

If you try to "get through the gatekeeper" at this point, are you making, 9, 12 or more dials to your decision-maker? Are you leaving multiple touches? Have you obtained any worth information or information that makes it more likely for you to speak or interact with your target in the future? "No," is the answer to all these questions.

Once told "we are all set" you really can't call back, can you?
Once you leave a message with the gatekeeper, you can't call back right away, can you?

So if you let the gatekeeper decide what your prospecting process is going to be, you are either stopped dead in your tracks or thrown off your highest-probability process path to achieve your business objective.

You need to complete your highest-probability plan to achieve your business objective. Only then might you decide to work a lower-probability path.

One lower-probability path you might try, but only once your highest-probability path has been completed, would be to try to "get through the gatekeeper." Which is desperation, Hail Mary pass, chosen when the odds of success are low, the reward is high, and you don't have any other viable options.

The Best Way To Deal With Gatekeepers

Ring. Ring.

"It is a happy day here at Sunny Industries. How may I help you?"

Hi, Charlene Jones, please.

"May I ask what this is regarding?"

"Oh, uh, well, it's no big deal. Voicemail would be fine."

If you get switched over to voicemail, you can hang up. You have dodged the high odds of being obstructed by answering that question and can still work your process.

Another option

Ring. Ring.

"It is a happy day here at Sunny Industries. How may I help you?"

Hi, Charlene Jones, please.

"May I ask what this is regarding?"

"Oh, uh, well, it's no big deal, well, maybe you can help me, I'm preparing a package for Charlene regarding _____, just so I know what to send, can you give me a ballpark idea of how many employees are at that location?."

"About 60."

"Super. Thanks. Hey, when I call back, is there a direct dial or extension I should use?"

"Charlene is at extension 1234."

"Thanks. Do you think it would be okay to email the info over? Do you know her Email address?"

"Sorry, can't give that out."

"Totally understand. You have been very helpful, thankyouverymuch."Click.

Another option

Let me share a slight twist to the above, which is how I chose to dodge the gatekeepers blocking question yet get some information that would assist me and keep me on the highest-probability path to success.

I would dodge the gatekeepers obstruction question by asking to be switched to voicemail. Once switched I would hang up the phone and then call right back.

Ring. Ring.

"It is a happy day here at Sunny Industries. How may I help you?"

"Hi, this is Scott again, I just called for Charlene Jones, and you were kind enough to switch me to voicemail, um thanks for that. But maybe you can help me, I'm sending some info to Charlene re your cleaning, just so I know what to send, do you have a ballpark idea as to how many employees are in your building?"

And then I would continue with sharp, concise, quick questions structured to extract as much worth and direct contact info as I could. It has always been my personal belief that people are more willing to share information with you if they think it is not very important to you. So, by not asking for what I want on the first call, and instead asking for voicemail, it is my belief that a gatekeeper may be thinking "huh, he didn't ask for this a minute ago and he seems pretty nonchalant about it, so it must not be a big deal, I'll help him and provide what I can." That approach fit my style and worked best for me.

What This Gatekeeper Scenario Illustrates

Remember that you are in charge of your calls and that you are the one who will decide how each step will be handled. A gatekeeper may request that you move off your plan, and you have a choice. Stick with the process that provides you with the highest probability of success. Or, because a gatekeeper asked you to, you can choose to vary from that plan and pursue a path with a much lower probability of success.

It's your choice.

Develop a plan you believe provides you with the highest-probability chance of success to book a discovery call or first sales appointment with a high-value decision-maker and stick with it. Or, abandon that plan and pursue a course of action that provides you with a much lower probability of success.

With the above interaction, you stick with your plan and with a good number of calls you will pick up info that is helpful to you — worth information and contact information.

After you have implemented the plan that provides by far, (there is not a close 2nd or 3rd option) the highest chance of success with your target, a conversation or reply and you reach the point of diminishing returns with that process, you could then choose a "Hail Mary."

Making 9 to 12 dials at a minimum with multiple touches of email and voicemail provide you by far your greatest chance of earning a meeting. Once you reach the point of diminishing returns on that process, then you might, might throw a "Hail Mary."

The Hail Mary

Having exhausted your best shot at earning a conversation or reply, you then can engage the gatekeeper. Here is how that interaction might proceed.

Ring. Ring.

"It is a happy day here at Sunny Industries. How may I help you?"

Hi, my name is Scott from SalesWeak and more than 3,000 companies including 130 of the Fortune 500 have chosen us to help them with sales productivity and closing net new accounts. Was hoping to speak with Ms. Big to determine if she would like to review our options at some point. Could you connect me?

"Why don't you leave a message and I will be sure that Ms. Big gets it and will call you if she is interested."

Thank you for that. How about this? I have a one-page pdf that summarizes what we do, the companies that have selected us and examples of the results achieved. Why don't I email that to you and you can share it with Ms. Big. Then I will call you back in 2 days, and you can let me know if Ms. Big wishes to schedule some time. That way I don't have to keep calling back.

"Um, okay. Send it over. My email address is trash@pretendmessages.com."

SELL THE MEETING

In the old days, I would run the Hail Mary using faxes. The same concept works today just with email and attachments.

Gatekeepers Cannot Sell Your Meeting.

Understand that there is no message you could leave with a gatekeeper that could sell your meeting. Not going to happen. A waste of breath to even try.

If you wanted to try, knowing that the odds of success are low, to put something in the hands of the gatekeeper that could sell your meeting, give it a shot.

My recommendation would be that you try your own variation of a "Hail Mary" only after you have worked your call plan to completion, and only with higher-value targets. This is truly a long shot, and the cost/benefit analysis only works with higher-value targets.

So Let's Look At The Big Picture.

To be successful, you know that you need to work a pool large enough so that there will be enough fish to catch.

You must constantly add new records to your target pool and therefore must "launch" a certain number every day or every week.

Once launched, you must have a plan and work that plan. Know what you are trying to achieve on every step, know what the next step is, and schedule it. You must schedule the next step every time.

You must complete scheduled tasks when they are due or pretty darn close to it.

As you work your process, you must continually try to improve the quality of the information you work with. You need to allocate your time by potential worth. As you work your process, you must know what to do to determine if a prospect has an average, above-average or below-average potential value. You must purposely allocate more time to those worth more time. You must be ruthless about identifying the low-value and low-probability targets as early as possible, coding them as such and spending no more time with them.

Remember, the name of the game is for you to be interacting with the highest quality pool you can. That means prioritizing records by what you KNOW and can confirm so that with a high degree of confidence you can say "this is an "A" value record or this is a "B" value record. They are worth my time. Or, this is a below-average value "D" record or a don't touch with a 10-foot pole worthless "E" record. Those records get bupkis and diddly squat. You constantly want to be improving the quality of the pool you call, identifying the higher-value records and spending time with them and kicking the low-value records to the curb.

What if you work a record well and can't determine its potential value. My best advice is to ditch them. If you have a group of records and after reasonable effort can't determine their value, the odds are that most of them are low-value, so ditch them.

You Win With Consistent Implementation.

You win at appointment setting and obtaining discovery calls by consistent implementation of a proven process. You continually seek to improve your process and make it more efficient, but you have to work your plan. Even when you vary from your plan, that is done for objective reasons and in accordance with your plan. You work off plan only within acceptable limits.

Here is the challenge

Here is the problem you face. "What to do" is not your challenge. Let's face it. There are a lot of people who book appointments and discovery calls very successfully. It is not rocket science.

Your problem is that once you figure out what to do, when to do it, and what to say, you have to do and say those things over and over and over again. It is repetitive, monotonous, and very boring. Asking smart people to do repetitive tasks do not mix well. Yet, that is what setting meetings is all about. You have to manage the monotony and boredom. Don't vary from your process; manage the boredom.

Don't Make This Mistake.

The good news is that there is a method you can follow to schedule more discovery calls and sales appointments. The bad news is that once you determine what that method is, you have to follow it. Step by step. Consistently.

Common Mistake #1 - Varying From The Plan

Too often I get calls from companies that established very successful plans that work for them to set more discovery calls. Sometime after things seemed to be going so well, the results slowed down. More often than not, the core reason is that they varied from their plan.

Those great scripts that were working were no longer used. The call process that was delivering conversations and positive responses were forgotten. The touches, the voicemails, and emails that were working changed or used inconsistently.

Once you decide upon a system, you have to stick with it. When you get bored, get sick of saying the same thing, can't bring yourself to dial the phone again, to endure another no answer or have the same conversation you have already had 500 times, you have to follow the system.

Follow your system. I am not telling you that you can't massage it, improve it, or test options. I am telling you that once you get a baseline of results, you must keep that going. If you vary too often from your plan, you don't have a plan. You have a mish-mash of exceptions to the rule and rationalizations as to why you are doing things different with this call, this conversation, this email, this voicemail.

Stick To Your Plan About 85% Of The Time.

If you vary from your plan more than 10-15% of the time, you don't have a plan. You are guessing, wishing, hoping, and winging it. You tell yourself you know what you are doing. That you are varying from your process for a reason. But that is a lie you tell yourself. The reality is that you get bored doing the same thing over and over and rationalize why it makes sense to do it differently.

If You Vary From Your Process More Than 10% to 15% Of The Time, You Don't Have A Process.

Good marketeers and salespeople always try to beat their baseline. You have an established process that consistently spits out a certain result. You always try to beat your control with something that will work better, but you can't abandon your control.

When you start, you seek to establish a core process which is your "control." You call a list with a certain profile, with a certain outreach process, you use standardized scripting and send certain templated emails. You launch a certain number of new records every day and week, follow your process, and consistently out pops a certain acceptable range of results. That is your control.

Always Try To Beat Your Control, But Don't Abandon It.

You should strive to play a game I call "beat the baseline." Very simply, if you are doing some basic tracking, you know your outreach velocity and know how your behaviors are converting at key points. So, for example, you know or should know how many records you are launching every week. You know how many conversations you have a week with decision-makers. You know how many of those conversations result in a discovery call or sales appointment being set. Over time you know what percentage of those appointments converted to closed deals and their average size. You should know these things.

As you work your process, you always try to beat your baseline by testing options and seeking to make marginal improvements but don't abandon your process.

Have a plan for each record and work that plan consistently.

Smile when you dial.

Worksheets, additional scripts, and periodic updates
are available to readers of this book at
ScottChannell.com/STM-book-extras

Chapter 22
What If It Is Not Working?

What if you are not getting results? Or you need to boost results?

The first question is to know what result you need to increase.

Is it the number of meetings you need to increase?
Is it the quality of the meetings?

Do you need to increase the percentage of first meetings or discovery calls that end up closing?

Is it the size of the average size of sale you need to increase?

Smaller accounts not only take roughly the same amount of time to sell as larger accounts, but they tend to churn faster and generate less margin so your cost of sale increases while profit decreases.

Do you need to adjust your target profile so that larger size accounts will pop out of your process?

Three Core Reasons For Poor Results

1. The List:

You are not interacting with enough high-value/high-probability targets. Too much of your activity is directed toward low-value no-value lower-probability targets.

If you were shooting fish in a barrel, you would not only want that barrel to have plenty of fish but for the barrel to be drained and the fish lying on the bottom. Those are good odds.

If you are working hard and not getting results, one reason could be that you have stacked the odds against yourself by allocating too much time, often way too much time, to targets that are not as valuable to you as others.

You need to do two things. Tighten the profile of your bullseye targets so that your time is invested with records that provide you with the highest probability of success. Also, be ruthless about discarding or pushing records aside that are lower value or probability or that with which you have reached the point of diminishing returns for your efforts.

Top producers are best at allocating their time where it will do the most good. Do not be like the knuckleheads who work hard with little to show for it with thoughts such as "you never know," "there are some good prospects in here," or "I don't want to miss one."

Work Probabilities, Not Possibilities.

Be willing to let go.

One of the quickest ways you can boost results is to make a concerted effort to stop calling all the low-probability records in your prospecting pipeline. Stop calling them immediately. That creates room for you to call fresh records that are more closely aligned with your bullseye best prospect profile.

You Want To JackHammer Into A Solid Vein Of Gold, Not Thrash Around In The Manure Pile Looking For A Few Nuggets.

If you are working hard and not getting results, the most likely culprit is that you are calling a list that is weaker than it has to be. Reevaluate your profile. Tighten your target bullseye. Get more aggressive about letting go at the point of diminishing returns. Don't try hard to rationalize a reason to keep investing time with a record. Let go.

Get to the point where you can say to yourself "I know this is the best list I can call with the time I have. I have done the research; I am using good list sources. I am highly confident that this is the very best place to be prospecting."

In my day I wanted to feel very confident that 85% of my activity was being invested with records that I had confirmed or had a very high degree of confidence were the best records to call. As to the rest of the records, I would only spend so much time determining if they were worthy. If after a certain amount of effort I wasn't sure of the potential value, buh-bye record, on to the next.

SELL THE MEETING

Records Being "Good Enough" To Call Isn't Good Enough

It is not sufficient for the list you are actively calling to be "good enough." If there are better records to call, higher value or higher probability, closer to your bullseye best prospect profile, you need to be calling them. Not the ones that are just okay.

Once you are confident that your list is the best it can be, look to the other 2 factors that may be dragging you down.

2. Your Process:

If you or your team are not getting decent results, it could also be that the call process you are working to earn a conversation with or reply from your decision-maker is lousy or non-existent.

You are trying to generate the most results by working a system of interaction — a system, pre-planned well thought series of interactions purposely chosen to provide you with the best chance to meet your business goals.

There is only one best call process for you to use to set the most discovery calls. There are not 4 best systems. The best way to achieve your goal does not change with every dial, the weather, or your mood and motivation. You don't have to work the "3 cycles of 3" system I believe in and have outlined in this book, but you do need to work a system. Your "system" will be responsible for 80% or more of your results. If you don't have a system, or you don't work your system consistently, or are quick to abandon it, those are very good reasons why your results are poor.

There is an activity component to your system. If you are not making enough dials on the right schedule and leaving enough touches (voicemails or emails primarily) when you should, then your results will plummet. But be careful, increasing activity levels using a poor call process is not going to solve your problem. Keep in mind that the most productive appointment setters/discovery-call setters do not make the most dials. They don't.

If you are not getting results and you are working in a reasonable range of activity, the problem is not your activity level it is your process.

Sorting And Ranking

There is also a sorting and ranking component to your system. Your system should enable you to identify the highest value targets so that you can spend more time with them. Even more importantly, your system enables you to identify the lowest-value and no-value targets so that you will *not* spend any more time with them. Time spent rolling in the garbage pile looking for something good is time you can't spend shooting fish in a barrel that has been drained.

If you are not getting results, be honest with yourself as to whether you have a decent system and whether you are working it properly. Time and time again I run into teams that retool and start generating a greatly increased number of discovery calls only to get a call a year later. "It doesn't seem to be working anymore. We don't know why?"

Often it turns out that the carefully thought out call process created and proven to provide the greatest chance of call success has been completely abandoned. Not enough calls are being made. They are not being made at the right times. The required number of touches are not being delivered. Qualification, sorting, ranking by value are not being done, so a tremendous amount of time is being wasted calling sludge.

If you or your team are not getting results, do you feel confident that you have documented an outreach process that gives you the very best chance of reaching your business prospecting goals? If not, tighten it up, massage it, upgrade it, then jump right back in.

If you have a process documented, is it being worked properly? Let's face it. The good news about prospecting is that you can figure out what to do. The bad news is that then you have to do it, again and again, and again. Sales prospecting is repetitive work. Once you discover what works you must do it over and over. There are not 10 different ways for you to achieve your discovery call results. There is 1.

80% of Results Are Generated By Working Your Process

There are exceptions to every rule. Crazy things happen. We deal with human beings that at times will act illogically and outside our expectations. There is a lunatic fringe element contained in any group of people we prospect and any system we use.

However, the vast majority of your results will be generated as a result of proper and consistent use of your call process. Eighty percent or more of results will spill out of the implementation of your core process. Less than 20% of results will be generated by exceptions to the rule, randomness, shit luck, serendipity, or the lunatic fringe.

There is a strong temptation to rationalize why on any individual call or with any individual record why you can vary from your core process. Fight this.

If you are not getting results, one of the main reasons is that your call/outreach process needs to be improved. Or, if you have a good process, a reason for lack of results is that you vary from your core process too frequently.

Even Variations From Your Process Are Part Of Your Process.

Even the variations in your system, the times you drive off the road and vary from your core process, is built into your process. When you choose to vary from your core process or cut it short, you do so for consistent objective reasons. You don't vary from your process because you are bored, that you dread saying the same thing over and over, that you can't bring yourself to leave one more voicemail that will not be answered. Your feelings of boredom and lack of motivation have nothing to do with what works. Nothing.

A Tale From The Cube

True story. I had a client who offered a unique environment service involving meters leaking mercury into natural gas fields. As a practical matter, only the top 50-100 oil companies were reasonable targets for this service. The contracts were worth millions if not tens of million dollars. Two good callers had tried yet failed to produce results. My calling days had long been over, but I offered to work the system to determine where the problem was.

So I was calling very top executives at very, very large companies. I worked the system and did the same thing over and over. I teach the stuff, and I was bored out of my mind. The same calls, the same corporate receptionists or phone trees, the same script routines, the same emails, the same roadblocks and rejections over and over. My tedium and boredom were occasionally rudely interrupted by a top dog that said "yes." I ended up getting my client meetings within the top levels of major oil companies. The system worked.

The drudgery of doing the same thing over and over was brutal. The temptation to skip steps or rationalize why for this call, for this company, it was okay to cut the process short was very strong. But I would think back to my early calling days when I would keep saying to myself "just work the system." When I was bored or began to doubt myself, I would "just work the system." When the thought of leaving that same voicemail one more time would make me want to vomit, I would "just work the system." Don't think about the system; work the system. I would play all sorts of mental tricks to keep me focused and working the system as efficiently as possible.

There is a time to take a step back and think about what your process should be. Most of the time you should be working that system.

If you are not getting results, it could very well be that your process needs to be improved. Or more commonly, that you are not consistently working your system.

Once you conclude that you are hitting the right targets and that your process is solid and you are working your process well, there is only one other core reason why you are not booking enough discovery calls or first sales appointments.

3. Your Messaging

If you are confident you are reaching out to the right targets, confident that your process is solid and that you are working it consistently, there is only one other key reason why you are not generating results.

Your messaging is weak.
Your verbiage is watered down.
You sound like the other idiots who have called and wasted their time.
You are not giving them reasons to listen to you just a little bit longer.
You are not communicating value and credibility worth their time.

Your verbiage is not enabling those who recognize a need and will be writing a check to you or one of your competitors within 3-15 months, to conclude that you are worth their time.

Most commonly, you are pulling your punches. You have things you could be saying that would connote credibility, value, and representative results you deliver, but you are not saying those things.

It might be because of feeling that being direct is being "too salesy," which is ridiculous.

It might be because you have some level of personal discomfort just laying your cards on the table and letting your prospect say "yes" or "no."

You might be afraid to be rejected, so you do mental backflips and rationalize that if you are "nice" and "not pushy" that people will listen to you longer. Wrong.

If you are confident that you are calling the right targets and that your process for calling is solid, the only other core problem is that your message is not resonating.

So you have to punch up your messaging. Be more direct. Push more value and credibility to the beginning of your pitch. Eliminate every moment and every syllable that is not communicating credibility and value to someone who has a need you can fill.

You need to get over your mental crap about being pushy, being perceived as rude, or interrupting someone. Those are your issues, not your prospects.

By choosing to prospect by phone you have already decided to interrupt people, so you need to get over that. Having decided to interrupt busy people, how are you most respectful of their time?

Do you call them up and recite verbiage and let second after second slip by without providing them information sufficient to conclude that you are worth their time? Do you fill the time between "hello" and " we are all set" with "I know you are busy," "won't take much of your time," "do you have a minute" and "I am not worthy?" If so, you deserve everything you get.

Or, are you most respectful of your suspect's time, a suspect you have chosen to interrupt, with a clear, direct statement as to what you do, why you are credible, the benefits delivered, and what they would get if they spent more time with you?

It takes about 30 seconds to deliver such a statement. The 15%-18% of the people you speak to who have a need will "get it" and can conclude that you are worth more of their time. Maybe a bit longer on the phone, maybe at a face to face meeting, or on a discovery call.

Those who do not have a need can also "get it" and say goodbye. That is a successful call for you, and you have minimized the interruption of your suspects time with a clear, concise, direct statement of what you do, why you are credible, and what they might get if they spent more time with you.

Just lay your cards on the table crisply, clearly, and with impact using the verbiage that most impactfully communicates your message. Roll out the big guns.

If your messaging is not getting the job done it is because your script lacks impact or you are holding back due to some belief that beating around the bush or being perceived as "nice" will get you more results.

You are always nice, you are always professional, but your messaging must communicate sufficient credibility and value to achieve your business objectives when you are speaking to a qualified prospect who recognizes a need on some level and will be writing a check to you or a competitor shortly.

Value Knocks Down Doors.

Communicate value up front. If you are talking to someone who recognizes a need, that will earn you additional talk time. If you are talking to someone who does not recognize a need, no matter what you say, how nice you are, how many times you say "I won't take much of your time" or "I am not worthy," they are still going to say "no." So put your best foot forward and let them decide.

Get over whatever is holding you back. Punch up your scripts so that they are clear, concise, direct and powerfully communicate your credibility and value.

Focus On The Component Parts Of The Process That Lead To Results;
Don't Focus On The Result.

Hang in here with me on this statement. When you wish to set more discovery calls and sales appointments, don't focus on the result. Focus on improving specific parts of the process that lead to the result.

Maybe you are getting a certain baseline result from a list pulled from multiple industries, but you notice that you seem to get better results from manufacturing companies or from companies that generate more than $5 million in revenue. Try to beat your baseline by launching more records from manufacturing companies and companies with more than $5 million in revenue.

Maybe you have an acceptable conversion rate of conversations with decision-makers to discovery calls set. Let's say that for every 4 conversations you have with decision-makers in which you deliver your "set the appointment" pitch, that you get 1 meeting. You could try to beat your baseline in this area by either generating more conversations with decision-makers or increasing the conversion of conversations to meetings set ratio.

Have More Conversations.

If you were going to try to have more conversations, you might make an extra effort to get direct dial and extension numbers. The more direct dial and extension numbers you have for decision-makers, the more conversations with them you tend to have. So every time you make a call and don't have a direct dial or extension number, have a strategy ready to try to get it. Implement a conscious, proactive effort to increase the percentage of records you are calling who have direct dial or extension numbers.

Or, if you were trying to have more conversations with decision-makers, you might try to do more of what I call "power calling." Very simply, when you have a direct dial or extension number of a decision-maker, you try to call that number before and after normal business hours. If you have your CRM set up correctly, and I feel pity for you if you don't, with a few keystrokes you should be able to create a filter to pull up all of your top-value decision makers that you have direct dial or extension numbers for. Schedule 3 or 4 sessions a week where you plow through as many records that you can where you have direct dial or extension numbers. Make those calls before or after hours.

Move Results By Increasing Conversations To Meetings Set Ratio.

Let's take another example. Let's assume that you have a good number of conversations with decision-makers, but not enough of them are agreeing to meet. A good conversation ratio would be 4 conversations to get 1 meeting. A top caller or calling in a very responsive situation might get a meeting with every 3 conversations you have, but that is exceptionally good and very rare. More typically you will need 5-8 conversations. If your conversation to meetings set ratio is 10 or more, you are definitely in the red zone. Something is very, very wrong. You are calling the wrong list, or your message is very weak.

What is the #1 reason why people don't agree to meet with you? You don't give them enough reason to meet with you.

If You Have the Right Targets, The Right Decision-Makers and Are Using The Right Process…

Assuming you have defined bullseye high-probability target companies, the right decision-makers within those companies, and you feel that your call/interaction process is solid, if you are not getting meetings it is because of your messaging.

If those other 3 things are right, you are not scoring discovery calls or more meetings simply because you are not giving people enough reason to meet.

Worksheets, additional scripts, and periodic updates
are available to readers of this book at
ScottChannell.com/STM-book-extras

Chapter 23
Finding And Hiring Appointment Setters

Turnover is the death of appointment setting programs. Finding a good appointment setter is not easy and when you find a good one treat them well.

Do everything you can to avoid making a mistake when hiring. Assume nothing. A wrong hire can set you back months, and you will get little for your investment. Remember, it is not only the out-of-pocket costs that are at stake. The much bigger issue and cost are the opportunities you lose when your program fails.

The buyers are out there. Hit the right targets and interact with them consistently in an organized manner while communicating credibility and value and you will pick up new accounts and increase your revenue.

Picking the right person or team member to work your system is crucial to your success. Here are my thoughts and suggestions on picking good appointment setters and avoiding a mishire and turnover in the position. Too much turnover in these positions is the death of an appointment-setting program. Turnover makes it nearly impossible to get a program off the ground.

Here Is A Generic Ad You Might Place To Find An Appointment Setter.

The headline might be "Sales Communicator" or something like "Inside Sales For Established B2B Company."

Do you seek a flexible high-paying part-time position in a professional environment?

If you are organized, have superior communication skills and are willing to follow a proven system, we would like to speak to you. Established growing firm services business clients and seeks communicator for phone outreach and follow-up to existing client base and new inquiries.

Superior people skills, positive attitude, and cooperative spirit a must. Experience in sales environments helpful but not required. Basic computer proficiency. Familiarity with contact management systems such as ACT helpful, not required. Must be goal driven and able to work independently. Training provided. You would be working a well established proven system.

Please be sure to reply with 1) Description of what you seek in a position 2) Hours available and 3) Compensation expectations.

Contact Horatio at 978-123-4567

The above hits many of the themes as to what you are looking for. Notice the use of "flexible position," "professional environment," and the directive to reply with the answers to 3 questions.

Many times what attracts and keeps good people are flexible work environments. You need X amount of meetings per week. You don't care what day of the week or what times they are booked. Look for the best person. Provide flexibility as part of the glue that will keep them and avoid turnover.

I feel strongly that these are part-time jobs. Productivity plummets after 3 ½ or 4 hours of working the phones. Plummets.

The 3 questions at the end serve a very important purpose. You are looking for someone who takes their job search seriously, pays attention, follows directions, and is prepared. If someone responds to that ad with very specific requests and either ignores the requests or is not prepared to answer the questions, that is a big fat clue they are not serious enough about a job with you, they don't pay attention, are not able to follow instructions, and don't know what they want. If you were to hire such a person, the odds are high that you will spend a lot of time and money to train them, and they will not stay with you very long or will be unproductive.

SELL THE MEETING

Qualities You Seek When Hiring An Appointment Setter

Good communication skills.
Seem smart.
Good personalities.
The situation fits a personal need. (Location, work hours, flexibility, etc.)
Not "in between" jobs.
Step up in pay for them.
No bad habits to break.
Positive attitude.
Money motivated.

Red Flags To Avoid. Higher Risk Of Turnover.

People in between jobs.
People making a lateral move.
People who just need a job and this is a step down for them.
People who have bounced around different call jobs.
People who can't articulate what they want and how much they want to make.
People who have worked in bad call environments. Have bad habits to break.
Negative people.

Some Comments On "The Situation."

Employee turnover is the death of these programs. You want to find a quality person who will stick with you. If you can offer a situation that fits someone's personal needs, that is a major factor in them sticking with you and digging in to get the results you need. There are a good number of intelligent, organized and good people skills workers out there who may not have worked call jobs before but would be great for your program. If you can provide training (this is not rocket science) and a situation that fits their personal needs such as flexible work hours, "the situation" is often the glue that will retain good people.

Articulating Expectations On Compensation

When you hire, you will know what you are offering for pay and what a decent person could make with incentives working for you. If someone performing decently for you can expect to make X and they want to make 2X, you have a problem. If you hire that person, they are unlikely to stay and will bolt when they find a job that pays better. I strongly recommend that you insist, INSIST, that they articulate to you what their expectations are for compensation. If their expectations are not in line with what they reasonably could make for you, it is not going to work out. Plus, and this is a personal thing with me, if someone can't articulate what they want my assumption is they don't know what they want. If they don't know what will make them happy, the odds of them being satisfied are low. The odds of them leaving your position for another job are high. If they won't tell you what they expect to make, move on.

Previous Phone Experience

If someone has previous experience doing a similar job interacting with the same level of an executive as you require, that is a positive factor. However, most phone jobs are lower level. Most phone jobs don't pay well, and the people are poorly trained with lousy management. They can come to you with a lot of bad habits. Many times their phone experience is not worth it. I'd rather find someone with a brain, where the situation fits, who has interacted with the public, is organized, and willing to follow a system and train them, than hire someone who has to unlearn everything they have been taught.

Process For Hiring

These are phone jobs. You seek someone who impresses over the phone. You need to spend time with people on the phone to make that judgment. Resumes and an in-office interview are not your best indicator of how someone is going to perform on the phone.

Here is a process I like. Place your ad with instructions to call a specific person at your company.

As that designated person receives calls, they should describe the position a bit, maybe even do a little selling themselves. If you are a growing company, have a professional environment, provide excellent training, offer flexible hours, all those things should be mentioned right up front. But most of all that person at this first step should listen and ask open-ended questions.

What attracted you to the ad?
What are you looking for in a job?
What is most important to you?

SELL THE MEETING

What questions do you have about the job?
What hours are you available?
What are your compensation expectations?

The person taking this first call should ask open-ended questions and just listen. At the end of the call, the applicant should be told that another person, Mr. Montypenny, will be reaching out to qualified candidates and they should send their information if they have not done so already.

At the end of the call, your first round interviewer should summarize their impression of the applicant. What questions did they ask? Did they answer questions asked? What was the general impression as to communication skills, phone presence, clarity of thought, preparedness, intelligence, etc.? They should rate them on a scale of 1 to 10.

You probably think that this takes a lot of time. Yup. You can spend time now and increase the odds that you will make a good hire. Or, you can save time up front and find out months later that the person you hired is a dud or decided the job wasn't for them. Your investment is wasted. The far greater cost is the new business opportunities you lost because things did not work out.

Whoever is going to make the hiring decision, Mr. Montypenny, should follow up by phone on the best candidates.

Questions would include:

What attracted you to the ad?
What are you looking for in a job?
What is most important to you?
Describe your best situation.
Have you worked a phone job before? Tell me about it.
Have you worked with the public before? Tell me about it.
What were the best and worst things about those previous jobs?
How do you feel about a job that involves making phone calls?
How do you feel about being rejected?
Do you consider yourself an organized person?
Can you follow instructions?
Are you willing to work a system? Follow a process?
How do you feel about using scripts?
What questions do you have about the job?

What hours are you available?
What are your compensation expectations?

Those 2 phone conversations are "the interview" and your best indicator as to whether they might be successful. If they don't impress over the phone, don't seem articulate, are not prepared to answer questions, then the odds of them working out are poor.

Have your best or final candidates in for an in-office chat and make your decision. Remember, your objective is two fold. Find the best person for the job and avoid turnover.

Worksheets, additional scripts, and periodic updates
are available to readers of this book at
ScottChannell.com/STM-book-extras

Chapter 24
Compensation And Incentives

When it comes to setting up a compensation and incentive plan, these are the core principles to adhere to.

The goal is to have a system that spits out first sales appointments and discovery calls that fit a certain profile consistently at a reasonable cost.

Your focus as an owner or manager should be cost-per-meeting.

Your incentive system should encourage behaviors that impact results consistently.

To summarize, your compensation system should support your goal of generating qualified appointments consistently, should encourage your lead generators to dig in and execute well, and your focus should be on cost-per-meeting.

Two Things

Your focus on cost per meeting is not to be confused with what the caller is making overall or what your overall costs are. Those are different issues. As an owner or manager, your focus should be on cost-per-meeting.

There is an assumption here that your program is well run. As an owner or manager, you are providing your lead generators with a list of targets that are bullseye targets for you. You have done the research. You have a very clear profile of your targets ranked in order of probability. You know what the acceptable levels of authority are within target organizations. You know the titles your lead generators are going after.

The job of your callers/lead generators/appointment setters is to deliver you a meeting that fits those parameters. Whether the meetings generated fit your desired profile is much more the responsibility of ownership and management than the callers. It is a management responsibility to provide callers with the targets to be called and the acceptable entry points (Titles and level of authority.) Management has the data; management has better access to information; management provides the callers with the list.

It is the caller's job to deliver a meeting within a company that fits your desired profile at an acceptable level of authority. When they do that, they have done their job and should get paid. Gaining the commitment of a decision-maker within a company that fits your desired profile with the mutual understanding that a substantive meeting is going to take place to share information about needs and capabilities has a value. When a caller sets that meeting, they should be paid that value and that money should hit their paychecks quickly.

Within well-run programs, it is easier to accept the concept that value should be paid when a meeting is set. Within well-run programs, there is more confidence that a meeting is worthwhile as there is more clarity about the profile they are calling. Within a well-run program, there is a history and knowledge that if a meeting is set within a company that fits a certain profile at an acceptable level of authority, that a certain percentage will result in a new account within a predictable period with an average sale of X and lifetime value of Y. Within well-run programs, you know what a qualified meeting is worth so you can pay for that value immediately, which encourages the setting of even more qualified meetings.

Within poorly run programs, there is no such confidence. The lists provided the callers have cast the net far too wide and include a large percentage; I'm talking 50%, 70%, 90% or more, of records that are a poor investment of time or a total waste of time. In the worst situations, callers are scrolling the Internet trying to find companies and people to call, which is insane.

If you are an owner or manager of a program where that is happening you should walk up to the nearest mirror and repeat "I have no clue what I am doing, I have no clue what I am doing."

In a poorly run program turnover is high and the quality of salesmanship is not great. Within poorly run programs the quality of meetings is much more of a crap shoot, so there is less willingness to pay for a meeting when set, which provides no incentive for a caller to do their job better.

SELL THE MEETING

How Much For A Meeting?

How much you would pay as an incentive when a meeting is set will vary by multiple factors including closing percentage, the average size of sale, and margin generated. But whatever the amount, it must be significant and it must hit the caller's paycheck quickly. Otherwise, you are not encouraging behaviors that will generate more meetings, lower your cost-per-appointment, and improve the quality of the meetings set.

Low spiffs do not impact behaviors. If someone who is working a system, honing their skills, and spitting out 5 meetings a week is not making significantly more than the person who is only spitting out 3 meeting a week, why should they bother? If the person who is digging in and generating 10 meetings a week is not making significantly more than the person generating 5 meetings a week, why should they bother? If someone is twice as good and generating you more qualified meetings at a significantly lower cost-per-meeting is only making an extra $50 a week, why bother? Screw that.

The Best Callers Flee Poorly Set Up And Poorly Managed Programs.

If your system is not set up properly, you will have a very hard time keeping good appointment setters. If you ask people to wade through crappy lists, waste their time trying to find good people to call, don't enable them to call efficiently with a properly configured contact manager/CRM, give them lousy scripts, then on top of that there is little difference in pay between a top producer, mediocre, and less than average producer, guess what? The good ones will leave you as they will get frustrated. You will be stuck with the mediocre and worse as they have fewer options.

The Compensation System I Like Best

I have helped companies where appointment setters are receiving a base pay of $60,000 or more with benefits and reachable incentives that would put them into 6-figure income territory. I have helped companies where people are working for $12 an hour (or less) with no benefits and at most, could hope to see an extra $50 or $75 in their paychecks. Whatever your reality is the concepts are the same.

Base Pay

In a perfect world, base pay would exceed or be very close to what someone could expect to earn in another job. If you find someone with raw talent, great communication skills, attitude and work ethic who is making $12 an hour and you offer $15 as a base, with incentives on top, you have a potentially very motivated appointment setter. You are offering something they would not otherwise have. Same concept on the other end of the earning spectrum. If you are hiring someone that could expect to earn $60,000, you will have to equal that or be very close to it, with incentives on top, for a quality person to take the job, stick with it, and dig in hard to get you results and earn the incentives that come with that. You want this to be a step up for people financially. If they could earn the same money elsewhere and not have to make calls and endure the monotony and rejection, they will.

Incentives Must Be Realistic.

Your incentives must be in the real world and reachable. If you want to demotivate someone or chase your best appointment setters away, structure your incentives to be unrealistic and unreachable. Or, as we will discuss in a moment, make their incentives based upon whether someone else does their job and pay them far in the future.

Incentives Are For Behaviors And Results Your Callers Control.

Appointment setters should be paid based upon what they can control. In a well set up system, they can control the quantity and quality of meetings and discovery calls set. They cannot control whether a meeting turns into an account. If you want to chase your best appointment setters away or demotivate them, pay them based upon whether a sales rep turns that meeting into a closed account, usually many months removed from when the meeting was set. Great animosity is created when good appointment setters feel that solid meetings are squandered by unprepared and lousy salespeople. Or, when an incentive is paid, it is so far removed time-wise from when the meeting was set, the incentive has little impact on improving the behaviors that would set more qualified meetings. Appointment setters, being human, think "why bother?"

Incentives For A Job Well Done Should Hit The Paycheck Quickly.

You want your callers to be motivated to dig in a little deeper, be prepared, make the extra effort, be sharper, work more efficiently, go go go. When they do that, and it results in more qualified meetings being set, they must sense the connection between their extra efforts, digging in, working smarter, making improvements, eliminating time-wasting activities, improving their messaging to get more meetings, and the impact those efforts have on their next paycheck.

When they see and feel the connection between improving their behaviors that impact the quantity and quality of meetings set, and what they see in their paychecks, they have constant motivation to make constant marginal improvements in their process, messaging, and time allocation. If their bonus or incentive is too far removed from the behavior you wish to improve, it has little or no impact on improving the behaviors that will result in more meetings.

The Best Callers Make More And More Money While Your Cost-Per-Meeting Goes Down.

As an owner or manager, you wish to have a compensation system where a good caller can make more and more per week while your cost-per-meeting goes down.

Your Comp System Should Encourage The Connection Between Increased Effort And Improved Results And The Size Of The Next Paycheck.

The next carrot should always be within reach. You want to have a system where a caller feels that no matter whether they are having a good week or a bad week or a good month or a bad month, if they dig in and get some meetings, they will see more money in their paycheck shortly. You want to avoid a system where incentives are calculated weekly or monthly, and when a caller has a bad run, they think "well, no incentive this month. I'll start to dig in next month (or next week) when I can make some extra money." That is human nature.

You want your callers always to have an incentive to improve the behaviors that result in booking more meetings and better quality meetings. That must be a constant mindset. You cannot turn off and on an attitude of improvement. It must be constant.

So Let's Look At A System.

So let's take a look at a middle-of-the-road example. Base pay for a caller is $30,000 annually, and reasonably someone doing a decent job should be booking 4 to 7 meetings per week.

$30,000 a year equals $577 a week.

If your caller averages 1 meeting per week, your cost-per-meeting is $577.
If your caller averages 2 meetings per week, your cost-per-meeting is $288.50
If your caller averages 3 meetings per week, your cost-per-meeting is $192.33
At the top of a realistic spectrum, if your callers are booking an average of 7 meetings per week, your cost-per-meeting drops to $82.42.

You can see that it is in your interest to have the average number of meetings set to be as high as possible. Without incentives, it is less likely that an appointment setter would focus on improving the behaviors that would increase the average number of qualified appointments set per week.

So consider this.

The first meeting set every week belongs to the house. They are getting a base pay. No incentive is paid.

2nd meeting booked in a week earns an extra $35.
3rd earns an additional $50.
4th earns an additional $75.
5th earns an additional $125.
6th earns an additional $125.
7th earns an additional $125.

Incentives are cumulative. So someone who books 3 meetings in a week earns an extra $85. $35 for the 2nd meeting and $50 for the 3rd = $85. When someone books 7 meetings in a week their incentive, paid in the next paycheck, would be $535.

Someone who is organizing themselves, improving behaviors and executing a system that on average spits out 4 meetings per week has earned themselves an annual 28% raise or $8,320. If someone improves their skill set, organization, and communication skills to the point that they spit out an average of 7 meetings per week, they have earned themselves an annual bonus of $27,820, a 92% raise over base pay.

As an owner or manager, you might be thinking "wow, that's a lot of money, I don't want to pay that." But oh you do. As your callers make more money per week on average, you get more meetings delivered consistently at a lower and lower cost.

Here is the cost per meeting using $30,000 a year as base pay and the incentive schedule discussed above.

Cost-per-meeting based upon an average number of meetings set per week.

2 = $306
3 = $220
4 = $184
5 = $172
6 = $164
7 = $158

The better job your callers do and the more consistently they spit out a higher number of meetings per week on average, the lower your cost-per-meeting is. You should know what an acceptable cost of sale is for a new account. Within that acceptable cost of sale, you should know how much you can pay for a qualified meeting.

With a system like this, the callers have a constant incentive to strive to execute behaviors that on average will spit out a higher number of meetings per week. The incentive for doing so is meaningful and hits their paychecks quickly.

What Happens If More Than 7 Meetings Are Booked In A Week?

If more than 7 meetings are booked in a week, the excess goes into a bank, to be applied to weeks when less than 7 meetings are booked. At the end of the month, if there are still meetings in the bank, they are paid out at the highest rate. In this example $125 per.

So if 1 week a caller books 9 meetings they are paid for 7 and 2 go in the bank. If the next week they book 4 meetings, they can take 2 from the bank and get paid for 6 meetings that week.

What If People Don't Show?

You should assume a show rate of 85% or better. Pay incentives assuming that 5 of 6 meetings booked will be held. If over time the show rate is less than 85% then it is a sign that the list is poor or the messaging is weak, and you should tweak the process. If your caller is booking drive-by's and glorified literature drops and calling it a meeting, that is something you should be aware of and nip in the bud before it becomes a problem. If you are listening, overseeing, and coaching behaviors that will not happen.

I would not recommend that you pay when a meeting is held. Again, the connection between the behaviors you wish to encourage and the reward is weakened. Plus, other people doing their job adequately impacts whether a caller gets paid, a situation you should avoid.

What Should You Pay?

What is reasonable for you to pay to encourage the behaviors that will deliver you more meetings at an acceptable cost, and consistently, will depend upon your acceptable cost of sale and cost-per-appointment. Those would be determined, in part, by your closing ratio, the average size of sales, margin realized, and lifetime value. The better handle you have on those numbers, the easier it will be to come up with the right compensation and incentive system.

Worksheets, additional scripts, and periodic updates are available to readers of this book at ScottChannell.com/STM-book-extras

Chapter 25
Management And Marketing Integration

But for a better management effort, many companies are losing out on new opportunities that would be theirs for the picking.

Companies that have the story to tell, the clients to reference, the results, and proof of a superior offering often are losing out on new business due to inadequate management of the appointment setting effort.

If you are an individual rep, the issue is the same; you need to manage yourself.

You can be great at what you do and know a lot about what you do, and yet be lousy at prospecting. Let me highlight the keys to successfully managing a "get the appointment" program.

Know What To Manage

Are you counting dials, pressuring reps to meet activity goals, urging them to call more and more leads? If so, you are among the clueless, and the odds are you are the reason why your team is not delivering the bottom line results you need.

If you are going to move bottom-line numbers, you need to know what moves bottom-line numbers and manage those efforts. "Whipping them harder" is not going to bring you the results you seek. Those who manage by spreadsheet and demand more activity are deluding themselves. Those "activities" have a weak relationship to results and the reports read are frequently fiction.

If your team is calling a weak list, with no defined process, messaging that is not communicating value and inefficiency is baked into practically every step your team takes, you are not managing. No matter how many times you bang the table and demand more dials or more meetings, that is not management.

You need to know what works to manage properly and impact productivity and the bottom-line results you seek. If you are wrong, you are doomed.

If your bottom-line numbers are not improving, be willing to admit that you might be very very good at what you do, yet know little or nothing about prospecting and appointment setting.

Set Standards

"If you do not do what this man says, you will not be working here long."

That is how a VP Sales would introduce me to new sales hires. Six or 7 times a year, over many years, as they grew from $20-80 million in revenue, I would hear the same thing at the beginning of training sessions.

This company did not grow because of me. They grew because they had a system. A system they believed in. A system they expected their reps to learn and implement. It turned out that my methods were pretty damn close to what they practiced; that is why I was there. But the beliefs and behaviors that were enabling them to grow so fast were there before I arrived.

To properly manage, you need to set standards of behaviors that will substantively impact your bottom-line goal. This company expected reps to call on companies that fit a certain profile, to interact with prospects a certain way, to respond to questions in a certain manner, to communicate the companies' credibility and value effectively. If reps met their standards or were on a path of learning how to meet their standards, they stayed. If not, they were gone.

As to every single step of the prospecting, get the meeting and sales process, there are behaviors that move you toward your goal, behaviors that move you away from your goal, behaviors that have no impact. You must educate your reps as to the behaviors, at every step, that will help them achieve your goals.

Now there are exceptions to every rule, crazy things happen, and reps have to deal with the lunatic fringe. Reps are not robots, and flexibility is needed at times. But remember this, there are sales behaviors much more likely to lead to the result you seek. You need to decide if a rep, or your team, are working the system and utilizing the behaviors that are most likely to lead to your growth goals.

You set the parameters, and you set the standards of behavior. You decide how much leeway is acceptable. You provide wiggle room and flexibility but remember this: if there are too many exceptions to your system, you don't have a system.

Management By Sitting Around

Inspect what you expect.

You need to observe what your reps are saying on the phone and out in the field. Too often, time and money are spent to develop systems and messaging that conveys credibility and benefits, and it is not used on the phone or in the field.

Management sets the standard. People are less likely to steal from you if they think they are going to get caught. Your reps are less likely to be unprepared, guessing, and winging it out in the field if they know that at some point you will be listening or observing. When reps are unprepared and winging it, you are losing opportunities. For every step and common scenario where their behavior is below standards, you are losing momentum and opportunities — slice, slice, slice. Every behavior of your reps that is subpar is moving you away from a close.

I love to sit among a group of callers and roll up and down the aisles to listen to what is happening on calls and to see how they move around the CRM. Do the reps seem prepared? Are they ready to handle the common scenarios they know they will encounter? Is there consistency as to how they handle repetitive situations? Do they sound confident? These are things you need to know.

There is absolutely no excuse, none, for reps not to be prepared to respond to questions and statements they hear over and over again. Does your rep have 20 different ways to start discussions? If so they are unprepared, guessing and winging it. Do they hem and haw, pause, seem uncertain as to what to say when they hear "send me some information" or "we are all set?" Absolutely inexcusable.

If this is happening, I blame management more than I blame the reps. You have created a culture where standards are ignored, and reps can go through the motions using behaviors that are not best. Behaviors that do not do the most to move toward a sale.

Assuming you have created a system and educated the reps as to the behaviors that are most likely to move them to a close, you should expect them to use them. You should inspect to make sure they are.

Your Reps Are Human

This may come off as negative. I don't mean it to be, but it is a reality.

Without proper management, supervision, and coaching, your reps will:

Do what is most comfortable for them, not what works best.
Drift down to the lowest common denominator of performance and behavior.
Resist accountability.

Your top performers are more self-motivated, approach selling or prospecting as a craft, and seek to improve constantly; they are proactive about improvement, keep score, and practice.

Your average and less than average performers, not so much.

Your greatest challenge as a manager is this: change.

People resist change. It is interesting to me that the poorest performers are those who resist change most strenuously. Among all the projects I have done, the teams that were the worst performers, had the most antiquated systems, had no standards for messaging, were by far the most inefficient, those are the teams that resist changing the hardest. The poorest performers are the ones who scream and yelp the hardest about even basic common sense improvements.

This is a lesson for management. The more your team has moved away from the best behaviors, the harder it will be to get them back on track. Management has been absent. Management has let the team get away with being unprepared and virtually winging it and not holding them accountable. Management has many times taught teams that if they scream and resist enough, they won't have to change. That is management's fault.

This is a call that comes in too often. Teams retool and lift performance, and all is right and well in prospecting land. A year later I get the call. "Scott, we don't know why, but results are not what they used to be. We can't figure it out." A little investigation determines that management and the team have drifted away from the behaviors that lead to improved performance. List criteria were loosened up, so more lower-probability suspects are being called. That great call process and touch system that was working are no longer being implemented consistently. Great messaging that conveyed credibility and benefits so succinctly has been watered down.

The lesson here is that left alone and not properly supervised and managed, teams will drift away from what works best to what is most comfortable for them and the lowest common denominator.

Management must set the standards, educate, expect certain behaviors will be used, and check under the covers to be sure it is being done.

Sales Leaders Don't Let Sales Team Call Crap.

I have beaten this point to death but due to its importance, choose to reemphasize it here.

There is no greater impact on results than the targets you or your team choose to call or interact with. No other factors come close. If you get this right and your team is mediocre or screwing up on other things, you can still make money. If you get this wrong, no matter what else your team does right, you are doomed.

Management has access to better information about whom to target than the callers. Management provides the list. Management should tightly define the prospecting bullseye based upon past and current buyers with a tight profile of SIC and/or NAICS code range, revenue ranges, and employee size ranges. Depending upon your industry and what provides clues to potential worth, other factors in your bullseye profile might be square footage, whether they currently have a vendor for your service, their level of spending on something or whether they use a certain marketing channel. The list goes on.

Management frequently assumes too much and does not spend the very few hours it takes to develop a finely tuned bullseye profile. Therefore your reps are doomed to waste 50% to 90%+ of their time (no exaggeration) calling or interacting with less probable suspects or total crap. That is managements fault.

If your team is searching the Internet trying to make educated guesses as to whom to call next, management has totally dropped the ball. If you require your team to turn in 10 or 20 leads a week they "think" might be good to call on, most of which fall far outside of your prospecting bullseye, you are the cause of your team's low productivity.

Words To Ban

Yeah, but...

You want your team to know and use the behaviors that are most likely to move them toward their goal in every situation. You need your team to work in the high-probability zone. Top performers are knowledgeable about and talk about behaviors, actions, words, scripts, which are the best to use in typical circumstances. That is what they think about — the best way to do things.

The mediocre and the wannabe's that never will be are at a loss to articulate how to handle common sales scenarios yet are masters at knowing the exceptions to the rules. They are quick to express a "Yeah, but" when the most successful behaviors are discussed. Ask them how they handle very common scenarios, and you will hear "well, everything is so different, it depends on the situation, you never know…." Lower performers are experts on all the exceptions to the rules. Every time you mention a high-probability behavior, a tried and true practice of the top sales high earning superstars, the first thing you hear from a never will be is "Yeah, but…."

We are in sales, deal with people, and crazy things happen around the edges. So what?
Keep your team focused on the highest-probability sales behaviors, not the exceptions to the rules.

Interested

A more meaningless, nebulous, tell us nothing, divert from the real issues, ridiculous sales word has never been invented. "Let's find out if they are interested." "They are interested in the gizmo." Does that tell us anything of substance that can be used to make better decisions to close a deal? NO!! It typically just masks ignorance of what is really going on and leads to wasted time.

As a manager, do those words do anything to help you determine whether a deal is real or fantasy or how to help your rep? No.

Do they fit your profile or not?
Did they express certain needs or not?
Did they describe a goal?
Did they relate specifics about what the status quo is costing them?

Were they specific about what they hoped to gain with a new vendor?
Did they share their buying criteria?
Did they relate their decision-making process?
Did they commit to moving to the next sales step?

There are a lot of things that give you clues as to whether a sale is on the right path. Whether they are "interested" tells you nothing of value.

As a manager, you need specifics. You need to know specifics to determine whether an opportunity is real and if your rep is prepared and doing the things that give you the best shot at realizing that opportunity.

You are doing your reps a favor when you ask specific questions as to matters that impact the sale. They know you will be inspecting, not assuming. Your reps will sharpen their questions and presentation skills knowing that you will be asking questions of substance and expecting real answers.

I'm different

We are different. This industry, this area, this side of the street are all different.

What they are really saying is "I don't have to change, listen to facts, learn anything, or be held accountable."

Many with average talent and drive get/stay very congruent with the behaviors of the top producers and make a lot of money. Many others with superior talent and drive shoot themselves in the foot immediately with the "I'm different" rationale for not having to listen or do what works. It is a very common self-sabotaging behavior.

Just step up to the plate and admit that you don't want to change, you don't want to learn, you're lazy, or you don't really care about making more money, but don't let your team use the "I'm different" excuse.

Demand Knowledge

There might be 20, 30 or 50 reasons why someone might buy from you, yet most sales reps would be hard pressed to name 5 or 6.

Are your reps fluent with the names of your top accounts in general? Your top accounts in each industry or vertical?

Do your reps have stories, examples, or statistics as to how your service or offering has improved business conditions at other companies?

Are your reps prepared and fluent discussing specifics, before and after examples of how your solution has helped others?

Are your reps prepared with the depth of knowledge necessary to remove the last elements of doubt in the way of a buy decision?

The sad fact is that too often reps' knowledge is not very deep. They might be great order-takers and able to skim the cream off the top and close what is easy but not able to remove doubt, educate, or demonstrate your offering to move those who would benefit greatly from your offering into the win column.

In this book, I push the creation of what I call the "pile of words." Very simply it is all the top verbiage, examples, names drops, specifics, stories, benefits, credibility factors that reps need to know to represent you in the marketplace. That document could be anywhere from 7 to 30 pages long. I don't care whether it is setting an appointment or discovery call, conducting the first meeting or managing an account deeper in the pipeline, there are facts, words, and phrases that best represent your offering and help prospective accounts fully appreciate how you might help them.

Without fluency in those basics, reps are left with superficial knowledge and the company is losing opportunities they otherwise could have had.

If it is not written down, it is far less likely to be used.

If it is not written down, I can guarantee you that only a small fraction of your credibility, experience, and how you have helped others is being communicated to your prospects.

Write down all the top verbiage and specifics that best enable your reps to communicate your credibility, benefits, and proofs of what you can deliver.

Check under the covers. Ask them how they handle opening a meeting, their top questions, handle or cut off at the pass common objections, illustrate your strengths, on and on.

It is management's responsibility to make sure that reps have all the top verbiage to properly represent your offering.

It is management's responsibility to make sure that reps are fluent and using that information to maximize sales.

SELL THE MEETING

Resource Allocation

One of management's top responsibilities is to properly allocate resources.

There is only so much money and time to go around. Management must allocate these resources properly to get the best results.

In setting sales appointments and discovery call land, there is usually a significant correlation between company size and the average size of a sale. If too much time is spent calling smaller size companies, average sale size tends to be smaller, and those accounts tend to churn faster. If too much time is allocated to larger potential accounts with longer sales cycles, that can lead to cash flow problems.

Here is a common example of misallocation of resources. The company provides the team with a list of targets that have not been properly profiled. The result is a massive waste of time by reps as they wade through a list filled with garbage that could easily have been weeded out before it got to them. Or, reps are left to scroll the Internet trying to decide who to call (which is insane) with the result that massive amounts of sales and prospecting time are wasted searching for people to call. A great list could very easily have been provided, but it wasn't, and a phenomenal amount of time is wasted calling targets far outside the bullseye profile.

The same concerns apply to how much time you spend chasing a suspect, how much time is too much time to spend in the pipeline? When does a rep need to let go and allocate that time to a higher-probability behavior or prospect?

It's is management's responsibility, management's sacred duty, to make sure that time and resources are being properly allocated to maximize results.

Maximize Your ROI With This Simple Easy Step.

This might be the highest ROI advice imparted in this whole book.

Your goal here is to turn Washingtons into Hamiltons, Jacksons and Grants. Ka-Ching, Ka-Ching, pile fat stacks and roll in the dough. You need to turn every dollar invested in prospecting into $10, $20 or $50.

One of the ways to bump your ROI is to leverage the data and intelligence you obtain through your calling.

One of the ways to leave a lot of money on the table is to NOT leverage the data and intelligence you obtain through your calling.

Why is it so important that you be highly targeted, set up properly, be able to code and segment, that you extract value and worth information about a suspect even if they don't meet or you never speak to them? So that you gather the most information possible about who is most likely to buy and their worth if they do.

If you are reading this book, you are likely selling something that is not purchased frequently. What you offer might only be purchased every 3, 5, or 7 years. So even if you do everything correctly, the odds of you bumping into a buyer at exactly the right time are pretty slim. My odds are that about 1 in 6 records you call will write a check to you or one of your competitors within the next 3-15 months.

As your team calls, you will identify higher-probability-higher value targets.

If your team calls 1,000 records, there may be 25 to 75 that are uber valuable to you, that represent your dream most-profitable lowest-turnover easiest to please and service Ka-ching fat stack accounts.

The small slice of your list that is super valuable to you deserves more attention. You need to touch them consistently with messaging that communicates your knowledge, experience, and credibility. These "touches" must go out on time, communicate helpful information as perceived by the recipient, and be devoid of the typical corporate yada yada that is discounted and ignored by the high-value targets you spent so much time and money to identify.

Think groups: Send a communication to a "group" that is easy to get out the door.

Think value from the point of view of the recipient: Communicate information that is valuable to your target audience and they don't get from other sources. You probably have stories from the trenches as to how common problems are solved, mistakes that can be avoided, and success stories with specifics as to how you have helped other companies. You probably know questions they have never thought of, consequences they have not thought of, and know how money can be misspent. Demonstrate your knowledge and worth by consistently sharing information that is genuinely helpful to your highest-worth prospects.

Think consistency of the touch: Consistency of the touch will deliver more results to you than the quality of the messaging. The targets of this very selectively sent messaging must have the sense that you are keeping in touch with them regularly. That consistent dripping earns you credibility and trust — drip drip drip. Don't get me wrong. You want your messaging to be as good as possible, but the consistency of the touch has far more to do with building name recognition and credibility than any "eureka" tidbit you might relate in your touches.

My personal favorite: Simple letters. One page. Three paragraphs with headlines. Simply share 3 short bits of info that are instructive, genuinely helpful to your target audience, and would not typically be found anywhere else. End with a simple invitation to reach out if you could answer any questions or to discuss options. That's it. Simple to get out the door. Low-cost. Perceived as informative by the highest-worth audience you discovered by investing a lot of time and money by calling.

Particularly if you are not touching your highest-value targets with anything consistently at the moment, the simple letter system is a great way to get started. You might use another tool at some time, but if you are not touching your targets nothing is happening, so particularly with your high-value targets, start touching them right away.

How this gets screwed up: Let me count the ways. You didn't set up your CRM correctly, so you have no easy way to select your highest value targets. When your team called, they didn't ask the questions that would tell you whether someone was top value, higher than average, average, or not worth any more time prospects. If you can select top targets, you go overboard on the messaging, convene committee meetings to review the content, and have too many people involved, so nothing gets out the door. Or, the messaging is diluted to the typical corporate lowest common denominator say nothing crap full of superlatives and promises of "best in class," "superior service," and genuine caring, which is discounted by 99% and promptly ignored.

From the recipient's point of view: They receive genuinely helpful information consistently from someone they come to believe has credibility and experience that may at some point help them. When that time comes, whether it be a one-time project, upgrade, or replacing a vendor due to service failure or lack of performance, who do you want to be top-of-mind and perceived to be worth talking to? You.

They reach out to you when they perceive a need. They are more receptive to taking a meeting when you do call.

If you are booking a qualified meeting at the cost of X. I bet that the additional meetings you book as a result of consistently touching your highest-value targets would be obtained at the cost of 1/10th X. Plus, the average size of these accounts is above average, so your ROI is through the roof.

Simple basic marketing consistently applied to your most qualified and valuable group of targets.

Think of your calling and outreach efforts as part of an overall effective system. Use the data and info obtained to utilize other effective marketing tools and formats.

Worksheets, additional scripts, and periodic updates
are available to readers of this book at
ScottChannell.com/STM-book-extras

Chapter 26
Selling With House Money:
Do You Make More Sales By Focusing On Overall Process or Individual Outcomes?

If you are in sales management or managing yourself, would you prefer to be the casino or the gambler?

Are you going to set more discovery calls and first sales appointments by focusing on your overall prospecting process or the result of individual calls?

In poker, there is a theory that when you make a bet with the odds in your favor, you have won something regardless of whether you win or lose that specific bet. And, when you make a bet with the odds against you, something is lost, regardless of whether you win or lose with that specific choice.

Can You Be Using Good Sales Techniques If Someone Says "No?" Yup! Big Time.

When you do the right things, you are going to be successful in the end. It doesn't matter whether on an individual play your script works, people agree, or you close a deal. When you are working a true system and you have the big picture in mind, your bottom line results will be multiples of trying to beat the odds pitch by pitch, proposal by proposal. You are not going to win every play, but you are guaranteed to win overall. You are the casino, you are selling with a system, and you are playing with house money.

Gamblers Focus On Outcomes.

On the flip side, if you are not selling with a system, you are much like a gambler. You think way too much about the outcome of each call, each meeting, each proposal. You are focused on the outcomes of individual plays rather than on executing on an overall winning system. You are trying to beat the odds stacked against you on every play.

If your sales methodology resembles a gambler, you don't stand a chance. You are going to win some; you may even win some big ones. But overall you will never be better than mediocre -- if you are lucky.

You Can Break The Rules Of Your System At Times, But Break Them Too Often, You Don't Have A System.

Having a winning system doesn't mean that you are a robot. At times, it is strategically wise to vary from your system. Let me relate an extreme example. In my early days, I was working for a client who sold employee relocation services. I called very big companies that moved employees all over the world. The white whale of the industry was GE at the time. They made more than 2,000 moves a year, and it was "impossible" to get a meeting with them. I heard it again and again. Bottom line, I booked that meeting with GE. I did it by varying significantly from my winning process. I actually, purposely, said swear words on the phone. I made a bet, and I won.

However, far more results are earned by sticking with your system when times are tough. I could relate many more examples of reps getting consistent results by sticking with their system even though there were stretches of failure. For a personal example, I had a client a few years ago who targeted very large oil companies for a specialized environmental service. The top 50-100 oil companies were by far the best targets. We had tried a few callers, and things weren't working so even though my calling days had long been over, I offered to jump in. Bottom line, Troy got about 8 meetings with top levels of the largest oil companies in the US for projects worth many millions. In that case, what got results was sticking with the system. When I was bored, didn't want to make the next call, heard "no" multiple times, believed it useless to keep going, I just kept saying to myself "Scott, work the system." I did, and the results came in.

In the oil company example, it would not have been a winning system to swear at the decision-makers when they picked up the phone, as I did to get the GE meeting. And if I had succumbed to boredom, frustration, or panic and varied my process I would not have booked 8 meetings for Troy; I would have been lucky to book 2 or 3.

In the GE example, I gambled and won taking a chance on strategies for that 1 target that would have been disastrous if used consistently on others.

Do What This Guy Says, Or You Can't Work Here.

Having your team working a system, having a company culture ingrained with the right way to prospect, handle a discovery call, move a prospect through a sales pipeline, and ultimately close the deal means that your team is working in the high-probability zone. It is your duty as a company owner, VP sales, or manager to know the difference between a system that works best overall versus gambling, guessing, and winging it.

Earlier in this book, I told the story of a client who flew me into company headquarters dozens of times to train new hires. They went from $20 million to $80 million in sales during that period, not necessarily because I was so special, but because they were working a system.

Every month before I started the training session for the new hires, the VP of sales would start the meeting by giving a speech about how well the company was doing, how quickly they were growing, and that there was a method to their success. It always made me uncomfortable, but he would end by saying "if you don't do what Scott is going to teach you, you can't work here. Do things your way, and you won't be working here long."

He didn't say that because I was so special. They were growing rapidly long before I came into the picture. But their system, their beliefs about how to sell their products, and their beliefs about what to do at each step of the sale to get the best results from their efforts was remarkably similar to what I teach. What that VP of sales was saying is "we have a system and ways of doing things that are working for us. If you are not willing to learn and work our system, you can't work here." They hired good people and paid them very well. They plugged their reps into a system and provided support for those who needed help in learning it. If the reps wanted to play outside the system, if they wanted to gamble, the company wasn't going to let them gamble with their money.

How Can You Tell If You Are Too Focused On Individual Sales Outcomes, And Doomed To Mediocrity (At Best) As A Result?

You Over React To Individual Calls Or Meetings.

My favorite extreme examples: Trainee thinks all the big thoughts and does all the prep work and is ready to start working what she has come to believe is a superior "get the discovery call" system first thing in the morning. She promises to let me know how it was going at some point. Eventually, I get the call, and the trainee says "Scott, it just isn't working, most people aren't picking up and the two people I spoke to cut me off. It just isn't going to work." Hmm, this call came in at 10 a.m. on the first day. She had been calling for less than an hour and was ready to abandon all the preparation and planning that had been done.

Another example that exasperates me. "Scott, I had a call, and they shut me right down. It won't work. It is _____. " Pick any of these to complete the statement. "Too long," "Too much info" "too salesy" "Isn't conversational enough." This one exasperates me as it is a pretty clear indicator that someone who takes the result of 1 call as indicative of what will work overall does not have things in perspective and is doomed to overreact to individual outcomes.

You Focus On "1 Thing" That Will Turn Everything Around.

It is human nature to want to hit the easy button. And often sales reps will believe that if only they had the right script, got better at objections, had a better story, could improve their elevator pitch (shoot me), or had a better list, all would be different. But the reality is that the answer is never "one thing." Never. It is always a combination of things that create a system that delivers superior results over time.

If you are bopping from 1 new idea or strategy to another, thinking it will make the difference, you are not tweaking a system, you are placing losing bets. You are selling like a gambler.

You Believe The "Everything Has Changed" Crap

Please excuse me if I go into rant mode for a moment. Whenever I hear someone say "everything in sales has changed," I sigh. I sigh because that person has stacked the odds against them. Those who believe that are typically shutting themselves off from learning something that will help them right now. Rather than learn from sales success, and that success might have occurred last year, last decade, they shut off opening their minds to examples that might help them by saying "everything has changed."

Now certainly some things have changed; Technology, our prospects' access to information, competitive environments, and more. But the drivers of sales success have not changed. You still have to target the right prospects, interact with them effectively, have good messaging, yada yada yada.

Don't let someone sell you the wonder strategy of the month by trying to convince you that "everything has changed" and you can't learn something from prior successful producers or even other industries. Be willing to learn from all sources and tweak the component parts of your system to win.

You Think Making More Calls Will Save You

First, let me say this. If you are a salesrep and work for a sales manager whose direction and coaching starts and stops with "make more calls," leave that job. You will never make any real money. If you or your manager are "activity focused" and really believe that more dials, more doors knocked on, more pitches or more proposals will turn things around, you are in denial and deluding yourselves. Assuming you are making a reasonable effort, "more" will never save you. You are not only selling like a gambler, but you are making very poor bets.

If Your Results And Income Have Not Changed Much Recently

Bottom line. You might think you are doing the right things and working hard enough in the right places, but if your results, your income hasn't changed much recently, it is a big fat clue that you are not working a winning system. If you think you are working a system, it's a pretty poor one. Certainly, if you can look back 2 or 3 years and your income or revenue needle has not moved much, you need to step up to the plate and acknowledge that what you believe in and have been doing isn't working. Put aside your rationalizations and excuses as to why. Admit that you are not working a winning system and have been selling in the gamblers zone. Be willing, be determined, to change.

The Probability And Payoff Of The Wins Delivered Also Matter.

When you focus on implementing an overall effective process your probability of sales success goes way up.

But the success of a sales or prospecting process is not just about the probability of wins and losses. It is also about the payoff of the wins delivered.

Everybody is familiar with the law of the vital few, aka the Pareto Principle. The 80/20 rule. 80% of success comes from 20% of our effort. 80% of outcomes come from 20% of the causes. 80% of the revenue and profit comes from 20% of the clients. 80% of sales are closed by the top 20% of the salespeople.

The 80/20 rule is a rough guide to the common distribution of cause and effect. Your number may not be "20" and "80." Your number might be 90/10 or 95/5. The point is that for most things in life, and in sales, not all efforts and inputs affect results equally.

When you work a winning system, you put more emphasis on the things that matter most to outcomes as a matter of process and habit.

The 80/20 Rule Also Applies to Screwing Up.

You should also be thinking about the 80/20 rule regarding what actions/mistakes have a disproportionate impact on achieving a bad sales result. What things can you stop doing or saying that are heavily contributing to your bad results? Rip those things out of your process.

If You Stop Doing Stupid Stuff, You Can Have An 80/20 Impact On Sales.

Sometimes it is not what you do, but <u>what you stop doing</u>, that contributes disproportionately to achieving superior results. If 80% of sales come from a small segment of your list, stop calling the low-return no-return parts of the list to get a big boost. Example: I do a lot of work in an industry where 50% of what is considered a "great" account comes from just 3% of target lists. If you don't know the profile of that 3%, you spend the vast majority of your time in knucklehead land. Identify and stop working on the 97% of your potential call universe that contributes little to no results. Just stop doing that, and you will immediately see a big impact on results. Very common.

You greatly improve your sales process when you make a habit of identifying and not doing stupid stuff as a matter of habit and process.

Why Does A Casino - "The House," Always Make Money Over Time?

Probabilities.

If you are a casino, you are working a system with the odds stacked in your favor. Overall, a casino has created a process that delivers good outcomes for them again and again and again. They do the things that most impact results as a matter of habit and have ripped out the stupid stuff that drags down results.

If you are a casino, you will have some bad results. Gamblers are going to win some bets. Some gamblers will "beat" the superior casino process fighting against them on individual bets.

Individual decisions can be based upon bad thinking and wrong assumptions yet be successful.

Decisions based upon sound reasoning can be complete failures.

But over time actions based on more thorough and reasoned decision-making, a winning process, will lead to overall better results.

Sales leaders make a strategic mistake by assuming that a "good outcome" must be the result of solid thinking and doing the right things. Not even close to being true.

Those who rack up the most wins and do so consistently all emphasize implementation of a superior process over prioritizing outcomes.

Gamble, and you will win here and there.

Work an effective overall system and you will win consistently. Ka-ching, Ka-ching. You will be piling fat stacks.

Even Basic Sales Systems Can Beat The Competition Soundly.

Everybody wants the quantum leap in sales results. I have seen far more quantum leaps in sales productivity from companies or individuals who get their basics in order rather than yet again, try the flavor of the month or the "one" new thing that will turn everything around. Getting the basics organized and implemented consistently is far more likely to vault your sales productivity forward than embracing the latest "everything has changed" strategy or technical innovation. And once you get your basics in order, you have a strong foundation upon which to layer all the more advanced strategies that will help you.

Even basic systems, implemented consistently, are usually good enough to run circles around 90% of the competition. I am not kidding.

If you are a sales leader, would you rather be "the house," working a system that will consistently spit out a high quantity of qualified discovery calls, or would you rather try to win a bet with every call you make, every suspect you reach out to?

When you are in sales, the only certainty is that there is no certainty. You deal with risk. You take a chance with every effort not knowing what the outcome will be. But when you are working a well thought out sales/prospecting process, you can have a high degree of confidence in what the distribution of outcomes will be. You can have a high degree of confidence knowing what the overall probability of winning will be, but also the payoff of those wins.

So if you are a company owner, VP of sales or account executive, are you prospecting with house money or are you gambling?

Worksheets, additional scripts, and periodic updates are available to readers of this book at ScottChannell.com/STM-book-extras

Chapter 27
Managing Your "Sales Debt"

Borrow by taking a quick and easy loan, and you get things you want now, no waiting. You pay the loan back — with interest.

It's a trade-off with a price. Sales managers (and sales reps self-managing) have the option of borrowing to get something now and pay the price later. But sales leaders and those who wish to be top producers must acknowledge the trade-off and what must be paid back.

Sales managers can run into serious trouble by borrowing too much.

Too much "sales debt" can cripple sales performance within an organization.

The More Common Types of Sales Debt

Choosing Sales Behaviors That Tend To Deliver Short-Term Results.

These are lower-volume, small-margin accounts with shorter sales cycles. The quick close is chosen too often over the larger longer-term sale and a price will be paid.

Lack Of Clear Focus On Targets More Likely To Deliver Great Accounts

Sales managers incur a huge debt of sales team inefficiency when they fail to spend time prioritizing target groups for best results. I have taken a lot of sales 911 calls and the #1 reason for the emergency is lack of focus on the most probable buyers by far. Managers incur a huge debt of inefficiency when they borrow time for quick closes by failing to keep their team focused on the highest-probability targets.

By failing to invest a little time and knowledge into selecting the highest -probability sub-segment of a list their team will spend a lot of time calling, they skip those few hours and pay the price of massive inefficiency as their team is doomed to wallow through sludge looking for something good.

Lack Of Sales Performance Standards And Training

There is a method to the madness. There are behaviors more likely to work and behaviors less likely to work. There is a right way to prospect and very ineffective ways to prospect. Scripts that communicate value and get meetings, scripts that don't. First meeting strategies more likely to lead to second and third interactions and a close, others more likely to ensure that the first meeting is the last. If an organization lacks those standards, or proper training and sales coaching are non-existent, time and money may be saved in the short run, but you pay the price of lower sales performance over time.

It can be OK to borrow, but be careful.

When you take out a loan to get something now, you plan to pay it back with interest. If sales managers don't properly acknowledge the sales debt being incurred and how it will be paid back, 2 bad things can occur.

1. The sales organization is financially crippled if not bankrupt.

The consequences of short-term thinking and borrowing against the future come due.

2. The sales team becomes a slave to the "sales debt monster."

Reasonable pursuits that are more profitable, yet take time, are shelved. The sole focus is finding business quick to meet the monthly nut.

Why Sales Executives Must Resist Taking On Too Much "Sales Debt."

1. Top talent will flee

When organizations take on too much "sales debt," they start to do stupid stuff. The short-term considerations are king. Well, top producers and those who could develop into top producers flee these environments. If a sales organization can't properly pursue profitable opportunities or sales reps must waste sales time with stupid tasks, they will go somewhere else. Top talent gets frustrated when they are not properly trained or must sell very inefficiently due to lack of proper systems. The mediocre and the bottom of the barrel reps have fewer options; they will stay.

2. The best most profitable accounts go to others.

Better accounts usually have longer sales cycles. Proper systems are necessary to be at the table when a buy decision is being made. It takes sales talent and a proper sales skillset to manage these opportunities to close. Those opportunities are not realistic for sales organizations with too much debt as they don't have the time, systems, or talent to win them.

3. The cost of sales go up.

Those accounts with shorter sales cycles. It sure feels good closing them. They may not be a perfect fit, the price concession pinched a bit, and they tend to be a little on the smaller side… but it's a close and new account on the board. But too much focus on short term wins come with a debt to be paid. A higher cost of sale and smaller margins.

4. Too much sales debt is a treadmill to nowhere or a greased chute to hell.

Debt is crippling. Whether it is an individual or a sales organization, too much debt can overwhelm you and narrow your choices with no end in sight. Just like the song that never ends, you will run hard on the sales treadmill to nowhere if you don't pay down your debt. Too much "sales debt" also puts you closer to the line of disaster. You have little room for error, market condition changes or losing a key account. A stiff breeze could put you out of your misery.

Sales Managers Can Avoid Or Pay Back a Lot of "Sales Debt" with Coaching Up-Front.

Managers most influence the quality and quantity of accounts closed at the beginning of the process. Are the reps calling on the right people? Are they prospecting correctly? Are they likely to conduct the first meeting with a solid prospect well enough? Do sales reps manage their pipelines well?

If managers do the proper coaching up-front and check under the covers once in a while, they can be assured that the reps are doing the right things. That pays off in higher closing ratios and account quality. But skip these steps or take it for granted that the right things are being done and you lose control. You borrowed some time by skipping training, coaching, and checking but the organization will pay a huge price in lower sales performance.

Summary: Sales Managers Must Avoid the Burden of Excessive "Sales Debt."

As a sales rep or manager, you are free of "sales debt" when you have taken the time to learn and hone the craft of sales, when you set up the proper systems to operate at maximum productivity and profit, when you have invested time and money to be able to compete and win the best accounts out there. You are selling with no debt. You have the freedom to think longer term and every week reap the benefits of the systems you put in place and training you did. You are operating debt free. Sweet.

Others Have Taken Some Short Cuts And Incurred "Sales Debt."

Maybe the suspects selected were poorly chosen so there is a price to be paid in low call efficiency and wasted time. Maybe the scripts and verbiage used has not been properly prepared so there is a price to be paid in fewer conversations and meetings set. Maybe developing sales skills and your craft has been neglected, so your sales bucket has holes in it and you pay the price of lower closing percentages. These are debts that must be paid. They are paid every week and every month.

When the "sales debt" piles too high you become a slave to your debt.

Your sole focus becomes meeting your monthly nut. So, short term thinking starts to dictate your actions. Your sales debt burden can be bone crushing.

Worksheets, additional scripts, and periodic updates are available to readers of this book at ScottChannell.com/STM-book-extras

Chapter 28
A Few Tips From Top Appointment Setters

Tip #1 From Tim O'Krongly

Scott's Intro:
In 2009, I got a call from an appointment setter seeking some help. After obtaining some background information, hearing about the high-level lead generation he was doing, the results he was achieving and the caliber of clients he had, I had only one question. "Why in the world are YOU calling ME?" He was that impressive. He responded that he wished to improve call efficiency, which he did.

That person is the author of the tip that follows. In my opinion, and with my 24 years of experience, with no hesitation, I can say that Tim is among the top 5 B2B appointment setters in the country. We have communicated as peers over the years and I am pleased that he was willing to contribute some of his insights to this book.

Secrets To "Securing The Meeting."
A tip from Tim O'Krongly, CEO of Prospect Link.

In most sales support books, the authors often write about managing the conversation with a prospect. Advice is often what to say when, how to lead the customer down the buying journey, and when to apply pressure to close the deal.

All good stuff, but HOW do you get that first meeting with a "suspect?"

In my career, I've been an entrepreneur, broadcaster, ad agency executive, client, and now I own a company whose only purpose is to secure that first meeting for customers. So, what's the secret to securing that meeting?

First, a backstory on a concept that may be familiar. It's the 4-P's of marketing. Something I learned from some of the best marketers in the world; Kraft Foods, Starbucks, Paramount Pictures, and Coca-Cola, to name a few. They are… Product, Placement, Price, and Promotion. Without that foundation, products do not sell to consumers.

As a seller in a B2B environment for the past 30 years, I've developed a sales version of the 4-P's. These are Preparation, Process, Persistence, and Patience. Let me explain how each of these works in the context of "securing the meeting."

Preparation: To sell (anything) you have to understand the product/service and the "why" it was created. Gathering that information is part of your first few weeks on the job. Understanding the value proposition from the buyer's perspective is the key to unlocking doors.

> **The outcome:** you should be able to identify the pain points your company addresses AND, equally important, the aspirations of the buyers. Then articulate how your company can address both.

Process: To do any job, you need to understand what tools are available — the same thing with selling.

> **Must haves include** a reliable email service provider, CRM tool, list building process, inbound lead generation, marketing support, social media program, LinkedIn coverage, thought leadership tools, white papers, blogs and… a phone.

Persistence: You know it takes over 12 touches to help a prospect understand your value proposition. Remember you want them to "invest" the one commodity they never get back… time… with you.

> **So, keep trying** until someone says no thanks (or worse).
>
> Never "give up" on a suspect… your job is to make them a prospect.
>
> You'll never know when their needs intersect with your product unless they tell you.
>
> Try every tool in your "process kit" to make that first connection (see number 2)

Use the phone but manage your team's expectations. People rarely pick up anymore. Today's phones have been relegated to participating in a conference call that YOU arranged.

Patience: Your boss, the owner of the company, your finance person, the board, stockholders, and YOU all need to know this "selling thing" takes time. Oh, and money. The tools in the process are an investment in your success. Make sure you use them so you can provide evidence of, and keep track of, your work.

> **Through all of this**, you have to be patient and promote being patient to all stakeholders. Too often companies look at Facebook, Google, Amazon, Uber and their success then think… wow, that was fast… why can't my sales team do this? The answer is simple; each of these companies had the patience for their vision and didn't let quarterly sales trends get in the way of annual goals.

So, there you have it… the 4-P's of getting yourself set up to sell the meeting. But WAIT… there's more. And this one is a biggie. DON'T hire the wrong people for the job of securing the meeting.

There are three types of sellers (and needs) … Finders, Minders, and Grinders.

Finders set sales appointments, and they are as relentless as pigs hunting for truffles. Minders are deal closers and have a special talent for understanding how to craft a scope of work for prospects. Grinders are account managers that have a respect for selling and are always looking for the next opportunity. They are organic growers.

When you need to grow your business, you can certainly rely on Grinders to capture more from current clients. But if you want exponential growth… put a Finder on your team and take off the leash.

I hope you get a great deal of value from Scott's book. I've found his writing/thinking to be in tune with current trends, and his ideas are very effective if you follow his process.

Here's to your success in sales. A profession as necessary as oxygen, because NOTHING happens until someone sells something. And no one sells anything without the first meeting.

Tim O'Krongly
ProspectLink.biz

Tip #2 From Sundae Johnson

Scott's Intro: In 2010, I got a call from the corporate headquarters of a large national franchise organization that depended heavily (still does) upon setting sales appointments for new business. The Chairman of the Business Development Committee related that in one year, a particular Master Franchise Territory had gone from ranking close to the bottom nationally for the number of sales appointments set, closing ratio and the size of the average sale, to ranking among the top tier nationally for those same categories.

When they inquired how they did it, the sales manager at the time related that they had found some training material (books and CD's – people listened to CD's then) from some schmo named Scott Channell and listened to a lesson every week. Those lessons and the principles taught vaulted them from the bottom of the pile nationally to the top of the pile.

The sales manager who managed that transformation, Sundae Johnson, contributes this tip. For many many years, Sundae had been a top producer nationally for her organization. Once her team was able to crack the appointment setting code, she was able to guide them to national recognition within the company.

Don't be afraid to be different. Decide to make it your life's goal!

The art of sales is truly dying. If you want to hone your craft and be more successful, become laser-focused on doing the things that feel uncomfortable until they are second nature!

Become relentless in seeking out those awkward moments when you sort of cringe inside and then do the things that no one else will do. Make a game out of it. Even when those things don't yield immediate scenario specific success, they WILL still make you more memorable in the back of your prospects mind, and guess what!? You still win long term because you're building a brand!

If you can't sell the appointment now, your goal isn't for everyone to like you; its for them to remember you when the time is right!

Go get em, Tiger!

Sundae Sisco Johnson

SELL THE MEETING

Worksheets, additional scripts, and periodic updates are available to readers of this book at ScottChannell.com/STM-book-extras

Bulk Orders And Customization
This book is available at a discount when purchased in bulk for corporate use or sales promotions. In larger quantities, this book can be modified with customized covers, content, and corporate logos. For information, go to ScottChannell.com or call 978-296-2700.

Speaking, Training, Coaching
Scott Channell is available for speaking engagements, training sessions and executive coaching. See ScottChannell.com for contact information.

Printed in Poland
by Amazon Fulfillment
Poland Sp. z o.o., Wrocław

29033664R00168